THE
STILL POINT

1

Also by Laurence Gonzales

JAMBEAUX
THE LAST DEAL
EL VAGO
ARTIFICIAL HORIZON

THE

STILL POINT

LAURENCE GONZALES

The University of Arkansas Press
Fayetteville London 1989

Copyright © 1989 by Laurence Gonzales

DESIGNER: *Nancy Burris*
TYPEFACE: *Linotron 202 Trump Mediaeval*
TYPESETTER: *G&S Typesetters, Inc.*
PRINTER: *Edwards Brothers*
BINDER: *Edwards Brothers*

The paper used in this publication meets the minimum
requirements of the American National Standard for Permanence
of Paper for Printed Library Materials Z39.48-1984. ∞

Library of Congress Cataloging-in-Publication Data

Gonzales, Laurence, 1947–
    The still point / by Laurence Gonzales.
      p.   cm.
    ISBN 1-55728-080-0 (alk. paper). — ISBN 1-55728-081-9 (pbk. :
  alk. paper)
    I. Title.
  PS3557.0467S75   1989
  814'.54—dc19   89-4655
                                                         CIP

To Fern Elise Howard

CONTENTS

The Rock

The Pit

The Sky

ACKNOWLEDGMENTS

Magazine articles are never the work of one person. This volume is no exception to that rule. I owe a great debt to my editors, many of whom thought up the ideas for these pieces, and all of whom helped me in the never-ending process of learning how to write. The list of names includes some of the best editors in the business: Asa Baber, Arlene Bouras, David Butler, Gretchen Edgren, Dan Ferrara, Rob Fleder, Don Gold, G. Barry Golson, Phillip Herrera, Arthur Kretchmer, Lewis Lapham, Hillel Levin, Walter Lowe, James McKinley, James Morgan, Barbara Nellis, Christine Newman, Kate Nolan, Geoffrey Norman, Patricia Papangelis, James R. Peterson, Reg Potterton, John Rasmus, John Rezek, Richard Rhodes, David Standish, David Stevens, Alice K. Turner, Craig Vetter, and Sheldon Wax, just to name a few.

But magazine articles really depend on the people who provide the information and the events—those who do brave duty as the characters in our stories. The stories—and the largest debt of gratitude—truly belong to them.

Articles are used by permission: "At the Still Point of the Turning World: Flying Jets with the Air Force" first appeared in *Harper's* magazine. "Deep in with David Carradine" and "The Rock 'n' Roll Heart of Robert Jarvik" first appeared in *Playboy* magazine. "Anatomy of a Drug Bust" and "When Doctors Are Addicts" first appeared in the *Chicago Reader*. "No Escape: The Endless Dreams of Elgin," "Marion Prison," and "The Executioners" first appeared in *Chicago* magazine. "Man in Captivity" first appeared in *Notre Dame* magazine. "The Flight of the Crystal Witch" first appeared in *Connoisseur* magazine.

Except for the point, the still point,
There would be no dance, and there is only the dance.

—T. S. ELIOT

The Rock

DEEP IN WITH
DAVID CARRADINE

It was the only car I saw on the MGM lot in Culver City that could stop a conversation just by cruising by. When he bought it, he had the engine rebuilt, but he wasn't satisfied with the way it ran, so he had it rebuilt again. He also had the body redone and now it looked as if it had just rolled off the showroom floor. It was a fire-engine-yellow 1967 Ferrari 330GTS with a Pinin Farina body, and with the top down, it looked like a special effect from *The Empire Strikes Back*, skimming effortlessly across your field of vision, a compact, featherweight sculpture of kinetic energy.

I slid into the passenger seat and he started the engine. The twelve cylinders fluttered softly beneath the mirror-polished hood like a caged flock of doves. I was reminded, as I sank into the seat, of the airplane I fly. I've always been impressed by its front seats. They are made for someone who, the entire time he sits there, has his life literally in his hands. In addition, the Ferrari could go a good bit faster than that airplane. The only problem would be finding the open ground.

A lot of people had told me that David Carradine lived on the edge, but that turned out not to be the case. Living on the edge is just a cliché. My dentist lives on the edge. Carradine has another way of describing it: "deep in." It has to do with commitment. For example, when a battalion leader shouts "Charge!" he is deep in—or at least he'd better be. It's so simple it evades most people. And when Carradine took off out of

Culver City, I knew we were deep in already, as Mar Vista whipped past and then Santa Monica and we entered onto the Pacific Coast Highway, weaving across the lanes like a slalom racer, by which time I had discovered that the car had no seat belts.

"I don't like 'em," was all Carradine gave by way of explanation in a style that could only be called mellifluous mania or pissed-off contentment or mellow fury or some other such oxymoron.

The only advantage to Carradine's driving style was knowing that it would be over quickly—we'd either arrive or we wouldn't in the snap of a finger. And so, without warning or ceremony, we found ourselves getting out at the house in Malibu where his wife, Linda, lived with their baby daughter, Kansas, and where we were going to stay until things got old or ugly.

The house was conceptual-ranch uni-level and was as cluttered as if they'd moved in that afternoon and couldn't quite figure a strategy for unpacking. The front entrance was partially blocked by six-foot-high stacks of movie film in cans and boxes—a picture Carradine had once made called *You and I.* Strewn around several rooms, there must have been fifteen or twenty serious guitars—Mossman twelve-strings and mellow old Gibsons, fat antique Martins—just piled around as if they were so much kindling. In the front room was a display of stills from his latest movie, *The Long Riders* (of him and his brothers Keith and Robert, posing; of him escaping, wounded, with Robert on the back of his horse; of him getting shot to pieces while riding full tilt).

If you are at all linear, or if you happen to be a control freak, hanging out with David Carradine can really make a mess out of you. Take something as simple as how many Carradine brothers there are. John Carradine, the famous character actor, is the father. In a biographical television special about the Carradine family, I heard him refer to "the four boys." The narrator also seemed to be laboring under the delusion that there were only four Carradine brothers—David, Keith (whose song in *Nashville* won an Academy Award and who played the lead in *Pretty Baby*), Robert (who has played numerous fine secondary roles in big motion pictures, such as *Coming Home*, in which he was the guitar-playing kid who killed himself, and who played a brilliant leading role in *The Big Red One*), and Christopher, a very talented and successful architect. Nevertheless, during a party I went to with David, Keith, and Christopher, I met Michael, allegedly another Carradine brother. And I saw a movie David made that featured yet *another* Carradine brother I'd never heard of. I asked David how many Carradine brothers there were and he said eight. I mentioned this to Linda and she said, "Oh, really? I thought there were only seven." If you happen onto an undisputed fact about David Carradine in your creep through this life, you hang on real right.

Reading David Carradine can be like reading the floor of the ocean. He owns the house in Malibu but apparently doesn't live there—or lives there only part of the time. He has another house in Laurel Canyon that is made of wood and glass. It must have two hundred tiny windows. Even the roof is made of windows. And they all open ("You have to be something of a monkey to do it," he said). He has six horses and nine exotic automobiles. He had ten, but he sold one recently—an O.S.C.A., built by the Maserati brothers.

Sitting in the living room in Malibu, drinking Bordeaux, I got my first clear look at Carradine in the subtle light of that sprawling house. He's forty-three, but he could just as easily be a lot older. He has wide, flat fingernails tipped by crescents of black, as if he'd spent the afternoon working on his car rather than on his next movie. He smokes cigarettes with a kind of delicate, implacable abandon, occasionally switching to a pipe of ancient briar for a hit of grass. His fine, straight hair is the color of a stone at the bottom of a stream; it appears never to have suffered the indignity of a comb or a brush.

He does not wear shoes. I spent a week with him and virtually the only time I saw him in shoes was at a wardrobe fitting.

You don't notice something like that right off, but it has an odd effect. It colors his aura, is somehow central to what he is. His first real fame came with the television series *Kung Fu*, in which he played a half-Chinese immigrant Shaolin priest named Kwai Chang Caine. Caine was a master of kung fu, a martial art. In that role, Carradine said almost nothing, except to spout an occasional mishmash of pseudo Zen aphorisms. His main activity was to walk into some unknown Western town where trouble was brewing and, while attempting to maintain a professional distance from it, become so involved in the very trouble he was trying to avoid that he would end up nonviolently kicking the shit out of a handful of big, heavily armed cowboys. He would do that, of course, without the aid of weapons. In a culture in which everyone is brought up to believe that the fastest gun in any town is the ultimate power, it was remarkable to see someone so fast that he could literally take the gun away before the man had a chance to pull the trigger. And in the winding-down days of the Vietnam War, it was frankly unbelievable to see someone with the unmitigated hair to program an alleged Oriental into that role, but there it was. Barefooted, rumpled, and unsmiling. Caine would shoulder his small cloth sack of possessions and walk (not ride) off into the sunset.

And now, with him in Malibu, I could see that perhaps that role had turned Carradine into a kind of second cousin to Caine. The clothes he wore were awesome in their decrepitude—beyond pity, really. During my week with him, at both of his houses, I saw no clothing that appeared to belong to him, and the only change of clothes I saw him make was in that wardrobe fitting, during which he seemed about as comfortable as a cat doing the breast stroke.

His jeans were too large and too old, the pockets stuffed and bulging, as if he carried his every possession right on his person, as if he'd been on the run for some time now and we just happened to light for the evening in this fabulously wealthy California neighborhood, like two outlaws sleeping in a barn before stealing our next pair of horses. I had the sense that he felt that way, too, as if the Bordeaux we were drinking belonged to someone else, who was going to be a trifle upset when he discovered it gone.

We talked about *Kung Fu* a bit—I felt obliged to—and I mentioned that in the early seventies, when the series had begun, I had been staying at Ken Kesey's house. It turned out that the only television show the ex–Merry Pranksters watched while I was with them (other than NBA finals) was *Kung Fu*. Carradine nodded. "Caine," he said, "was made of, by, and for those people—the Pranksters. It was what they were all about."

Since *Kung Fu*, Carradine has been in a dozen or so movies, including *Bound for Glory*, about the life of Woody Guthrie; *The Serpent's Egg*, directed by Ingmar Bergman; and *The Long Riders*, a brilliant film about the James-Younger gang in which Carradine plays Cole Younger and, along with Pamela Reed, walks away with the picture.

Carradine was born and raised in Hollywood (or near enough to it), and he appears obsessed with it, constantly defining himself in terms of his differences from it, eternally taking his own temperature against the chill and paradox it throws off like a spoor. As we sat in his living room, he began talking about William Faulkner's going to Hollywood to write the screenplay of Hemingway's *To Have and Have Not*.

"Halfway between Hemingway and Faulkner," he said, "is Hollywood." He poured some wine and lit the briar. "You want to know what Hollywood is like? I had offers to do two movies once. One was set in Hong Kong. The other was set in Chinatown in San Francisco. The company that was doing the Hong Kong movie decided to shoot it in San Francisco in order to save money. The one that was doing the Chinatown movie decided to shoot it in Hong Kong to save money. And at that point, I realized that it doesn't make any difference what you do. You just do anything you want."

That was one of the reasons Carradine decided to make his own films. He knows Hollywood (meaning the film industry) so well that he simply operates on parallel tracks with it, jumping over from time to time to collect a check to keep his own work going. His latest production is called *Americana*. He started it in 1973 and finished it while I was with him. He has an annoying habit of making films on budgets that contradict everything that is accepted as Gospel by the industry. A sound mix they might do for seventy thousand, he does for thirty thousand. Where they shoot a thousand feet of film, Carradine shoots one hundred.

I asked him how he does certain things that seem to require great expense. For example, in *Americana*, the main character (played by Carradine) fights a dog in a pit for the entertainment of some rural Kansas locals. The scene is very realistic—and quite disturbing. I envisioned stunt men, multiple cameras, highly trained dogs, make-up artists, and scores of takes to get that eerie, close-in feeling he got.

"It was one of Dan Haggerty's wolves," Carradine explained. "We borrowed this wolf and then starved it for two days. Then we just smeared me with dog food and I got into the pit." He smiled a thin smile that I would come to recognize as characteristic. It was a smile you might see on a man who has a bazooka pointed at his head and has just been told to start shitting Tiffany cuff links or die. "I got injured," he added. "I got the scars."

Deep in.

❖   ❖   ❖

Carradine is covered with tattoos and loves great wines. He is a faithful husband and a grandfather. He has taken hundreds of acid trips and a few other trips, as well. Bob Dylan studied kung fu with him. ("Dylan looked like this really dead-on master, and he didn't know what he was doing. He was great.") He wants to seed the Santa Monica Mountains with wild animals—fox and lion, deer and possum and quail ("I stop short of rattlesnakes"). David is not his real name (it's John) and he likes Jose Cuervo gold tequila in pint bottles (the better to run with). He is four years into a fifteen-year shooting schedule of a movie about his eighteen-year-old daughter's life. He is full of secrets, and just when you think you have a fix on one thing, he's got another for you.

On his left nipple is a tattoo of the Sufi symbol, which is a pair of wings attached to a red heart surrounding a yellow star and moon. Above his dick he has a butterfly tattoo and on his right rib cage and abdomen, a tiger, moon, and tree. There is a hawk on his left wrist. I wondered how many tattoos he had in all.

"They're all sort of one," he said. I guess only his proctologist knows for sure.

I also wondered if that didn't make it difficult as an actor when he had to take his shirt off.

"Yeah," he shrugged. "But classy actors don't take their shirts off. Laurence Olivier never took his shirt off."

The clutter of the Malibu house is astonishing in its thoroughness, but it is not the clutter of some posthippie pad. It is the clutter of a sunken ship, where every cloud of sea dust drifts away to reveal some new treasure. Getting out of bed that first morning, I practically stumbled over some of his wines. Château Pichon-Longueville 1945. Château Giscours 1929, Labarde-Margaux. In another room, cases of Haut-Brion 1961. "I went broke last year buying wine," he said.

When I arose, no one but Kansas was up. She was spreading yogurt around (and eating some of it, too), so I wandered outside to sneak another look at the Ferrari. A tan Honda Civic pulled in behind Linda's Mercedes and Keith Carradine unfolded himself from the driver's seat. A few minutes later, David got up (wearing the same clothes) and the two brothers hugged and kissed each other on the mouth, held each other at arm's length, as if to see how they'd grown over the years. They slammed each other on the back with detonations of manly affection and generally caused a jubilant uproar, with dogs barking and children squawking and the sun leaking in to coat everything morning rose and yellow and send little diamonds of white creeping across the floor.

"Family is the only real thing in all society," David said. He adores Keith and it isn't difficult to see why. One of the first things you notice about Keith is that it would take a lot of bother to get to dislike him. He has a smile as clear as a temple bell, a boundless energy and affection. He immediately got into it with David's old hound, Buffalo, talking to him, growling at him, sliding his hands through Buffalo's fur like a cartoon pirate running his fingers through a chest of doubloons.

Half an hour later, we sat in the dining room, eating a strange California concoction that was supposed to cure all ills. It tasted OK but was more like something you'd feed to a pet rabbit than to a human. I think the recipe called for using only fruits and vegetables whose names ended in consonants. David had gone on a diet of that back when he was doing *Kung Fu*. He said he had never felt better, had limitless energy, and needed only three or four hours of sleep a night. Keith went on the diet for three weeks, too. His weight plummeted to 123 pounds, which didn't sit too well on his 6'1" skeleton.

"He cured himself by eating roast-beef sandwiches and drinking Pepto-Bismol so he wouldn't barf," David said with a laugh. Sitting across the table from me, Keith still looked needle-thin at 157 pounds. "But I don't care what you say," David added. "It worked for me."

After breakfast, Keith began doing Lord Buckley routines, and in about four minutes, he had us on the floor. He recited from memory such infamous bits as *God's Own Drunk* and *The Nazz* and turned his long, mobile face into that of a sixty-year-old black man without apparent effort. It was startling and convincing, and Keith such a superhonkie when it comes to appearance. Then, abruptly, he left to go about his Saturday errands, reminding David to be sure to be at his house the next day for the barbecue.

When he'd gone, David sat shaking his head in admiration. "Keith has total recall," he said. "Amazing, really. He's deep in." A little bark of a laugh escaped. "Keith does crossword puzzles with a *pen!* Fuckin' *New York Times.*" Another beat. "He's a virtuoso guitarist, too. Very shy about it."

They say that time speeds up and slows down, depending upon what is happening. It was only twenty-four hours until we were supposed to arrive at Keith's, but it took us about a month to pull it off. I've never seen a man take so long to get through a day in my entire life.

❖   ❖   ❖

The weather was severe-clear as we screamed out of Malibu in the Ferrari. Soon, however, we were stuck behind a Mercedes sports coupe chewing along at seventy miles an hour. "Get outa the fast lane, baby!" Carradine shouted, and sent the Ferrari dancing all over the road at 198 kilometers per hour (123 mph), missing the parked cars on the right by so little that if the car had had another coat of paint, we wouldn't have made it through. I was trying to decide whether my chances of surviving the impact would be better if I got down as low as possible in the seat or if I stood up so that I'd be thrown clear. There was so little to the car, just that craneload of engine and a windshield the size of a cafeteria tray.

But then, through that Einsteinian magic of high-speed travel, the trip was over and Carradine was parking in a no-zone. "Isn't this nice?" he asked with that thin smile. "They've got all these special parking spaces marked out for me in red."

We entered 9570 Wilshire on our way to his wardrobe fitting for a new movie. "Watch," he said. "I'll just say, 'OK, OK, fine, fine,' and it'll be over with." I wondered why on earth anyone would even think of asking him to choose clothes. That's like asking Stevie Wonder to give you a haircut.

But in a small, paneled office, producer Arthur (*White Lightning, Gator*) Gardner had racks of clothes waiting for Carradine and didn't seem at all fearful of letting him make the choices. As advertised, the fitting was quick and simple. Carradine chose a red-checked shirt, ordinary-looking new blue jeans, his own Stuntmen's Association belt buckle, a conservative beaver hat with a little bit of a rake to the brim, and a leather jacket.

Just to complete the picture, he even put on a pair of new cowboy boots.

It was remarkable how a few moderately priced clothes could clean him up. And I realized then what the effect had been when I first saw him barefooted and wearing those destroyed blue jeans. It hadn't been a surprise at all. I had *expected* him to look that way. If he had been dressed in clean, pressed designer jeans, then I would have been shocked. "I'm an Irish-American hippie," he had told me and others, and while that was not the central truth, it certainly helped explain his choice (or lack of choice) in clothes.

"This is just right," he was saying, looking in the mirror. "I don't want to look like the urban cowboy." He examined the jacket with guarded approval. It looked like something a cop might wear. "I'll have to get the George Hamilton out of this."

"Pee on it," Gardner suggested.

Then he was supposed to shuck back into his thirties hobo outfit and leave, but somehow they decided he should take the boots to break them in. Before it was over, Carradine walked out without getting back into his own clothes. He was in costume for his next movie, and he stayed in costume the rest of the week. Maybe he still hasn't changed.

❖   ❖   ❖

Carradine's Laurel Canyon house commands a dizzying view of the haze above the city. It makes you feel as if you're in a space capsule, descending into an orange jello mold. The floor of the main room upstairs is actually the deck of the U.S.S. *Los Angeles*, which Christopher Carradine somehow got hold of. He also designed the house ("Somewhat reluctantly, I think," David said). With its half-empty tequila bottles and marijuana debris, the house had the general air of a place that had been hit by a ferocious bust just before we got there and had been stripped bare by hungry narcs and not by any selection of the owner.

Actually, the Laurel Canyon house is the *Mata Hari* house, *Mata Hari* being the movie with the fifteen-year shooting schedule. Carradine's eldest, Calista, plays Mata Hari, and the schedule was created to cover her life from the age of fifteen through the age of thirty. They shoot two weeks each year. "The reason I chose Mata Hari," Carradine said, alternately sipping from a pint of tequila and hitting the briar full of grass, "is because it's a woman, and if there is one thing I don't understand, that's it. And I've got a daughter, and it's really difficult to be a father to her. The only way we can really get together is to have this picnic every year. Also, it's such a yin character, with all the excesses you associate with that."

Carradine, of course, plays her father. "It's a very subliminally sexual relationship," he said. He threaded a reel onto the Moviola in his editing room, and we watched the tiny, flickering screen. Calista was stunningly beautiful, sitting at a desk, reading a letter, and I couldn't help thinking of Vermeer. Nothing really happened during the nine minutes on that reel, except that she read a letter at a desk, but it was almost unbearably erotic. It was fascinating to speculate on the depth of Carradine's motivations for setting a fifteen-year shooting schedule with his first-born daughter, thereby more or less capturing her for the most critical portion of her life.

"The film is erotic as hell," he said. "You've got eleven-year-old girls *in flagrante,* and we just recently shot Mata Hari pregnant—and she really *was* pregnant." He was referring to Calista's new baby, who had just made him a grandfather. "I think it's a first—a nude pregnant scene. Or a pregnant nude scene, I don't know which." He smiled. "We shot the pregnancy partly because I didn't want to miss a shoot."

The tequila and grass had made him thirsty, and he went into the kitchen, which was outfitted with the brass fixtures from yet other once-noble ships. He stood at the sink, trying to open a can of fruit juice with a great butcher knife, taking arm's-length swings at it. I just turned away, thinking how very deep in it would be to have the opportunity to tie off an open arterial hemorrhage and then drive Carradine's Ferrari to the hospital while he bled to death beside me. When I turned around at a sound I took to be metal gouging bone, I found that he'd wrenched two jagged puncture wounds in the can and was unsteadily pouring us juice.

I had already had plenty of time to wonder if being deep in was a pose with Carradine, and I was beginning to believe it was not. I remembered back in September 1974 seeing an item in the newspapers about him. It seems he broke into a neighbor's house and left his piano covered with blood, his furniture upset, and his windows broken. Carradine told me that he had been at an Indian peyote ceremony and had taken "something like eighty buttons" before the thing really got cranked up proper. Leaving aside the question of whether or not anyone could survive taking eighty peyote buttons, he related the following: "I suddenly felt like General Custer and had to get out of there; I certainly wasn't worried about the police."

So he went tearing up and down the neighborhood, looking for company. "I didn't want to be alone," he said. He broke into several houses, but nobody was home. Finally, he arrived at that last house and cut himself when he put his hand through the window. He started playing piano (of course) and then broke out of the house again to get home. And the whole time he told me that story, he didn't seem to think there was anything strange about it at all.

I was beginning to see that that very fact was what made Carradine so strange and threatening to most people. Not so much that he did those crazy things but that he didn't consider them the least bit odd. There was no remorse or embarrassment, no attempt to conceal what he had done. You know the story: If you commit the crime intentionally, you're a criminal. If you commit it without getting a filter of self-consciousness over it, you're crazy. If David Carradine had been just an ordinary fellow and had pulled that stunt in, say, Watts—or even in Akron, Ohio—he would right now be either dead or in jail. Or he would have gotten off on an insanity plea. But he is not an ordinary fellow. He is a star. The magnitude of his stardom should not be underestimated, either. *Kung Fu* is still shown all over the world.

And now I was with him alone in Laurel Canyon. I can't say he was drunk, but his eyes were taking turns doing the work of moving left and right and of focusing, and I learned (after all the 115-mile-per-hour driving he'd been doing with me in the right seat) that he does not have a driver's license—hasn't had one since 1977, when he let it expire. "I've got something like one hundred tickets outstanding," he said.

I couldn't help wondering if having those court battles going on all the time didn't make him a little nervous. "Look at the shah of Iran," he said. "He's got cancer, he's a deposed monarch. There are all these people out to kill him. And he still goes to a ball game, he leads a life. That's how you have to do it." I was going to say something, but I didn't. And two weeks later, the shah of Iran was dead.

❖   ❖   ❖

"A musical instrument," Carradine was telling me, now convincingly drunk, "is a physical metaphor for the universe. It takes this thing right in the frontal lobes"—he tapped his forehead—"and sends it through the nerves to these clumsy devices—these *fingers*—and then to this *machine.*" He shook his head, as if he'd been punched from his blind side and was going to get up and fight. "If you could eliminate the body, you'd have pure philosophy."

I decided that he was trying to explain about being deep in. "The camera," he said, "can see when you're making faces as opposed to acting. It looks right into your eyes and right through you, and when you're doing it right, it can't see anything wrong. You can't hide. You have to be completely transparent. My father used to tell me that you had to be opaque, but I think you have to be transparent. And I've been trying to be that way ever since." In other words, you approach the point where the musical instrument is eliminated.

Still, he seemed to think I needed more of an explanation.

He grabbed a large blowup of a photograph taken during the shooting of *The Long Riders*. Three Carradines, two Keaches (James and Stacy), and a Quaid (Randy) rode their horses full gallop, shooting their way out of a hopeless situation in Northfield, Minnesota, where they'd been boxed in while robbing a bank.

Carradine explained that at first he hadn't wanted to make the movie, that he did it as a favor to the brothers involved. "I just thought I was supposed to make a personal appearance, that I was there because I was bankable. There wasn't even much of a part for me in the script." He smiled as if even I would know better than to believe that bullshit. "Then I stole the show."

He shook the photograph in my face. "Look at Jim," he insisted. "Look how hard he's working." Indeed, I hadn't noticed it before, but there was something about James Keach's expression, as if he were making a face. "Now, look at Stacy." Stacy Keach looked great. Of course, he always does. "He'd hurt his leg. He was in terrible pain, and he was just trying to stay on his horse. Deep in. See it?" I nodded.

"Now, look at me. See that hat?" In the photograph, the wind whipping past him had flattened the brim up, like an old military hat, and Carradine was riding hard. He looked significantly fine in that picture. "I wanted that effect. It was on purpose. One of the problems you run into in cowboy pictures is your hatbrim is stiff and when you ride hard, the wind gets up under there and blows your hat off. Then you've ruined the shot, because it won't fit with the next shot if you don't have your hat on. I chose this soft hat, and they said it would never make it through the picture. But it just folded up when I rode." He smiled that thin smile. "I'm just tryin' to stay on my horse and keep my gun loaded, that's all."

A beat. "And my horse, of course. That's my picture horse; I use him whenever I need a horse in a picture. He's an old cow pony. Most movie horses are ex-show horses. Mine is a real cow pony. He had to chase cows all his life until he met me, and he thinks movies are the easiest thing he's ever seen."

There is a scene in *The Long Riders* in which the gang is holed up in a cabin and the Pinkerton men outside shoot it to pieces with so much firepower that, as wrapped up in the movie as you might be, you can't help wondering how they did it. "We used five thousand squibs in that scene," Carradine explained. A squib is the little explosive cap that makes it look like a bullet is tearing into the wood. "To photograph the bullets from the inside of the door coming through, we got a lot of locals together and gave them real bullets and had them shoot the shit out of the door for a while." When that part of the filming was over, everyone went about his business and the rifles were stacked with the other props. Girls came and went, picking up the guns and playing cowboy off camera, goofing around and pointing them at one another. "And when the prop men broke down the rifles at the end of the day, they all had live ammo in them," Carradine said. He smiled that weary, shit-eating smile again. "Somebody could've got her head blown clean off." He said it as if it would have been just delicious.

I don't know whether Carradine already knew what was going to happen or if it was just a coincidence. You hang out with him for very long and you'll begin to believe his connections are good downtown and maybe even better in other worlds. But he insisted I drive the Ferrari home to Malibu, as if I might as well get a hand in before the entire trip went to hell. It was full night when I flipped on the auxiliary fuel pump and headed out. By the time we hit Kanan Road up in the mountains, I more or less had the feel of it ("I liked the way you got into first there," he said, "most people can't do that"). But I wasn't about to attempt anything like the way Carradine drove. I hit maybe ninety-five in places—real flat, open places. Anyway, I don't have the chops for it: I've handled only one other machine vaguely like that 330GTS and it went straight up.

As I drove, Carradine kept talking about how careful he had to be with his Ferrari, because his eight other cars were in the shop and this was his real everyday car now. He said he drove it slowly (*slowly?*) because it got nearly ten miles to the gallon that way.

When we got home, we were only about four hours late for dinner and Linda wasn't speaking to us. She went to bed, and we drank a 1975 Château Margaux with the reheated chicken and rocklike potatoes.

❖   ❖   ❖

Sunday morning we were supposed to get ready and head over to Keith's. It was going to be a big deal. Other Carradine brothers would be there. Walter Hill, who directed *The Long Riders*, would be there. But already the day wasn't going as planned. For one thing, Carradine was not awake. Linda decided he needed the sleep and, besides, there were errands to run before we could leave for Keith's. Wednesday there was going to be a big screening of *Americana* for the industry heavies, who would decide whether or not to distribute it. Some invitations had yet to be delivered, and it fell to Linda to do it, only she could not find the keys to her Mercedes. As the morning slipped away and we ransacked the already ransacked house, looking for her keys, she decided with a reluctance that bordered on trepidation to take the Ferrari.

She could not stop talking about what Carradine would do if she so much as got a scratch on it, and I was beginning to think we should have walked, as, mortified and duty-bound, she crept around Malibu from Robbie Robertson's house to Rick Danko's house to Bob Dylan's house, delivering invitations. Linda told me that things had been very strange in Malibu recently. A perfect stranger, she said, had wandered into the Dankos' house the week before and blown his own brains out all over their floor.

"Jesus," I said, "how are they?"

"Oh," Linda shrugged, "they're fine."

As we pecked our way back to her house, my only feeling was gratitude that she was driving at about the same speed as everyone else on the road and that we got home safely.

The afternoon was well on its way by the time Carradine got

up, and right off I knew something was wrong. He said hello as if nothing were going on, but I could see that it was a front. He was still dressed in his movie outfit from the previous day's fitting, and it was beginning to look pretty rank already. The writer for *Mata Hari* was sitting at the dining room table, and Carradine asked him, "Where's the nearest place to buy cigarettes?"

The writer was from Paris. Carradine was in his own house, so the question did seem a little odd. Nevertheless, the writer mumbled something and Carradine started out the door, past the stacks of movie film. Inasmuch as I had gone everywhere but to the bathroom and to bed with Carradine since I'd arrived, I got up to accompany him to the store. Then I thought better of it, given the sense I had that he was feeling a bit uncharitable. I sat back down and had to wait only ten minutes for the payoff.

He stumbled in out of the hot, bright sunlight, gripping his solar plexus as if someone had kicked him in the stomach. I thought it was an act until I saw the blood. His face was the color of the moon and he was bleeding from the head and neck. His mouth was open and he was making a sick, glottal sound, gulping air as if something were caught in his throat. As he lurched across the room, I jumped up and ran over to him.

"I just had a wreck," he gasped, and went right past me to find Linda in the bedroom.

There was a pause, like the seconds between lightning and thunder, and then Linda came rushing out, grabbed my arm, and said, "Come on," in a way I knew meant trouble and also meant I could not refuse. I followed her out into the driveway toward her Mercedes and stopped the minute I saw the Ferrari. The driver's side was demolished, the left rear tire blown open, pieces of it hanging off, and the car sat at an odd angle like a cripple. The left window had been up when the collision occurred and had been blown into the cockpit with such force that it looked as if someone had spilled a basket of ten-carat emeralds in there. The universe that stood between what that little car was and what it had been was so vast it was heart-breaking, and I was convinced, looking at it, that Carradine was far more seriously injured than he realized.

"Come *on*," Linda was saying, and I jumped, following her into the Mercedes, to which she had apparently found her keys, for she drove out of there with vicious purpose.

"David had an accident," she said, staring straight out the windshield, her teeth locked together. "He hit another car and hurt some people. It's a hit-and-run."

We were already on the Pacific Coast Highway, heading north, and if I'd had any thoughts of maintaining a professional distance, I had no reason to entertain them any longer.

"I want you to listen," Linda said. "You're going to leave me there. I want to make sure they know that he's not running from it. Take down this number." I got out my pen and she gave me a phone number for Carradine's doctor. She instructed me to get the doctor to the house right away to look at Carradine and then have him taken to the house of a friend, where he could stay until everything cooled down. I didn't bother asking her what to do if David needed to go to a hospital. I had a feeling he'd rather die than submit to that.

It wasn't far to Paradise Cove, where a crowd had gathered around police cars and a little red foreign sedan that was more or less destroyed. Linda jumped out and I was busy getting the awkward Mercedes out of there, but I did see a woman bleeding and looking around in that vague, awe-struck way people do when they've been injured so suddenly that it may take weeks for them to comprehend exactly what happened. Fortunately, the police didn't see Linda get out of the Mercedes, so I blended back into the crush of Sunday traffic and raced to the house.

Carradine sat on the couch, looking very ill. He had mopped some of the blood off his face and neck and was holding his chest and abdomen. He tried to smile as I went in, but it didn't work out too well. I asked him how he was, and he just raised his eyebrows and flicked the corners of his mouth, as if to say, "How the fuck do you think I am, asshole?"

I explained to him what Linda had instructed me to do. I mentioned the friend's house where she said I should take him.

"That's a very intelligent idea," he said, as if I'd just suggested a particularly good change in the story line of the movie in which he and I were starring.

Then we heard the first radio outside.

"Police," I said.

"I'm going out the back door," Carradine said, and he got up like a wounded gazelle and was gone. I had to stop for a second and wonder if he had ever been there to begin with, so complete and abrupt was his disappearance. The house was utterly silent, and there was no one home but me; a police radio was was barking so close outside I thought the car was coming through the house. And at that moment, I remembered what I was doing there. I put on my press credentials. I'm not sure what made me do that, but I did and I walked out into the sunlight to greet the single police car with two men getting out of it. When they saw me, the man in the passenger seat just sat back down, hugging what appeared to be the barrel of a shotgun. The other crouched down a little and pointed at me as if he had already drawn his gun.

"Who was driving that car?" he demanded, pointing to the demolished Ferrari. He was genuinely scared and very young, and they are the worst kind. The young ones haven't learned enough about the world to have equanimity. And the scared ones . . . well, that's what the guns are for.

"I don't know," I said. My mouth had gone dry the moment I heard the radio, and it wasn't all that easy to talk. There is certainly one thing about being deep in. When you find yourself there, you aren't going to mistake it for any other place.

"Where's David Carradine?" he shouted.

"I don't know," I said again. He straightened up then, seeing that I hadn't started shooting yet. He unhooked his revolver and loosened it from its holster. My heart sank.

"Who are you?" he demanded.

"Look," I began, taking a step forward, then thinking better

of it and taking another step backward. "I'm just a reporter."
I tapped my press badge in case he hadn't seen it already. "I'm
looking for David Carradine, too."
He looked at me in such a way that I knew he was convinced
I was lying. "No, you're not!" he screamed—he did not seem
capable of saying anything except at top volume. "You're an accessory to a felony!"
"No," I said as calmly as I could. "I just flew in from Chicago. I'm a reporter. I'm looking for David Carradine."
"Shut up! Shut up!" he screamed. His buddy in the car was
fidgeting, and it was making me almost as nervous as they
were. "You stay right there! Don't move!" Two more police
cars arrived as he was screaming at me. "Now, don't move!"
I was thinking of all sorts of things at that moment, but
moving was not among them.
Numerous other cars began arriving and discharging police
as the young cop growled, "If he wants to play it this way, this
place is going to be crawling with cops." And he was right. If he
had just had the presence of mind to turn around, he could have
seen them, too.
California Highway Patrolmen began filing by the fire-
engine-yellow Ferrari as more and more cars arrived. They'd go
around to the driver's side, inspect the brutal folds and creases
and tears in the sheet metal, peer inside at all the glass, poke a
finger into the exploded tire, and then just shake their heads
and hustle their sidearms to a more comfortable position. It was
well known that the cops around Malibu wanted Carradine's
head on a platter. And now they had their chance.
Except that Carradine was nowhere to be found. And they
did not have a search warrant.
The nervous kid who wanted to bust me rested his foot on
the rocker panel of his car and called in the license-plate number. "Freddie Ocean Ocean Lulu," he said, embarrassed by what
he'd just spelled out and looking more pissed with each passing
moment.
The radio coughed and crackled. "Ferrari, yellow," it said,

"one niner six seven. Carradine, David," and so on. Carradine had told me that the FOOL on his license plate was the tarot-card fool. At this point, however, it could have been any old fool.

Part of Linda's plan for me was that I get the doctor to look at Carradine, effect the escape, and then return to get Linda. Of course, I would never participate in a crime to such an extent, but now I had no choice, being detained as I was by a growing swarm of highway patrolmen. Fortunately, at the scene, Linda heard a police radio say that they had a witness at the house (that's me—apparently my status had degraded somehow from accessory to witness without the young cop's say-so) and she walked back the quarter mile or so to intervene.

The crowd of policemen maintained a very professional, courteous front with her. As she told me later, "They know that I'm not afraid of them and that I'm not going to shoot them." She politely declined to answer questions, and they politely allowed as how they were going to impound the car. Directly, a tow truck arrived and Linda gasped, "Oh, God!"

"What is it?" I whispered.

"He's towed us so many times, he's practically like family," she said and went over, smiling, to greet the young bearded man with the tow truck. She explained that the Ferrari could not be towed. It had to be carried on a flat-bed. I don't know how she thought towing could do it any more harm, but the man shrugged and left with his tow truck, anyway.

By that time, things had calmed down all around, except for that one young cop who had wanted to arrest me. He did not look at all pleased with the way the drama was progressing. He looked like a mean dog who'd had his bone taken away by a meaner one. During the course of events, almost every cop there had walked up to him, pointed to me, and asked. "Who's he?"

Each time, the kid had shrugged, embarrassed, and admitted grudgingly, "He says he's a reporter." It seemed to irk him to no end.

The flat-bed arrived, took on the Ferrari, and departed. The police began to get back into their cars and disperse. The show was over. The young cop couldn't get his car started, and each time he cranked it, he seemed to get more and more angry, until it finally turned over with a sound like a safe falling down a fire escape and he squealed up the sloping driveway and raced away before a rooster tail of dust and gravel.

As the last car was pulling away, the cop behind the wheel stopped at the head of the drive and signaled to me. I walked up to him and leaned in the window. "You want a ride outa here?" he asked politely. I didn't know what he meant at first. Then I realized that he correctly assumed I was just a reporter, stranded out there, and that I might need a ride somewhere.

"I think I'll just stick around and see what happens," I told him.

"Suit yourself," he said, and drove off.

❖   ❖   ❖

The black truck a quarter mile ahead of us had three people in it. The one on the right—the lady with the sun hat, who appeared to have just come from the beach—was David Carradine. The two other people in the truck were friends doing a favor for a buddy in trouble. Deep trouble. Steel château, felony trouble, the kind that makes you realize that, in this society, you can pay someone to do almost anything for you, but there is no one you can pay to serve your time.

"David watched the whole thing," Linda said, driving the Mercedes with the abrupt, jerky movements of someone who was scared and trying to be careful. "He was across the street, hiding out and watching the whole thing come down." I couldn't tell whether she thought that was terrific or awful or both.

We were finally on our way to Keith's house up in Topanga Canyon, taking the long, scenic route through the mountains to avoid detection. "The cops never come up in here," Linda assured me as a police off-road vehicle whipped past us going the other way. "See?" she said, and laughed nervously, as if to say, They're on their way *out.* "David and I had a fight," she explained. "Whenever we have a fight, he goes off like that." It seems Carradine was very upset that he had not been awakened early enough to get to Keith's on time. He blew up at Linda, who thought she was doing him a favor by letting him rest and by delivering his invitations for him. He lit out in his Ferrari to burn off a little venom, and when he was turning the car around in Paradise Cove, he pulled out onto the Pacific Coast Highway and didn't see the car coming. He got T-boned.

By the time we were riding along through the mountains, we knew several things. The entire coast line was crawling with cops out to get Carradine. The doctor had examined him and pronounced him badly banged up (separated ribs and what not) but probably not ready for a hospital stay. The people in the other car were also banged up, cut a little, but at least Carradine wasn't staring down both barrels of an involuntary manslaughter charge. And finally—perhaps most important— the party was being held over on Carradine's account. Even Walter Hill was waiting ("Have you ever known Walter to stay at *any* party for more than an hour?" Carradine had asked Linda earlier, when he was angry).

"I don't understand it," Linda mused, almost to herself.

"What?"

"He asked about the car." She frowned and shook her head. "He didn't ask about the other people. He was concerned about how the *car* was."

The welcome Carradine received at the mountain hide-out was as expected—the wounded warrior returning. Keith put his hand in David's hair and just looked at him with tenderness and despair, as if he'd seen it all before and knew he'd see it all again, until one day they came and told him that his brother had finally gotten so deep in that he wasn't coming out again. Death and dismemberment in a cowboy picture is one thing. Everywhere else it's another matter entirely.

Carradine was clearly hurt. Just to watch him try to move was painful, as if he were four hundred years old or a master of t'ai chi, practicing for the last battle. On Keith's shoulder, he barely made it to the front door and then sat on the first thing that presented itself—the piano stool. Someone brought him watermelon and he began eating slowly.

"He's begun a fast," Linda explained, and informed me that the doctor who had examined him was holistic and didn't approve of drugs. "But he's got a real M.D. and all," she hastened to add.

"Uh-huh," I said.

Everyone wanted to know what had happened. Carradine had gotten that old smile together again, the one where he has the bazooka pointed at his head. In his bloodied, rumpled, and ripped movie costume, he now looked like the baddest slunge of a modern-day cow-puncher that ever spat blood. I don't know, maybe I'm just not deep in enough to appreciate such subtleties, but I couldn't help wondering how come nobody had put two and two together and figured that if Carradine was in such bad shape, there must be some other people out on the highway, too. And what were they doing right now? No one asked. It didn't even seem to matter.

"The best part," Carradine said with quiet, pained relish, "was going out the back. I was going through the bushes, shot in the side." Then he told a story about a movie he'd done in which he was climbing onto a moving train, escaping, and was shot in the process. He lay on the floor of a cattle car, and his line was, "Oh, God, I'm gonna die in a cattle car." Now he said that was just what was going through his mind as he crawled and stumbled through the bushes, escaping the police: "Oh, God, I'm gonna die in a cattle car."

Then Linda launched into a rather embellished description of how I'd "held off nineteen police cars by scaring them" with my press credentials. Keith turned slowly toward me with a smile that seemed to say he knew a damned sight better than to believe that crock of horseshit. He arched his eyebrows.

"Long Rider, eh?" he asked.

❖   ❖   ❖

Monday morning, bright and early, found us in dubbing room seven at MGM in Culver City, remixing some of the last fragments of sound on *Americana* for the big showing Wednesday night. An engineer sat at an enormous computer-operated mixing console facing a full-size movie screen at the bottom of which was a digital readout of footage and frames. He seemed concerned about Carradine's condition.

"Time," Carradine assured him, "is the cure for everything but lies."

The rerecording took a couple of hours, and then we retired to editing room 151 to finish the job.

"At least you got to drive the car," Carradine allowed.

"Yeah," I agreed, "but why did you leave the scene of the accident?"

"I was just hurtin' so bad," he said. "I'm not gonna let a little thing like the law stop me."

In the tiny editing room, barely big enough for the Moviola and storage racks, Carradine's editor worked silently and expertly, cutting the film. And the only time I saw even the vaguest glimmer of something you could call regret was when Carradine unscrewed the cap on a pint of Cuervo gold and took a thoughtful sip. He was standing and had been trying to sit down, but each time he began to sit, it was too painful and he'd straighten up again. Finally, he just stood there smiling, as if to say, Ain't I a sorry shitass? Then he shook his head sadly and said, "I wish I lived a little better."

So did I. Word had come through the lawyers that he would be arrested on sight.

Upon my arrival in California, I had abandoned my rented AMC Concord in the MGM lot, but by Monday night, it had taken the place of the Ferrari in the driveway at the Malibu house. Carradine stayed up in the canyon with Linda, while I continued to sleep at the beach house, making forays into the mountains or out to the city to keep up with David. I had been told the police were watching but saw no sign of them. Up at Keith's, things were quiet, Lord Buckley rapping softly in the background ("And that's when I first saw the bear"). Linda told me, "David said he was glad he got the wreck over with here so he didn't have to have it in Africa. We fought so he could have it here." That made about as much sense as anything I'd seen so far, so I just nodded.

Linda had gone to a veterinarian with some cock-and-bull story about one of her horses having a sprain and her own vet having died and got the man to give her some DMSO—dimethyl sulphoxide, a drug not approved for human use but said by some to have analgesic properties. She began treating her husband with it for his soreness, and he wandered around Keith's living room and kitchen, his shirt off, his wild map of tattoos agleam with the oily salve.

Wednesday night, the screening of *Americana* took place as planned, a great affair at Paramount, a packed house and a warm reception. "It's not a movie," Carradine later told me Hill had confided to him, "it's poetry." And Carradine hastened to explain that Hill was being neither coy nor complimentary.

Then something very strange happened. The entire problem of the hit-and-run just went away. As if it had never happened. I'd never seen anything quite like it. And soon even the facts began to change. The story began to go like this: "Hit-and-run? *What* hit-and-run? There was just an accident, that's all."

As the week drew to a close, the story had changed so much that it seemed Linda had also been in the Ferrari at the time of the collision and Carradine had been so injured that he had left her at the scene to attend to the others while he went to seek badly needed medical attention. And as far as culpability was concerned, Carradine had merely been poking the nose of his car out of Paradise Cove on a busy Sunday when some unlocal yahoo broadsided his beautiful automobile. Fault? Whose fault? It was an *accident*, plain and simple.

At the end of the week, Carradine was still in costume for his next picture and hadn't worn the boots enough to muss up the brand-name tag that still hung from one of them. He was getting set to fly to South Africa and right into the teeth of the

Screen Actors Guild strike, which would cripple the business during the summer of 1980 and fuck up the fall television season. He was still staying up at Keith's house. "We'll have to move out of Malibu," Linda had said. "They're really down on us now."

I asked Carradine what would happen. He said nothing at all would happen.

"Why?"

He shrugged. "My lawyer worked it out."

"But how?"

Carradine shrugged again. Linda couldn't explain, either, and when I called her back over the next few months, the trouble about the wreck had disappeared and Carradine was off in Africa and there was still no explanation of how it all had happened. Linda was back in the Malibu house with Kansas. No one had picked up *Americana* for distribution. No one wanted it.

All through my stay, I had tried to figure out whether it was a pose with Carradine. And in wondering, I had remembered a story a friend of mine once told, about a kid whose parents got him a trombone. He learned to play it and became fairly good at it. So he joined the high school band and did all right. Then, in college, it seemed they needed a trombone player, so he got into the college band and did four years of it. By the time he got out of college, he was a pretty damned good trombone player and, since jobs were scarce, he began taking jobs playing trombone. Well, that went on and one day he woke up in a cold sweat in the middle of the night. He was forty-five years old and he was terrified. "Oh, my God," he whispered to himself, "I'm a trombone player." And that was really the closest I could come to explaining the things David Carradine did.

THE ROCK 'N' ROLL HEART OF ROBERT JARVIK

> *Strange as my circumstances were, the terms of this debate are as old and commonplace as man.*
>
> —ROBERT LOUIS STEVENSON

On good days, he seemed normal enough. About eight in the morning, his black Toyota Celica would pull into the parking lot at Symbion headquarters at old Saint Mark's Hospital, an institutional red-brick building on the northern outskirts of Salt Lake City. He'd stride in, carrying his briefcase, collegiate and neat in his dark blazer and bright tie, and he'd even get his own coffee from the little lunchroom. Then he'd sit in his office in an arctic blast of air conditioning, signing letters and glancing now and then through black Levolor blinds at the first five hundred-foot ripples of the Wasatch mountain range— yellow, rocky hills that seemed to become incandescent in the growing heat of the day.

He'd talk on the telephone with potential customers— usually the directors of heart-transplant programs—and he would charm them, being by turns witty and sober. He had a way with people.

His office walls were covered with awards and with pictures of the people who had played significant roles in the develop-

ment of the artificial heart, most of all himself. (From William
A. O'Neill, governor of Connecticut: I AM PLEASED TO DESIG-
NATE FEBRUARY 14, 1985, AS DR. ROBERT K. JARVIK DAY IN CON-
NECTICUT.) On a bookcase behind his desk, various hearts and
pieces of hearts lay in disarray, like the castoff idle tinkerings
they might have been, had he not had a compulsion to design
and build things—not only the artificial heart but the artificial
ear, a surgical stapler to replace stitching, and an internal power
pack to run an improved artificial heart.

On good days, Dr. Robert K. Jarvik, president of Symbion,
Inc., the company that manufactures the Jarvik-7 artificial human heart, had the appearance of a successful entrepreneur
who had everything—intelligence, style, money, talent, good
looks, youth, and a sense of humor.

Then there was the weekend I spent watching him design a
new dildo.

True, I had seen hints that there was more to this man than
met the eye. The ties, for instance. The blazers and slacks and
shirts were ordinary enough. But the ties. . . . They were sometimes lavender or lilac, sometimes shiny, sometimes almost—I
don't know—*punk*. There was also the high-pitched giggle. Dr.
Jarvik had a way of delivering a line, deadpan, and then following it with a little squeak-cough that turned out, upon close
examination, to be a laugh. And he had a crooked smirk that
pulled his upper lip way back over his teeth; it could be coy
or menacing, depending upon how he used it. He also had a
quirky sense of humor, as when he gave me a T-shirt showing
the human heart and turned to tell his secretary, "Look, he's
got a heart-on." Giggle.

Still, it was nothing I could put my finger on when I first
went to visit him in Utah. It was the second time I met him,
when he came to Chicago, that I saw the other side of Dr.
Robert Jarvik.

He had been on a tour for Symbion, visiting hospitals, uni-
versities, and scientists around the Midwest. Public relations
for the artificial-heart program takes up a lot of his time these

days, and it gets wearying, traveling from hotel to hotel. Besides, not everyone wants an artificial heart. Some people would rather stick with their own hearts, no matter how pesky the darned things get. It's hard to believe, but some people would rather die than have an artificial heart.

So Jarvik was traveling around, proselytizing; and one day, in an airport in Arkansas, he met a woman—call her Joan of Ark. I don't want to use her real name, because she may not want to know Jarvik after she finds out that he's thinking about mass-producing the dildo he designed for her, the one with the unicorn on the end. Besides, she's got her own children, and they may not want everybody to know that Jarvik fell in love with their mother in an airport in Arkansas. In fact, I've changed the name of the state, too, just to be on the safe side.

"I feel like a teenager," Jarvik told me when he phoned to say he would be arriving in Chicago with Joan of Ark for the weekend. "I've only known her for a week. She's great, though. She likes to go camping when there are tornado warnings out."

"Hey, cool," I said.

They were going to spend a romantic weekend in that Toddlin' Town, hitting all the best restaurants and (presumably) hoping for heavy weather. Then Jarvik was scheduled to go off to Milwaukee to visit the heads of a new artificial-heart program there, and Joan of Ark was scheduled to go back to the rest of her real life. Jarvik suggested that maybe we'd go out to dinner Saturday night, he and Joan of Ark and my wife and I. It sounded like a good opportunity, journalistically speaking.

But tragedy struck: Joan of Ark couldn't make it. Something had come up at home. Jarvik was left alone in Chicago for the entire weekend with *nothing to do.*

He called again: Could I maybe find him a nice, interesting, beautiful lady companion to take to dinner Saturday night? I told him he could dine at my house. "Well, if you think of any interesting lady who might like to accompany me . . . ," he suggested again.

"So," I said to my wife as I hung up the phone, "guess who's coming to dinner."

❖   ❖   ❖

The assignment had begun normally enough: Interview Jarvik and find out what sort of man manufactures hearts. He was the principal designer of the Jarvik-7, which is now the best known of several such devices in the burgeoning field of artificial internal organs. I flew out to Symbion headquarters in Salt Lake City and met the man and had the grand tour of the plant. True, there were undertones that led me to believe I wasn't getting the complete Dr. Jarvik; but I was willing to let him present himself as he chose. That was his prerogative, and I wasn't there to overturn his soil, just to interview him. Indeed, while at Symbion, I discovered the serious, competent side of Robert Jarvik. He did, after all, develop the first workable artificial human heart; and he did raise twenty-five million dollars to start the company that manufactures it; and without him, a number of people who are now alive and extremely grateful would almost certainly be dead. But where Jarvik is involved, no matter how grave the issue, there is always another twist; and it takes a while to catch on to that. Take the case of the second implantation of a Jarvik-7 in a human, that of William Schroeder. (The first recipient, Dr. Barney Clark, lived 112 days.)

With Jarvik, things must always be just so. If they are not just so, he becomes irked and changes them. It is that compulsion, along with his ability to block out all but his own goals, that may have allowed him to complete work on an artificial heart that had been under development by dozens of others for decades. So it was nothing out of the ordinary when Jarvik moved into a hotel room near Humana Hospital Audubon in Louisville, Kentucky, and decided that he had to rearrange the furniture. He wanted a desk to write on, and it had to be in just the right place, by the window, for the early light and the view: writing desk, mirror, bed, window, muted pastels, a cup of coffee at 9:45 A.M.

Jarvik keeps a diary. He carries it with him and writes of the most minute and seemingly trivial matters, right next to what he hopes will one day prove to be profound theories of the universe. He made sure I read excerpts from his diary when I went to visit him:

> I think Bill Schroeder is going to do very well. I still see him clearly in my mind's eye, overwhelmingly stronger than Barney ever was. I can see him stand up and walk down the hall with the portable driver. This is possible and this is now where I set my hopes for him: that he will do well—be home from the hospital in less than two months—and find himself feeling well and able to walk outside when new leaves open next spring.

If physicians had read that diary at the time of Schroeder's operation, when Jarvik wrote it, they might have been more than a little worried by his optimism. They knew there were many problems with the artificial heart, and Schroeder would be lucky to live as long as Clark had lived. But Jarvik is an optimist, not a realist. His optimism stems, in part, from his ability to make the wildest of his dreams come true. That childlike quality circumscribes and defines his life. Asked where he'd like to live, he said, "I'd like to live in Seattle, if we could get rid of the clouds." The remarkable thing about Jarvik is that if he moved to Seattle, he might very well get rid of the clouds.

When I first met him, we spent half a day discussing the most esoteric, mystical, artistic, and scientific subjects imaginable, from his desire to fly in space (preferably with Sally Ride) to his conviction that he has discovered, by logic and without the aid of higher mathematics, the ultimate nature of all matter in the universe. Jarvik is not a surgeon; he is not even a practicing physician. He received an M.D. but never did an internship or took a residency. When the talk turns to matters of biochemistry, his eyes appear to glaze over. What, then, is he? Alchemist? Artist? Entrepreneur? As I read Jarvik's journals, passages from a Robert Louis Stevenson novel kept coming back to me:

> Though so profound a double-dealer, I was in no sense a hypocrite; both sides of me were in dead earnest; I was no more my-

self when I laid aside restraint and plunged in shame, than when I labored, in the eye of day, at the furtherance of knowledge or the relief of sorrow and suffering.

Observing the surgery on Sunday morning, Jarvik wrote in his diary:

> Now 8:17—Mr. Schroeder's chest has just been opened. . . . Things are very calm. No one is talking. Surgery is proceeding very directly. There is the presence of cold air and the hum of the video recorder. . . . No talking.
>
> 8:35—Opening the pericardium. There is a major difference compared to Dr. [Barney] Clark. Then we had the feeling that he might arrest and not survive the last few minutes while he was being put on bypass.
>
> 9:25—Progress is steady but slow. The chest and pericardium are now widely open. The heart is beating—the right stronger than the left, but both ventricles are moving only slightly.
>
> 9:50—Now on bypass. The heart went into V-tach and now is stopped. The aorta is cross-clamped.
>
> 9:56—Apex is clamped. DeVries is beginning to cut out the heart.

It was two days later before Jarvik could fully relax; after the operation, Schroeder began bleeding heavily and had to be cut open again.

Somewhere along the way, through the extremes of elation and disappointment there in Louisville, the wild swings of emotion, Jarvik had met a woman. That special electricity had passed between them, and they had sworn they'd try to get together. Of course, the ultimate in optimism is to find love in the midst of adversity. It's the stuff of which classic novels are made. Stevenson described a similar feeling this way:

> There was something strange in my sensations, something indescribably new and, from its very novelty, incredibly sweet. I felt younger, lighter, happier in body; within I was conscious of a heady recklessness, a current of disordered sensual images

running like a millrace in my fancy, a solution of the bonds of obligation, an unknown but not an innocent freedom of the soul.

After days of medical emergencies, during which Schroeder was snatched back from the brink of death time after time, Jarvik sat at the writing desk by the window in his room and took a photograph of himself in the mirror—for posterity. Jarvik fasts and does sit-ups and rides a bicycle in the Wasatch foot-hills to ward off the transformation of aging. A man of thirty-nine years, small and thin, with boyish good looks and black hair touched here and there with gray, he snapped his picture again. And again. Only now he looked haggard in the hoary No-vember light.

Stevenson wrote:

> I lingered but a moment at the mirror: The second and con-clusive experiment had yet to be attempted; it yet remained to be seen if I had lost my identity beyond redemption and must flee before daylight from a house that was no longer mine; and hurrying back to my cabinet, I once more prepared and drank the cup, once more suffered the pangs of dissolution, and came to myself once more. . . .

That day, Jarvik shaved and dressed and visited Schroeder, who was finally out of immediate danger and breathing on his own. The Jarvik-7 artificial heart clicking away in his chest felt better than his own heart, Schroeder said. At one point, Jarvik became so confident in his achievement that he promised Schroeder he'd take him fishing one day. Schroeder believed him, too, so they set the date.

Jarvik reassured the television reporters as they were drawn to the bizarre event. He looked good on camera. He'd been on the cover of *Time*.

The next night, Jarvik sat in his hotel room, waiting for the mystery lady. He wrote:

> It is ten at night and I have a bottle of champagne with two glasses waiting for a phone call or for the lady with the kiss in

the dry-ice bubble to show up at my door—as she said she would
if she can get away. This is the way life goes—to celebrate such a
moment so long in coming with a new friend.
    OK, telephone.
    OK, doorbell. . . .

❖   ❖   ❖

For some time, I had been promising my four-year-old daughter
that we'd go to the Field Museum of Natural History. So when
Dr. Jarvik came to town unexpectedly early, we invited him to
go along. Then, on the way, he announced that he had to have
some Polyform modeling compound, a special white-plastic
material that looks like Spackle and can be molded and then
baked in the oven until it hardens to the consistency of wood.
There was a sense of urgency about his mission. Having visited
Jarvik at Symbion, I knew all about special modeling materials.
I knew he had made the first Jarvik-7 hearts by hand, pouring
Lycra plastic, layer after layer, over a mold. In fact, the hearts
were still being made that way by technicians in a special clean
room when I took the tour; so I naturally assumed that he now
needed Polyform to make a model of some sort for his trip to
the hospital in Milwaukee. Or perhaps he had just been struck
by an inspiration and was going to invent some new medical
device before our very eyes. This was important, I thought.
This was medical science.
    We stopped at the largest art store in our area but had no luck.
All the way downtown, Jarvik inquired about other stores;
by the time we reached the Field Museum, I had begun to wonder if I might be standing in the way of some vital medical
invention.
    In the Field Museum, I observed Jarvik for signs of stifled
scientific creativity. From afar, dressed in blue jeans, a dark
suede jacket, and white Reeboks, he looked like a student—
short, intense, emaciated, hands jammed into his pockets, in
close examination of the elk and antelope horns on display in
the mammalian-fauna room.

When we left the museum, we were fortunate enough to find a large art store that was still open and sold Polyform. Jarvik bought himself a load of it and bought my daughter some colored modeling clay as a gift. When we got home, she and he spread out on the kitchen table to make their models.

They had a similar method of working, except that Jarvik was more demanding, sending me down to the basement for iron wire for the core of his model and upstairs for carving tools and here and there for kitchen knives, *satay* skewers and whatever struck his fancy as he massaged the white Polyform into a long, thick roll. I didn't mind all this; after all, I might be able to say I had had a hand in making the Jarvik-9 or something.

They both worked all afternoon, side by side, heads down, muttering now and then, conferring with each other, commiserating, concentrating on their work, smearing the clay around.

My daughter nibbled on snacks to keep from getting hungry while she worked. Jarvik fasted, as was his avowed habit. In fact, the only sustenance he would take was diet Coke and Tylenol. I offered him regular Coke, but he said, "No, it has, you know, *nutrients* in it."

Only when he could stand it no longer, just before I was about to serve dinner, did he begin roaming the kitchen like a hungry cat, rummaging in the refrigerator and the cabinets, grabbing whatever he could find to put into his mouth. At one point, he even took a piece of lettuce that I was in the act of pushing down the garbage disposal. He rescued it, rinsed it off, and popped it into his mouth.

By the time dinner was ready, it was clear that he was not making a scientific breakthrough in my kitchen. No doubt about it: It was a unicorn dildo.

He explained that when he was in high school, his parents had gone to Japan and had brought him back a piece of an ivory tusk that was about the right size and shape for what he was now modeling in Polyform. Years later—after a marriage and two children and the artificial heart and a divorce and all that sort of stuff—he had promised a girlfriend (call her Lilly of the West) that he would carve her something from the tusk (and we are not talking here about carving scenes from the Sistine Chapel but, presumably, something long and stout). But he had never gotten around to it, and he and Lilly had eventually broken up. Now, looking at his prototype for the ivory carving, he shook his head and emitted a high-pitched giggle. "Lilly of the West would kill me if she knew I was making this for Joan of Ark," he said with a smirk.

After dinner that night, one of the guests who had seen the dildo sculpture confided, "I don't trust men who like unicorns."

"Yeah," I said, "but what about men who like dildos?"

Someone who had known Jarvik when he was in college later asked, "Does he still sit in the corner at parties? I used to go to these parties and see him. He'd just go into the corner and sit. No chair. Nothing. Just him in the corner."

Yes, sort of.

He squatted on the floor by the fireplace most of the evening after dinner, hugging himself, talking about himself, speculating on where he might move if he could leave Salt Lake City, land of the Mormons, where no antelope dildos roam. He brought out his video tape of a Swedish recipient of the Jarvik-7, and we watched the man make history by talking and walking and eating a huge meal and then thanking everyone because he was alive.

"That," Jarvik said, "is the richest man in Sweden." The Swedish press also said he was a gangster—now an artificial gangster. Imagine the moral questions that brings up.

Finally, Jarvik brought out the artificial heart he carries in his briefcase, and we all handled it, sipping our port by the fireplace in the living room of my turn-of-the-century house. The trees we were burning had grown to maturity before any of us had even conceived the possibility of such an invention as we now held in our hands.

The Jarvik-7 looks like a Tupperware carburetor with long, thin fuel lines coming off it. The only really exotic-looking parts of it are the Bjork-Shiley tilting-disc titanium-and-carbon-steel valves. They are as beautiful as jewelry; instead of the familiar old lub-dub, they go click-tick. The Jarvik-7 is a spooky thing to hold, though, because it has the general shape of a human heart; and you know that a man who is dangling between life and death will have his chest wrenched open and his own beating, liver-colored heart snipped out with silver scissors and forever stilled, while this wobbly plastic apparatus is shoved down into that bloody cavity to take its place.

Holding the Jarvik-7 in my hands that night, after seeing Jarvik work on his dildo all day, I stood watching him squat by the fire and hug himself and talk about himself; and I couldn't help wondering what it would be like to have one of his inventions inside my body. Joan of Ark was about to find out.

❖   ❖   ❖

The holy secrets of the body were revealed to Robert Jarvik as a youth; his father was a doctor, and he let Jarvik watch surgery when he was still in high school. It was while watching surgery that Jarvik perceived the need for a way to close off blood vessels faster than the traditional method of hand-stitching them. He invented a surgical stapler. That patent, which was bought by a large medical manufacturer, still pays him royalty checks.

It may well be that the moment it was decided that the Jarvik-7 artificial heart would be built occurred when Jarvik was a freshman architecture student at Syracuse University. "It was in the spring; I remember that very clearly," he said. He was studying for an exam in the library when someone called him to the telephone. Jarvik knew something was wrong; freshmen at Syracuse did not get paged in the library.

What was wrong was that his father had just been diagnosed as having an abdominal aortic aneurysm and was being rushed to Houston's Baylor Medical Center to go under the knife of heart surgeon Michael DeBakey. Jarvik went home and for the next few days followed his father's progress by phone, learning of the new and radical techniques being used: DeBakey sewed a Dacron patch over the delicate blood vessel that had ballooned out and threatened to burst.

The surgery worked. Technology and flesh were wed. "That made a big impression on me," Jarvik said. (Later, he would buy Dacron in a downtown Salt Lake City fabric store and use it in constructing his artificial heart.) "That's when I decided to go into premed. My parents had always wanted me to be a doctor. I didn't quite want to do that. I wanted to be an artist or something."

"Were you pressured into medical school?" I asked him.

"Yeah," Jarvik said with a smirk. "I don't think he had that aneurysm at all. I think they went to the Caribbean." Then he giggled.

In fact, he was unable to get into medical school because of his grades. He was rejected by two dozen schools before he went off to Italy, where acceptance standards were not so strict. He daydreamed his way through a year of medical school there. When he came back, he enrolled in the biomechanics program at New York University and eventually got into the University of Utah artificial-organs program, run by Willem J. Kolff, who had developed the artificial kidney and was the first man in the West to implant an artificial heart in an animal. (The dog lived ninety minutes.)

Jarvik was immediately put to work trying to improve upon the artificial heart, which was under development by Dr. Clifford Kwan-Gett, Kolff's assistant. The Kwan-Gett heart held the world's record—ten days—for keeping an animal alive.

Jarvik plunged himself into the task, working obsessively, sometimes forgetting to eat or sleep. He redesigned the device to make it fit more neatly into the chest. Before he had been there half a year, the world record was up to two weeks.

Jarvik redesigned the heart several times during the next year, and soon it was known as the Jarvik heart. But he had run into a major problem with clotting. The machinery was rough on the delicate and complex components of the blood. This caused many clots to form, which used up the chemicals in the blood that make clotting possible. Hemophiliacs have no clotting factors; that's why they don't stop bleeding. The animals that received Jarvik hearts were dying not from the artificial hearts but from uncontrolled bleeding.

Then, in early 1973, the Cleveland Clinic, where Kolff had worked before he moved to Utah, set a new record with an animal that survived seventeen days. Kolff put the pressure on Jarvik, whose talents as a designer he had come to appreciate over the months.

A Jarvik-3, as the most recent design was being called, was implanted in a calf named Betty. She lived only six days. Kolff grew even more anxious, because the American Society for Artificial Internal Organs was about to have its annual meeting. Being in second place for that meeting would mean losing his primacy in the artificial-organs field.

In April, the Jarvik-3, with some improvements, was put into a calf named Burke. The A.S.A.I.O. meeting took place in Boston, and the announcement was made that the Jarvik-3 heart had kept an animal alive for nineteen days. There was a buzzing in the crowd: Who is this Jarvik? The answer was, a twenty-seven-year-old kid from Connecticut who was not even licensed to practice medicine.

Unfortunately, by the time Jarvik succeeded in perfecting the invention, his father had died of an aortic aneurysm.

In spite of that (or perhaps because of it), Jarvik wanted his medical degree. He went to his University of Utah Medical School interview armed with his degree in biomechanics and the latest model of his artificial heart to impress the admissions officer.

"I come to you with my heart in my hands," he said.

❖   ❖   ❖

When I was out in Utah, Jarvik showed me the animal lab. In a red-brick room with a high ceiling, we watched half a dozen calves with artificial hearts standing in steel cages. Their heads stuck out between the bars so they could eat from plastic containers of hay and feed. The concrete floor was awash in urine and manure, and every now and then, a lab technician in rubber boots would hose it down the drain. The room was a cacophony of hissing and clicking sounds from the Jarvik-7 hearts and their pneumatic driving units. (William Schroeder described his as sounding like a threshing machine.) On the newer Utah-drive units, a Compaq computer traced each beat of the heart graphically on a green phosphorescent screen.

Each calf was connected to its console by one-inch clear-plastic tubing. Life flowed invisibly through that tubing: air to power the Jarvik-7. The concept of the artificial heart is elegantly simple: Air pushes a diaphragm, which changes the volume of a ventricle. As the volume gets smaller, blood is pushed out; as the volume gets larger, blood fills the ventricle again. There are two ventricles, two pneumatic hoses.

On top of each cage was a sheet of paper on which a cute name for the animal had been scrawled in black marker. Below that, a digital timer showed days and hours since the operation. They ranged from a few days to a few months. On the newer calves, I could see the stitches where the chest had been opened; but on the older ones, it looked as if the polyurethane tubing issued quite naturally from a smooth expanse of seamless hide. Jarvik reached into one of the cages and jerked on a tube to demonstrate the attachment he'd designed to prevent infection. The calf flinched in pain and tried to kick him but could not, being tethered in the cage.

"See, that doesn't pull on the skin. The force is transmitted to the deep tissues."

The calf kicked at him again.

"How long can they survive like this?" I asked.

"Months and months," he said. "But usually, we don't keep them that long. It's pretty expensive to keep these animals alive. Most of them we sacrifice before that."

On video tape, I had watched a calf receive a Jarvik-7 heart.

Like tightrope walking, it looks so easy: With a smooth stroke of a tiny silver blade, the taut skin is slit and falls away like an unzipped overcoat. The chest is split open by steel spreaders, and the big blood vessels entering and leaving the heart are tied off with loops of ribbon. The animal is put on a heart-lung-bypass machine, which pumps the blood out the jugular vein and into the carotid artery, bypassing the heart.

Then the surgeon grips the heart with silver tongs and hauls it out of the chest.

The surgery is deft, and there is surprisingly little blood up to this point. But then the surgeon plunges a pair of scissors into the beating heart, and the blood pours out. It is quickly siphoned off, as the snipping continues, until half the heart is gone—the pumping part, the left and right ventricles. That is the point of no return.

Four plastic quick-connect cuffs are sewn into place on the *vena cava*, the aorta, and the two remaining valves. The Jarvik-7 heart is actually two separate mechanical pumps (ventricles) that fit together with a Velcro attachment. The left one is snapped into place first. The air is sucked out of it with a fat hypodermic syringe; and as someone hammers on it with a hemostat to make sure there are no air bubbles, fresh red blood is pumped in to prime it. The right ventricle goes in the same way, and the two are pressed together so that the Velcro holds.

Now the animal is doomed to be part flesh, part machine, for the rest of its short life. Stevenson wrote of the duality of human nature, "I saw that, of the two natures that contended in the field of my consciousness, even if I could rightly be said to be either, it was only because I was radically both. . . ."

❖   ❖   ❖

The second day that Jarvik was in Chicago visiting me, we got up bright and early, and I told him I'd have to go shopping for food if we were going to have breakfast.

"I'll go with you," he said.

We bought all the usual breakfast foods—eggs, *The New York Times*, coffee cake—and when we got home, Jarvik clipped stories about the most recent artificial-heart recipient while I unpacked the groceries. The *Times* gave ample space to the University of Pennsylvania's achievement. It was the first serious competition for Symbion.

When asked what he'd like to eat, Jarvik said, "I think people eat too much." He refused to eat anything. I urged him to have a bite so he wouldn't get so hungry, and without looking up from the success story of his competitors, he said, "Eat whatever the hell you want."

So we fixed breakfast for three instead of four. Just as we were about to sit down to eat it, Jarvik popped into the kitchen, sat down, and started eating everything in sight. "I always do that," he said cheerfully, "refuse to eat and then pick at someone else's plate."

After breakfast, he took one look at his Polyform unicorn dildo and decided that it was all wrong. He shoved the breakfast dishes aside, got more wire, and spread out on the kitchen table again to start over from scratch. He wasn't going to rush through this thing; it was too important.

I said this must have been how it was when he was working on the artificial heart.

"The artificial heart was never this interesting," he said.

I admired his tenacity, his stamina, his single-minded sense of purpose. My daughter glued herself to his side, asking questions, offering him bits of blue modeling clay, but he managed to work around her distractions.

My wife remarked that it was a lot of work for someone he'd known only a week.

"You haven't met Joan of Ark," he said.

Apart from that, he spoke little that day, unless he needed something.

I went out for a jog. Later, my wife told me that while I was out, Jarvik had taken her aside and, giggling like a teenager, had explained to her what the sculpture was, to make sure that she knew it was a dildo. He ran upstairs and got his journal and let her read the good parts, where he described making it. He was already writing about it, though it was not finished or tested. He insisted that it was not a unicorn but an antelope. Evidently, even he thought there was something weird about guys who like unicorns, and so he gave the new model more definition to show that there were two horns, not one. ("I got a good look at those horns in the museum," he said.)

In spite of Campbell's soup for lunch, Jarvik turned up starving again that evening, right about the time dinner was ready to go into the oven. He began to root, first asking my wife, then me, if we had peanuts.

This dinner had been planned before Jarvik had announced his arrival. It was a family affair, but I thought it would be fun to have everyone together, especially since my father happens to be a biophysicist. I thought maybe Dr. Jarvik and Dr. Gonzales would say something quotable in biophysics. My mother was making enchiladas. One of my brothers was in from out of town. I envisioned this homey autumn scene as Mozart played on the Victrola.

We explained that we did not have peanuts, but Jarvik insisted. "Come on," he said, "*everybody's* got peanuts." And he started going through the cabinets. He found some walnuts and said, "See! Look!"

"Those are walnuts," I said.

"Same thing," he said.

He then decided he didn't want the walnuts and settled into a bag of raisins, stuffing handfuls into his mouth. My daughter happily joined him in that, her favorite food.

The ovens were heating up for dinner, and we were about to begin when Jarvik insisted that his dildo be baked first.

"Couldn't we bake it after dinner?" I asked. "We're about to put the food in."

"No," he said. "It only takes thirty-five minutes."

As it turned out, we all stood around for half an hour—my wife, my parents, two of my hungry brothers and I—peeking into the oven, watching the dildo turn from a snowy white to a toasty brown, until Dr. Jarvik declared it finished.

❖   ❖   ❖

During my trip to Utah, Jarvik told me about an exercise device he had invented. It was like a jump rope, he said, only weighted. It was actually a tube of heavy nylon mesh filled with birdshot. He had devised a series of exercises to be used with this Ae-rope-ic, as he called it, "almost like a dance." He showed me the prototype one day when we stopped at his apartment in the hills near Salt Lake City.

Jarvik brought up the mail and slit open a letter from Lilly. She had sent him two pages torn from *People* magazine, featuring the inventor of something called the Heavyrope, which happened to be the very thing Jarvik had invented. As I sat in the living room, I could hear him shouting from the bedroom. "Shit! I hate that! That pisses me off! Goddamn it!" From where I sat, I could see his study. In it were a weight bench with about ninety pounds on it, an artist's easel and oils, a lightweight pink racing bicycle, and a fly rod with a Pflueger reel.

Jarvik came stomping out of his room, waving the magazine pages. "Thanks a lot!" he shouted at the absent ex-lover. And to me: "You know he invented this goddamn thing in 1968? Shit! I *hate* that."

The apartment, he said, was a temporary measure. In January 1985, he had divorced Elaine Levin, a real woman with a real name who had been the real Mrs. Jarvik for seventeen years. Jarvik had lived with Lilly for a while after the divorce but moved out. Now the apartment where he lived looked lonelier than a highway motel room: a bathroom with no soap, no towel, no wastebasket. An injection-molded shower with no curtain. The kitchen was equally bare. The refrigerator was bare except for a few Heinekens.

It was, after all, only temporary.

Up the hill, there was a piece of land on a crest overlooking the Great Salt Lake. There Jarvik would build his real home, as soon as he could find the time to finish the design. (He would, of course, have to design it himself.) Then he would become the real Dr. Robert K. Jarvik. It was as if, having transformed himself once from husband and father and scientist into this new creation—this famous and dashing miracle worker, jetting around the globe—he could not find the concoction that would change him back.

I had seen it before in young rock-'n'-rollers who had suddenly come into great wealth and power: Their lives changed suddenly, and what at first seemed wonderful soon ceased to seem real to them. Unable to unlock the combination and return to normalcy, they started running. They ran toward the mirage of their real lives or away from the specter of their unreal lives; but either way, they could not stop running. Traveling in airplanes and limousines in great luxury, they found themselves filled with a dreadful sense of being lost, of drifting in space.

On the day Jarvik received the *People* article, we were to meet his ex-wife at a Little League game in which his eleven-year-old son, Tyler, was playing. On the way, Jarvik stopped to pick up something at his family's house. Although he had been divorced more than half a year and separated even longer, he still had the garage-door opener. He pulled his dusty, black Toyota (license plate UP-N-UP) into the garage at his former house, strode inside, ran quickly through a wicker basket of mail, and began to rummage in a kitchen cabinet.

"You know, she's got every kind of vitamin on earth in here, but where the hell's the aspirin?" Perhaps he had a headache from not eating.

At the ball park, Jarvik sat in the bleachers, thinking, while Elaine and their daughter, Kate, hollered encouragement at Tyler, and Elaine occasionally nudged Jarvik in the thigh when something exciting happened. "We're just hoping he hits the ball," she said. "That would be enough."

Rob and Elaine, as they were once known to their friends,

seemed to fall back into the easy familiarity of husband and wife, as if they'd never been apart. There was a gentle intimacy in the way they sat touching each other. Elaine said that if Jarvik moved, as he kept talking about doing, she would move with him.

"Do you like Salt Lake City?" I asked.

She laughed. "Do I like Salt Lake City?" she asked Jarvik. He smirked.

Some weeks later, as we were driving around Chicago, searching for Polyform modeling compound, Jarvik told me, "You ought to find some nice guy for Elaine. She's really a great person. She's just not for me. But she keeps meeting these Mormon guys, and then it just doesn't work out. Don't you know some nice guy for Elaine?" A nice guy for Elaine, an interesting lady for Rob. Sounds like they should get to know each other.

At the Little League game, Jarvik kept coming back to the article in *People* about the Heavyrope inventor. He was thinking hard, and every few minutes another strategy for making the best of a bad situation would rise to the surface. "Maybe I should just compete with them," he said.

Elaine, momentarily distracted from Tyler's attempts to hit the ball, said, "Hmm?"

The visiting-team coach threw a fit on the field.

A lady in our section of bleachers got beaned with a pop-up foul.

Jarvik was off in his own world. "He's got them jumping rope," he mused. "My rope is heavier. You can't jump rope with it. I've got a whole series of exercises worked out. Maybe I could do a book."

"Hmm?"

Tyler finally hit the ball and was thrown out at first base. There was a moment of excitement, then Jarvik went back to his reverie. An hour and a half into the game, he had arrived at this: "Maybe I should just give that guy a call and see if we can work something out. . . ."

❖   ❖   ❖

It was the final night of Dr. Jarvik's Chicago visit. The dildo had come out of the oven, piping hot on a cookie tray. The enchiladas had gone in, and we were finally seated around the big table. Mozart was playing in the background. I was at the head of the long table, with Jarvik on my left, my mother at the opposite end, my father next to her, my brothers and wife and daughter. Not much biophysics was spoken at the table. Jarvik was curiously quiet as he made quick work of his enchiladas.

We were nearly through with dinner when I wondered out loud whether or not I should have a second helping.

"Sure, have one," Jarvik said, scooping up a generous portion of enchiladas with a spatula and flipping it across the table at my plate. It missed the plate and landed on the tablecloth, splashing reddish-brown chili sauce this way and that. I saw my mother's fork pause halfway to her mouth, which remained open for some time. My father's eyes had shifted to the left as he followed the arc of travel of the flying enchiladas, and now they seemed stuck there—the eyes, that is. It was so quiet you could have heard a Bjork-Shiley valve click-ticking.

"Well, it would have been neat if it had worked," Jarvik said.

"Rob's drunk again," I said. Pause. "No, the sad part is Rob's *not* drunk." There were a few hollow laughs.

Then I was out of the room, serving chocolate cake, when I heard someone explain to Jarvik that the white stuff in the glass bowl on the table was not whipped cream but sour cream. He knew that, of course, because it had been part of the dinner. When I returned to the table, Jarvik had piled sour cream on a piece of chocolate cake and put it at my place.

"I made you a special dessert," he said. Smirk.

I went to get another piece of chocolate cake to replace the piece he'd spoiled; and when I returned to the table, Jarvik had put a second slice of cake on top of the mound of sour cream.

"I made you a sandwich," he said.

I carried both pieces away for the garbage disposal, thinking about a dinner he and I had had in Salt Lake City with his (then) girlfriend, a TV reporter—call her Electra. We were at one of the fanciest restaurants in Utah, built like an ancient

French manor house; and because Jarvik is famous in Salt Lake City, he was recognized by a number of people as we dined. After the dinner, he grabbed two long loaves of bread from a nearby shelf and made Electra fence with him as the people in the restaurant stared incredulously. Jarvik wouldn't stop fencing until he had broken Electra's loaf and knocked it to the floor.

I thought, Here is a man who is truly fearless, acting this way in front of not one but two reporters. In fact, his former wife is a reporter. Doesn't he know what reporters do? I wondered. I could only conclude that he frankly didn't care what anyone thought of him.

Or perhaps, like Stevenson's hero, he was a scientific genius who had begun to experience involuntary transformations:

> I was led to remark that whereas, in the beginning, the difficulty had been to throw off the body of Jekyll, it had of late gradually but decidedly transferred itself to the other side. All things therefore seemed to point to this: that I was slowly losing hold of my original and better self, and becoming slowly incorporated with my second and worse.

❖   ❖   ❖

On the night Jarvik finished his unicorn (now antelope) dildo at my house, after airborne enchiladas and chocolate-cake surprise, we sat around watching the news for word of the artificial-heart implant at the University of Pennsylvania, the first implant of a non-Jarvik heart in which the patient had an appreciable chance of survival. The patient was doing well, in fact, and Jarvik expressed his hope that the man would survive a long time. The success of another artificial-heart group would give Symbion that much more credibility. Moreover, he was interested in watching the news because news anchor Faith Daniels might come on. "I really like her," he said. "She's really cute." We also talked a lot about the dildo. He kept asking for paint.

"Don't you have any white spray paint?" he asked, incredulous that my home could run without it. As with the peanuts, I think he believed I was concealing white paint from him. "How about black? It would look great painted black."

I said I had none.

We watched the news and poked at the fire.

"I've got it!" he said a while later. "White nail polish. That'll work great."

I regretted that we had none. Not only did my wife not paint her nails, she most especially didn't paint them white. Not even my four-year-old daughter painted her nails white. I wondered if, in addition to sitting out in tornado weather, Joan of Ark painted her fingernails white. Maybe she was a really New Wave woman.

Later, Jarvik was speculating on how difficult it was going to be to carve the dildo out of ivory, now that he had the prototype done nearly to his satisfaction. He was talking about using some exotic reduction grinding machine at Symbion to make a copy of it. "The only problem is that you can't copy things one to one with it. It only reduces models, so this would come out about one fourth the size." We talked for a while about how it would be to sell tiny ivory antelope dildos. Then he decided that it would be better to send the thing overseas somewhere and have Micronesians or Orientals carve them out of ivory— cheap labor but the real thing.

"It would cast really nice in bronze," he said, admiring the horns, the detail, "but it would be too cold."

And later, just before going to bed: "I've got it! I can have them made of polyurethane."

"You mean Lycra?" I asked.

"Yeah, that's what the artificial heart is made of."

I envisioned the red-brick Symbion building in Salt Lake City churning out flesh-colored Lycra antelope dildos within sight of the Mormon Temple. I imagined an outpouring of chagrin and dismay.

Maybe, I thought, just maybe, Jarvik is a New Wave artist, and this is not medical science at all; it's just art so avant-garde that we can't even recognize it: all these people with artificial hearts and antelopes.

Before going to bed that night, he worried about how he would transport the protodildo without breaking it. I offered him Styrofoam peanuts, but he shook his head, deep in creative thought. He went upstairs, muttering to himself. A few minutes later, he came rushing back down, carrying one of his white Reebok gym shoes.

"Look!" he said excitedly. "It fits!" He tipped the shoe so that we could see. The dildo was nestled neatly inside.

❖   ❖   ❖

The next day, at breakfast, after Jarvik had left, we were talking about it, and someone said, "He's just inconsiderate."

"No, he's not!" my daughter piped up. "He fixes people's hearts. He's *good.*"

And therein lies the baffling thing about Dr. Robert Jarvik: He does what he sets out to do. It's difficult to argue with success. He and Schroeder actually went fishing in the summer of 1985. Schroeder caught a fish, too.

CHARIOTS OF FIRE:
THE PENSKE RACING TEAM AT
THE INDY 500

*"Roger loves to go to the track with everything
spic and span and just blow their doors off."*

—DERRICK WALKER
GENERAL MANAGER
PENSKE RACING TEAM

Rick Mears is the golden boy. Always grinning, the handsome, thirty-year-old lead driver for the Penske Racing Team has the most successful record in racing history with the single exception of Mario Andretti. Team owner Roger Penske dotes on Mears like a father with his favorite son. Sometimes they lock themselves away in the garage or sit out on the pit wall away from everyone else, and they bow their heads and talk. They speak in tight, light whispers with slight farmboy accents— Penske's from Ohio, Mears's from out in Bakersfield. Then Mears stops grinning and listens intently, nodding, gesturing when he speaks. They talk about a lot of things out there, about the geometry of oval tracks, the intimacy of rubber and road, the conservation of energy, the second law of thermo-dynamics. But most of all they talk about the meaning of life: blowing their doors off.

Mears, a slight man, no more than 150 pounds, almost always wears the same thing: soft brown corduroy pants, a brushed cotton shirt, Topsiders—earth colors—and black socks. Out at Michigan International Speedway one April day last year, he stood at a relaxed angle, squinting at the track, and then kind of drifted along, gentle, apparitionlike, his hands hanging immobile at his sides, slightly supinated, those million-dollar hands. His walk was a shuffling, almost sideways gait, as if he'd broken an ankle or a knee once or twice, but he'd never been in such a bad wreck. In that regard he'd been extremely lucky.

"Knock wood," he said, rapping his head.

Mears's voice, his handshake, the way he walks, his clothes and manner, all contribute to the overall impression: He never seems to hurry, never makes an abrupt movement; everything is smooth and controlled. I watched him drinking one night after he'd been driving at two hundred miles per hour all day long. Even his drinking was the same, sip after sip, beer after beer, never off the pace, never out of control.

In preparation for the Indianapolis 500, Penske had brought Mears to Michigan International Speedway (which Penske happens to own) to run a five hundred-mile endurance test. The stadium was empty except for Penske and Mears, Penske's other driver, Al Unser, Sr., and a few crew members. The test was a dry run to make sure the brand new car would actually go five hundred miles at race speeds without breaking something.

Mears slipped into his fireproof socks, Nomex nylon long underwear, and his red-orange Simpson fire suit with PENNZOIL stitched across the chest. Undyed Nomex is a soft, ivory-colored material. Its slightly slippery texture makes it seem not quite real. Mears has worn it all over his body ever since a pit fire in 1981 nearly burned his nose off. Mears picked up a pair of orange Simpson fireproof gloves and patted them in the palm of his hand.

"Let's see now, have I got everything?" he asked himself.

He put his black socks inside his Topsiders and placed the shoes neatly side by side. He picked up his Bell helmet, carefully wrapped the Nomex balaclava back over the impact-resistant plastic, and placed the gloves inside the helmet.

When he reached the car, he stopped and regarded it for a moment before proceeding. It was a Penske PC-11, the latest in a series of cars designed for Roger Penske. It looked superficially like most other Indycars. We've all seen them, four fat, black, open wheels surrounding a hot slash of color, in this case chrome yellow, Pennzoil yellow, Hertz yellow. Rocket shape with front and rear wings. Broad pods of body work on either side of the driver. That particular yellow picks up better on long-lens videotape machinery. Exposure is the name of the game. Speed and exposure.

But these surfaces aren't merely decorative; they act as wings. If it were possible to turn the PC-11 upside down and accelerate it to 150 miles per hour, it would take off. It might not fly very well, but it would get off the ground. Right side up, the car is forced into the road, giving it holding power in the turns. The previous year the PC-10 had been the fastest Indycar in the world, and with it Mears took his third national championship. The PC-11 was supposed to be better still. It was Mears's job to prove that it was.

He put an earphone in his ear so that he could hear Penske's voice. In his other ear he put a plastic tube that led to the pop-off valve. Thus, physically connected to a component of the car itself, Mears would hear a hissing noise when he reached cruising speed, an escaping of gas, and the tone and timbre would tell him when he had reached the limit of the machine. "Going full chat," they called it.

He put his helmet and gloves on, gingerly climbed over the fragile body work into the yellow car, and sat with his hands on the tiny steering wheel until all was ready. Steel hasps clanked together as someone strapped him into a blue, web-belt harness. The aluminum and carbon fiber tub in which he sat was so small that both his left and right shoulders could touch the sides at once.

He was at knee level to the crewmen who moved about, fueling, adjusting, tweaking, massaging. Mears's eyes moved neither right nor left; his orange gloves remained perfectly still at the four and eight o'clock positions on the soft, black, suede-covered steering wheel. In the center of the wheel it said PEN-SKE. It was Penske's car, and this was Penske's golden boy, and with the grace of God and a little luck, he was going to blow their doors off at Indy.

The black-and-yellow-uniformed crewmen faded, and only one remained, Peter Parrott. Sandy-haired and sad-faced, he stood in front of the car, signaling Mears: not yet, not yet. There was a noise behind Mears, and he moved his foot. The starter whined. Flicking his eyes left and right, he could see in the rear-view mirrors the crewmen ready to push him out. The air was shattered by the catastrophic clatter of the engine, uneasy out of its element of speed.

Parrott gave the frantic hand signal: Go, go, go! Mears put his foot down, and the roll began.

The car was nothing at slow speeds. It clanked when it walked. The engine didn't work, the wings didn't work, the aerodynamic body panels were just slabs of exotic fiber. The motor behind him thundered unpleasantly as he went through the gears, zero to sixty in 2.5 seconds, a twitch of the foot. In another second the car was poking along at a hundred. All around the track, warming up, it was awkward and unresponsive. The space shuttle strapped to a 747.

But then he put the hammer smoothly, gently down. He turned the black, knurled turbocharger boost knob on the left side of the steering wheel, and as he eased through 130, 140, 150, the controls gradually began to stiffen, and the car settled into the track and slid up into the black groove made by the whistling passage of a million tires. The sound of the engine grew smoother, more gentle, and soon Mears could hear a hissing in both ears, radio static in one, the pop-off valve in the other.

Now the car locked itself down onto the road, and Mears was forced into his seat, everything solid and deliberate, in control. The aerodynamics were working, and the noise was all behind him. Silence and soft vibration. A signboard appeared outside the pit wall. It was a tiny yellow thing like a postage stamp from a foreign land. One second it was there, the next it was gone, in the past tense. The first few times he couldn't read it, but then, like an astronaut circling earth, he grew accustomed to its rhythmic passing and finally grasped its meaning. It said he was going two hundred miles an hour.

He looked deep into the oncoming curves, aiming along the black groove in the fluid, hissing silence. Behind him the engine made its gentle vibration, massaging his back. The day was sunny and bright and quiet as he went around and around, leaving everything behind. Mears floated into time present, the past at his rear wing, the side of the cockpit gently tapping his right shoulder, the muscles of his face pulled into soft, centrifugal contours.

Then something happened. It happened so fast that he would never be able to say precisely what it was, but the cocoon of silence was broken, and the time-present world tightened down all around him. One moment he was looking at a place on the wall fifty yards ahead, deep into the next curve. The next moment the car was in the wall—of the wall—and then time seemed to slow. Suddenly it was no longer the golden, silent flying machine, it was fifteen hundred pounds of berzerk metal and plastic, and a hellacious double handful of it.

Mears steered the car into the wall, trying to keep it there, to spend all that energy and pray the contraption didn't fly upside down and scrape his Bell helmet away on the concrete. There was no sensation, only the terrible noise, roaring, thundering, Kevlar-aluminum-carbon-fiber ripping, tires exploding in air, wheel rims and turbo snails, and the long howl along the concrete wall, wondering how many of those pieces flying through the air are pieces of you and how many are the wild razor blades of the car.

Then there came a place where the wall made a little angle, an outward jutting of concrete—who in God's name designed this thing?—and when he hit that, the car ricochetted into the infield, and everything stopped.

There was a fearsome pain in his legs as he struggled to get out of the carbon fiber-aluminum tub. The PC-11 that was going to win the 1983 Indianapolis 500 lay scattered over half a mile of oval track somewhere west of Detroit.

❖   ❖   ❖

The Indycar season, sanctioned by Championship Auto Racing Teams (CART), comprises thirteen races from March through October. The Indianapolis 500 is usually the third race, and although it is not sanctioned by CART, it is still part of the circuit. Since the mid-seventies one of the greatest threats on this circuit has been the Penske Racing Team. In 1977 Roger Penske decided to open his own Indycar manufacturing plant. When his driver, Tom Sneva, got into the new PC-5 on May 14 of that year and cut it loose, his first qualifying lap at Indy was clocked at 200.535 miles per hour. It was the first time anyone had gone two hundred there. Motor sports were changed forever.

In fact, every time a major change takes place, if you look closely, you'll probably find that Roger Penske had something to do with it. He made the first plastic Can-Am car. He introduced the four-speed Indycar transmission and the four-bolt wheel and the tall gravity-fed fuel tanks with wide-mouth hoses that make pit stops so quick (and potentially so lethal, as Mears learned in that 1981 pit fire). Penske is even credited with turning racing into a big business of big sponsors. John Mecom, Texas oil millionaire and legendary race team owner, said, "Roger pioneered the business of getting sponsors involved."

Most important, however, is the fact that Penske's team wins. It has three Indianapolis 500s to its credit along with five national championships. It has taken two Can-Am Challenge Cups, six NASCAR Grand Nationals, Daytona's twenty-four-hour race, the 1976 Australian Formula One title, and two U.S. road-racing championships.

To find out what goes into making a Penske car and getting it ready to win at Indy, I followed the team through the spring of 1983. It was a little like being assigned to NASA during a two-month countdown, and the similarities were more than incidental. The PC-11 was made of some of the most exotic materials on earth, such as the carbon fiber used in helicopter blades and fighter planes, the aluminum honeycomb used in passenger aircraft, and the Kevlar plastic used in the space program. Its chief designer was not a racing mechanic but a British aerodynamicist, Geoffrey Ferris. Its fabricators were from the British aircraft industry. And like the space program, the testing of the PC-11 was not without its setbacks. The total destruction of the prototype at Michigan was just one.

The racing season was supposed to begin at Phoenix in March. When the PC-11 was brought out there for testing, however, it proved not to be as fast as the previous year's model, the PC-10. It was hastily sent back to Ferris's drawing board in Poole, England, while two quicker cars, modified PC-10s, were prepared for competition. They were never run due to rains that damaged the track and cancelled the race.

Atlanta was the next race, the only one remaining before Indy. When Mears won the pole there and set a new track record just shy of 205 miles per hour, hopes for the redesigned PC-11 ran high. At the start of the race the next day, April 17, the wild yellow blur Mears was driving pulled away from the pack so quickly that he almost lapped the field. He blew their doors off.

But halfway through the race the PC-11's ignition system melted, and Gordon Johncock drove his Patrick Racing Team Wildcat to victory. It was a bitter defeat for Penske and Mears. It had been arch-rival Johncock, driving for arch-rival Pat Patrick, who beat Mears by twenty feet the previous year in the closest race in Indy history. Worse, the Patrick team was largely a clone of the Penske team, with former Penske designers and chief mechanics giving it whatever edge it had. The Patrick Wildcat was an original design, as was the Penske car. Each had virtually identical Cosworth engines, identical Goodyear Eagle tires. Each had one of the best drivers in the world.

The real competition would be in the design of the suspension and the aerodynamic surfaces that held the car to the road— the ground effects, as they are called.

But the car that had been so quick at Atlanta in mid-April was destroyed in Michigan at the end of the month. With little more than two weeks left before qualifying trials at Indy, the Penske Racing Team regrouped at headquarters in Reading, Pennsylvania, to do the impossible once again. By May 4, general manager Derrick Walker stood in the ten thousand-square foot shop admiring two brand new PC-11s. The shop was a cinderblock structure as unassuming and functional as can be. Places where race cars were prepared used to smell like gasoline and grease. This place smelled like Kevlar, the honeycomb plastic bodywork, one of the most exotic materials on earth. It is not an unpleasant aroma: Imagine a wooden closet that's been closed up for a long time.

I sat in one of the new cars. Getting out of it was like trying to get out of a stainless steel body stocking. Laughing at my plight, Walker said, "Don't worry, when it's on fire, you find you can get out rather quickly."

He should know. He was in the 1981 pit fire. The flames went up his back, burning off his pants and shirt and hair. His recovery took nearly a year.

An intense and affable Scotsman, Walker, thirty-seven, swings his arms high when he walks, looking quickly left and right, leering, always chewing gum. He seems to be hurrying away from something. When he leered at me, his eyes showed white above and below the iris. He had curly, dark, receding hair. His face was weathered from two decades of standing in the wind and sun beside a race track. It was a marvel he could hear anything at all after listening to engines for so long. While Roger Penske was the visible force, the emblem of the team, Walker was the day-to-day brains that made it work. Penske, a multi-millionaire-entrepreneur running several major businesses at once, was a weekend warrior. Elusive most of the time, he took over in the pits when Mears drove. Walker became pit manager for the second car, driven by three-time Indy winner Al Unser, Sr. But here in the Reading shop, Walker was sovereign. Because if it didn't happen here, it couldn't happen at Indy.

Now as he stood admiring his handiwork embodied in the two yellow cars, he laughed as if he didn't quite believe it. Fluorescent tubes made uneven bars of light and shadow on a spotless red concrete floor. "Two new cars in two weeks," he said. "Pretty fantastic, if I do say so myself."

It was a little confusing. There was the original PC-11, the prototype, which had proved inadequate at Phoenix. Then there was the revised PC-11, which had gone so quickly at Atlanta and had been destroyed in Michigan. Finally there was the second revision, embodied in the two new cars on their metal stands before us. There were two cars because the Penske Racing Team is actually two teams in one, Al Unser's and Rick Mears's. Both men run each race, each with his own crew responsible for preparing and maintaining his car. In addition, a third PC-11 would be prepared as a backup in case one of the primary cars failed before qualification.

I asked if the PC-11 was going to be faster than the PC-10.

"With the PC-10 we had it sussed," Walker admitted wistfully. "The eleven is still a question. It would be nice to be further ahead, but we're not."

In fact, they were out of time altogether. The cars were to be shipped the next day to Indy, an eleven-hour drive in a specially-built semi trailer waiting at the back end of the building.

At the other end, packed for shipping, a bundle about the size of a garbage can waited on the loading dock. It was the wrecked car from Michigan, ready to be sent out for analysis, just like the wreck of an airplane would be. It was literally a bucket of parts. Yet Mears's only injury had been badly scraped shins and a broken Rolex. Already a modification had been made to prevent that from happening again—a thicker suede-and-foam wrap for the steering bar that had done the damage.

Mears's post-crash comment to me was: "Well, my Rolex came off when I hit the wall going a hundred and eighty-five. I was pretty mad." His best guess about the cause of the crash was that there had been debris on the track. At two hundred miles per hour an acorn could lay open a tire like a straight razor.

After the crash the car was redesigned, and my obvious question was: What did Geoff Ferris do that was supposed to make the PC-11 faster than the PC-10? The body work was lowered somewhat, Walker said, but whatever was done to the tunnels was cloaked in black security: No one was saying.

The underbelly of the car is the major secret. The body work on either side of the driver creates two tunnels that force air beneath the car faster than it can travel over the top of the car. This creates a low-pressure area below that holds the car down. The greater this force, the faster the cornering speed. Anyone, it is said, can go 220 in a straight line. So far no one's been able to do it all the way around the track. In April of 1983 Rick Mears was the man who had come closest, having gone 208 at Indy the previous year. Geoff Ferris did it with the PC-10 tunnels. I remembered the first time I walked into the trailer that carries the cars. Walker and I stood beneath the two PC-11s, which were suspended above us in their racks. I had a camera around my neck. He eyed it suspiciously, his eyebrows jumping. He leered at me and in his best Scottish accent asked, "You wouldn't photograph the underside of our cars, would you?"

I didn't even know what I was seeing then. The engine and transmission were housed in a long, narrow, multi-angled sheet metal shape. Its shape, coincidentally, was that of an old-fashioned coffin, laid out along the length of the car from nose to tail. The design of this engine tray was economical and clean, and where someone had bothered to make it that way, someone had also taken the time to polish the surface so that I could see the hazy image of my face in it.

On either side of this tray were the graphite gray tunnels. They were nothing more than gently curving carbon fiber surfaces, radically elongated S-shapes that would ride several inches above the track.

A mechanic walked in and saw me staring up at the car's

belly. "That's where it makes it or breaks it," he said. "Right under there. A lot of people think what makes these cars go is on top."

So when I asked what had been done to the tunnels, I was given a little smile. A nod's as good as a wink to a blind horse, Walker seemed to say. The pressure curve was moved around, massaged.

I watched the crew setting up Mears's car one day at Atlanta. Every few laps Mears brought the car into the pit and the crew, under the direction of chief mechanic Peter Parrott, swarmed over it while Geoff Ferris stood by nervously and watched. The crewmen wore black corduroy trousers, black athletic shoes with yellow stripes, and matching yellow shirts with Penske racing patches stitched on the pockets. One man measured the circumference of the rear tires, while another took the temperature of the rubber and wrote it down. Two men, working together, measured the weight being exerted by the two front tires and wrote down the results. Everything was written down. Meticulous records were kept. It was not unlike the testing of a new aircraft in that regard. To the extent that the PC-11 wasn't working, Ferris meant to know why and to fix it.

Each time Mears pulled in, Walker, Penske, and occasionally Ferris leaned into the cockpit to talk to him. He explained to them what the car was doing. Was it under-steering (pushing) so that when he turned left, the car kept going straight for the wall? Was it loose so that the back end was sliding out? A car going over two hundred miles per hour doesn't handle in response to anything you or I would recognize as steering. It flies along in a silent, super-gravity world. Sometimes you can turn left, and the car can go right. Beyond two hundred miles per hour, you've stepped through the looking glass.

Minute adjustments were made in the suspension in an attempt to get the elusive qualities that would make the car respond correctly. Tires, dampers, wing angles of attack were all changed. With each set of alterations, Mears ran a few laps, "looking for the numbers."

In the pits, a large fireproof blanket was thrown over the rear of the car to help safeguard the secret. At one point a spectator came over to peer at the exposed rear of the car. Ferris, a slight, almost ghostly Englishman who looks as if he stepped out of *The Wind in the Willows*, became agitated and discreetly nudged one of the mechanics, who covered the car's privates. To peer at the secret—it was almost blasphemous. Ferris shied away. I remembered his first reaction when I introduced myself and said what I was going to do. He looked horrified. He nearly gasped at my first few questions about how the car was designed, saying, "I can't tell you that," or, "I don't want to reveal too much." It was insensitive of me, but I had no idea, not then.

But watching the machine go, I could see what Ferris meant. The thing was only perfect on the drawing board. There or at two hundred miles per hour, and then everyone could watch, but no one could see the secret. You couldn't even read the numbers. The car was just a yellow blur. It was beautiful.

But all the secrecy may have been unnecessary. The truth is that no one can explain the difference between 199 miles per hour and 209. The "numbers" are "found" or they are not, Ferris might as well be an astrologer as an aeronautical engineer. It's Einsteinian guesswork, voodoo calculus. Tweaking a suspension, massaging a tunnel, chasing the conditions on the track with the setup of the car—it's an existential act of engineering, and when the right setup is "dialed in," the driver knows it. In 1982 it looked as if Mears were headed for that magic 220 mark. But since Atlanta (where he went almost 205) he'd lost several miles per hour. Where did they go?

Now at Reading headquarters the new cars were almost ready, and a fourth car, a PC-10 with some updated equipment on it, would be brought along to sell. And perhaps right there is a larger explanation of many mysteries concerning this sport in general, concerning the problems with the PC-11 in particular. For why, if Penske had it sussed with the PC-10, would he want to give away all those secrets, sell the car (six copies of it at that point), and start over from scratch?

"That's the sad part of it," Walker said. "That you give away a whole year's work." His look went far away. His eyes narrowed. "Last year we gave away the best car we'd ever had. The customers came in and we laid out the sheets, and there were all our secrets on the table." His voice had that resigned sadness you might hear listening to a cold-war-torn intelligence officer tell how a satellite design had slipped into Russian hands.

Penske claims that selling cars is necessary to offset the cost of racing. Perhaps that is true. But at a deeper level, coming out with a new model every year is just part of the game. The sponsor isn't buying any used cars.

The central paradox of Indycar racing, in other words, is that it has become such a technical feat that the only way to win is to make something you can't afford to hang onto.

"It might have been better to stick with the ten," Walker said, "because it's a known quantity. But you can't race against your own car. And all this puts an unbearable pressure on the team to outperform itself. Sooner or later we're going to be in a position where we find that we haven't done the best job we could have done. But we have the drive. If the car we've got now isn't the car we need to win Indy, by the end of May we'll have a revised car."

Walker spoke of his cars as if they were lines of poetry one could rearrange—delete a word here, add a metaphor there. Indeed, that was the PC-11, the poetry of fluid mechanics, form drag, vortex generation. The poetry of blowing their doors off.

❖   ❖   ❖

By 7:30 A.M. on the day the cars were scheduled to leave for Indy in the big yellow semi, more than a dozen crew members were all over the shop, massaging the new PC-11s into glittering, yellow reality. The shop was an acoustical nightmare of whining drills, hammering, compressed air screaming, coping saws, the pop of acetylene torches being lit. The Penske motto is: Whatever it takes to get the job done. And not the disappointing performance of the PC-11, or the failure at Atlanta, or even the cataclysmic destruction of their number one race car was going to keep these men from exerting the maximum effort. The vast room stayed clean during all that hectic work because every team member was involved in a continuous process of cleaning up after himself. It was the Penske touch, the last inch in the foot, as he called it.

Late in the afternoon the three cars were polished and sprayed and Windexed and Brakleened, fixered and buffed one last time until the PPG urethane paint job radiated yellow light. Then (and only then) they were wheeled into the hazy sunlight.

There was a new truck to carry the new cars. Penske had just bought it. It had never been taken on the road before. And now the cars were lifted on a hydraulic platform and carefully wheeled into the trailer's roof racks. Everyone came out to stand in the sunlight and watch. It was the first time I'd seen any Penske team members idle. Behind them the shop was so clean it looked as if no one had ever worked there.

The following day they pulled into Gasoline Alley at the Indianapolis Motor Speedway, ready to wheel out the radiant machines. When they opened the doors to the trailer, however, they found that the cars had gotten loose during the ride.

"It looked like someone had thrown a bomb in there," Walker said.

The new truck's suspension had been too stiff and had transmitted enough vibration to the cars to set them free. During the eleven-hour ride from Pennsylvania, they began jumping around, crawling up over one another, chewing up body work. The four thousand-pound damper springs exploded. By the time it arrived at Indy, suspensions, body parts, springs, struts were all over the truck. Fixing the three cars required what they call a major massage.

Later—about twenty-four hours later—a massive team effort had been exerted, and the cars were rebuilt yet again. No one even seemed to realize what a frankly unbelievable blunder it had been to take the new cars in an untested vehicle. It was all the more surprising of the Penske team, known for its constant testing.

❖   ❖   ❖

John Mecom, a legendary racing team owner, stood out on the deck of his fourth floor suite overlooking the Indianapolis Motor Speedway. Just below him in turn two was the spot where Sneva had walloped the wall his first year driving for Penske in one of the most pyrotechnic wrecks ever seen at Indy. Upside down, his car hit the wall twice, and the engine and transmission rocketed two hundred yards. The crash sent a sheet of flaming methanol roaring through the debris fence, missing the first floor suites (Penske's among them) by a few feet.

Mecom, a large, rugged Texan, leaned on the railing and stared down at the spot. "Roger drove for me," he said, recalling Penske's career as one of the top drivers in the nation in the early sixties. "At first people didn't respect him because his words didn't all run together properly. But he won, and he won a lot. He really changed this business more than anyone else. First of all, he came in thinking. Then he made friends where others might be stirring the waters. He wasn't like A. J., calling people long-haired British fags. And he didn't always have grease under his fingernails like some of us."

Mecom turned his hand palm down to inspect his fingernails, which were impeccably manicured. The Penske influence, he seemed to be saying. "R. P. was the antagonist and the mediator. And people found they had to listen to him. They still do. He goes first class, and he can afford to, because he's done the work to get the sponsor behind him. If it's a one-hundred-thousand-dollar project and he spends one fifty, the sponsor gladly picks it up because the sponsor is getting more than his money's worth."

Penske, now the recognized crown prince of American motor sports, is all business. He takes weekends off from his five-hundred-million-dollar-a-year Penske Corporation to oversee his race team, but that's business, too. He can stand in front of the television cameras and say a few choice words, but for the most part it is obvious that he considers the press superfluous.

"Basically, we don't like to talk to anyone," one mechanic said. "That's why we cover the cars. That's why we close the garage doors."

Penske puts a finer point on this xenophobic attitude with his unnerving habit of walking away right in the middle of a sentence. Karen Unser, Al Unser's wife, said, "Roger talks in half sentences. He'll be just getting to the point and he'll turn around and walk away."

Walker explained: "When R. P. walks away, the ground where he's been standing is smoking." High strung.

One day in May at Indy, I listened to Penske tell Unser about modifying the PC-10 they'd brought with them. He thought it might be a good road racing car if they didn't sell it.

". . . put that oil tank back there, huh? What do you think? Move that engine back just about that much, huh? That'd put more force here. We're shippin' that Ten-B next week, maybe sell this one or I don't know—we'll have the same bell housing and, hey, what do you think? Say, that engine wasn't leaking any or blowing or, huh?"

Al: "No, I didn't hurt it."

"So we could just move that back there and he'll make that oil tank, and huh? What do you think?"

"Yeah."

I asked Penske a question, and he turned on his heel and walked away.

Later I saw him corner a Cosworth engineer and talk him right into the garage wall. The Cosworth engineer made the mistake of suggesting that he could build his own winning race engine for a million or so dollars. Penske practically jumped down his throat with both feet.

"Do you really think you could build something, huh? That—something that would compete with this? Because—hey, I'm dead serious—do you think? Because I'd love to build our own engine. I'm serious, hey listen, do you really think? Because I'd—"

The engineer backed around the garage, muttering that he wasn't exactly in a position to take Penske up on his offer, being employed by Cosworth and all. I came back forty-five minutes later and Penske was still gnawing on him.

The first day of qualifying, two weekends before the race, Penske and his team members may have thought that the worst had already happened, but it hadn't. It hadn't rained yet. And now, shortly before Mears and Unser were due to go out and blow everyone's doors off in time trials, it commenced. Umbrellas blossomed on Gasoline Alley.

A crucial decision was made when qualifications were postponed to the next weekend. Because of Mears's crash, the five hundred-mile endurance test had never taken place. The team could stay at Indy and try to get the car going quickly only to learn too late that it wouldn't go the full five hundred miles. Or they could go to Michigan and make sure it would go the full five hundred miles only to learn that it wouldn't go quickly enough to win anything. Penske chose to run the five hundred-mile test. It went off smoothly, while other teams closed the technical gap between their cars and Penske's. Penske could have guessed that at least one or two of them would pass him.

The weather remained good enough to qualify that last weekend before the race, and when the track opened for practice, Mears was the first man out, turning 201.3 right off the bat. Penske stood at the wall, timing him, nodding his head in approval. Then Mike Mosley's Kraco March came smoking past, and Penske did a double take. "Hey, Mike, goddamn, Mosley . . . er . . . Simon . . ." The mechanism that made words for him had fried a valve.

Even to the uninitiated ear there is a noticeable difference between the sound of a car going less than two hundred miles per hour and one going more than two hundred miles per hour. In Mosley's case this ineffable difference tightened just one notch more, and all up and down the pits the attention turned toward the track as car number eighteen blurred by. Coming at us, it made an ominous Niagra Falls-Doppler sound. But its passage was like a cannon going off, ten million cubic feet of air moving all at once. Mosley was going 206.856 miles per hour. If Mears wanted the pole, he was going to have to pray that Mosley blew up his engine.

In the meantime, Unser's car burned a piston during a practice lap. Now with a little less than two hours before time trials, Walker did something remarkable, something, perhaps, that had never been tried before. He ordered an engine change for Unser's car, to be performed in ninety minutes. If that didn't create sufficient challenge, the only engine they had on hand was the one from the PC-10. It had the 1982 fuel system on it. Changing a fuel system was a major massage.

"Can we do it?" Penske asked.

"We can try," Walker said.

The Cosworth engineer Penske had chewed over the previous week, co-author of the engine in question, was pressed into service by Walker. Then the entire team, every hand available except for a couple of men needed on the other car, were put to the task of changing an engine in an hour and a half. Without a fuel system change, this process normally took better than three hours.

Garage seventy-six filled with yellow-shirted Penske men, eighteen hands on two motors, turning bolts. Suddenly all the fancy aerodynamics meant nothing, and these men were reduced to grease monkeys, elbow deep in the oily guts of the beast. The talk was constant, mostly necessary.

"We'll have to get the trumpets off."

"Just stabilize this and I'm going to twist this jack."

"Half inch."

Outside, a sound like jet engines filled the bowl of the Speedway as practice went on, turbochargers screaming.

"Does the polarity matter?"

"That is just like an oil pressure . . ."

"Is that what the diode is for?"

The work proceeded at a scarcely believable pace but never recklessly. Like Mears, they were smooth, in control, extremely quick. Records may have been set; we'll never know. In twenty minutes, the old engine was off. The transmission, rear axle, wing, and wheels sat outside the garage. Tools were scattered everywhere, nuts and bolts in trays. A small crowd had gathered to watch.

"Got some jism to put on there?"

"Where's the other bomb gone? The alternator assembly?"

The fuel system, like an artificial heart of aluminum, magnesium, stainless steel, and black rubber hoses, was lifted, wriggling, into place.

"Can we come over?" It was the new engine, ready to go. The old one was shoved aside, the new one positioned so the bolt holes matched up.

"One more lifter . . ."

"Here we go . . ."

"Pick a tool, any tool."

"Hey, who designed this thing, anyway?"

The Cosworth man, thin and British, laughed softly. He was covered with grease from his own invention.

"Peter, did you tighten all the trumpets on the right side?"

Walker, rapidly chewing his gum, returned to tell them that the car had to make an appearance on the track in order to be official. Otherwise, it wouldn't be allowed to qualify.

"OK, Nick, let's go, screw it on."

The transmission was rolled back, rear suspension and wing attached.

"Down in the back just a hair. Ooo, that's it."

"Nuts, nuts, get 'em on . . ."

Air guns whined as tires were put back.

With ten minutes to go, they buttoned up the body work and cockpit, concealing unattached hoses and partially assembled engine works, and rolled the car out into traffic on Gasoline Alley. With two minutes to spare, Al Unser's car was officially recognized. Although Unser went on to qualify the backup car, the team had just created a new spare in about an hour and a half, and you could see the satisfaction on their faces.

I remembered Penske telling me about their victory in a pit stop contest held by Miller High Life the previous week. It wasn't a very long story. He just smiled and said, "We blew their doors off."

❖   ❖   ❖

Mike Mosley went over 205 miles per hour on his qualifying run. This, it was assumed, would give him the pole position. When Mears went out to warm up his tires, he gave a little orange-gloved wave as he motored by, poking along at 100 or 110. When he cut it loose, it sounded awfully good, but the clock told the tale; at 204.301, he was a full mile per hour slower than Mosley. After a few more cars qualified, the arrangement was becoming obvious. Mosley would be on the pole, Mears in second place, and maybe one of the faster guys on the outside of the first row—Bobby Rahal or Tom Sneva.

The sixty-seventh running of the Indianapolis 500 was being called historic because it was the first time a father and son had ever been pitted against one another. Al Unser's twenty-one-year-old son, Al, Jr., was driving the Coors Light Silver Bullet, and his Eagle-Cosworth had been quick in practice. Before Al, Sr., knew what was happening, his son had taken the middle spot in the second row and the old man found himself in seventh place. And that wasn't the last surprise of the day.

By a peculiar slip, someone had drawn up the qualifying order sheet with one entrant's name misspelled. The "I" had apparently been dotted upside down. It read: Teo Fab! The young downhill ski racer came out in a brand new March car owned by the Forsythe Racing Team. Painted an unusual green color, emblazoned with the Skoal snuff trademark, it looked precisely like the little tobacco tin that Rick Mears kept in his locker. He didn't smoke, but he did dip a little Skoal from time to time. Green, as Mears and other old hands at Indy knew, was bad luck. But Fabi wasn't an old hand; he was a rookie, and besides, he was an aeronautical engineer from Milan, Italy.

When he turned up the boost and came honking out of turn four to take the green for his qualifying laps, all activity stopped in the pits as we turned to watch. It was something about the sound of Fabi's car. The sound and the fact that he was going so quickly that it was impossible to see him. When he crossed the finish line on his first lap, he was just a green smudge, a flicker of light, and that fighter bomber sound. About a minute and a half later he had officially seized the track records from Mears, one lap at 208.049, four laps at an average speed of 207.395.

The drivers, mechanics, and owners hung on the wall, their mouths open. Up and down the pits one phrase was heard repeatedly that afternoon. It was whispered with a sad shake of the head: "Fuckin' Fab!"

❖   ❖   ❖

Saturday, the day before the race, everything that could be done had been done, and Walker sat in a garage with a few crew members, watching the rain come down outside, telling pit fire war stories and chewing his gum faster and faster.

". . . fuel roarin' out the vent onto his leg . . . if that had caught fire he'd-a been finished, 'cause he'd-a gone roarin' down that pit lane, and they'd-a never stopped 'im . . ."

And later, as the day pressed in on him: "There's never been this strong a field, not for a number of years. There are eight cars out there that can do it. Teo's team has done everything right so far." The threat of the Patrick team seemed somewhat remote now. Number two driver Johnny Rutherford had crashed car forty twice, the second time sustaining serious leg injuries when he hit the wall exactly where Gordon Smiley had died the previous year. Patrick brought in Bill Whittington to drive, and he crashed, too. Johncock in number twenty simply couldn't go as quickly as he had gone before. The magic numbers were not to be found. But there were Rahal, Sneva, Ongais, and Foyt, always Foyt. Walker paused, sighed. "You can't believe you've fucked around for a month just to lose."

The entire field had a case of nerves (everyone except Rick Mears, who was perpetually unperturbable). Karen Unser called it "Jickie Day." I asked her what that was. She grinned provocatively and sort of jickied around a little to demonstrate.

Sunday morning the weather held, and Clive Howell, chief mechanic on the backup car, sat in the empty garage, patiently scanning the radio channels, writing down the frequencies for each important team so he could intercept their transmissions during the race. The 500 was taking on the character of a major military operation.

Just before ten o'clock the cars were pushed out onto the track and lined up in their starting positions. In garage seventy-five, Mears opened his cluttered locker to find a little green box of Skoal sitting on the top shelf. Hanging below was an orange driving suit with a note taped to it: "Wear This One." He did as he was told, first removing his brown corduroy slacks and rubbing ointment into the cracking scabs on his shins, his souvenir from the Michigan crash. He placed his black socks neatly inside his Topsiders, which he set side by side next to the gray steel locker. I couldn't help thinking about those shoes and socks, sitting there all the time he was out on the track. How if he didn't come back for them, someone would have to remove them. What would you do with them then?

"Let's see now, do I have everything . . ."

A few minutes later Mears was getting into his car in row number one. It is worth noting that defeat for Mears means being in row number one and not on the pole. There were people all up and down that track who would have given a lot just to be in row number two. Al Unser, Sr., for example.

Two rows behind him Walker stood looking at Unser, who stood looking at his car. For a backup car it was not working badly. With a little luck, with a few fast cars crashing or blowing up, he could stay near the front of the pack. Maybe even pass his son in row two.

"I guess you've got to get in now," Walker told him. "I don't know what for."

He didn't shake Unser's hand or anything like that. He just walked away. Derrick Walker had done everything he could do. He couldn't drive the thing, too. I asked if he'd ever been tempted to try.

"I don't have the courage," he said.

I knew at the time that it sounded odd. Courage isn't a word you hear much out there. You don't hear it around NASA or around aerial ballet troupes either. You fall from grace or you don't fall from grace. To comment upon your elevated status is considered bad form. But Walker was too intelligent to put it from his mind altogether. He had been thrust into the flame once as it was and knew full well where he stood.

The pits were now cordoned off with chain. The rules had changed since the pit fire that nearly took Mears's nose off and very nearly took Walker's life. Those of us inside the chain had to wear fire suits. Mine was blue, like Unser's team, and said BOB SPROW on the pocket. Sprow was Unser's chief mechanic. I felt kind of odd then, but I think what really brought the danger home to me was paying $11.40 for a pair of Simpson Nomex fire socks.

Mears's refueler, Bill Murphy, had said, "You gotta have the socks. That's really important, because when the fuel spills, see, it goes all over your feet." The idea of losing my feet impressed me. Now in preparation for the race I asked if Murphy had any advice about what to do in the pits.

"Yeah, wear this," he said, handing me a Nomex balaclava to keep the flames off of my hair and face. "And if anything unusual happens, run like hell."

At first I just held onto the headgear, looking at the setup in the pit. There really wouldn't be anywhere to go. Although Mears's pit, just to the left, was run by a crew separate from Unser's, it was all one chained-in box. My back to the chain, I faced the pit lane, the track beyond. Behind me was a solid wall of people, then another fence, then the howling half million who'd paid to get in. Inside our enclosure were some forty-four fat Goodyear Eagle tires, two fuel tanks holding almost five hundred gallons of methanol, hoses snaking everywhere, fire bottles, racks of brakes, wheels, spare shocks, wings, mirrors, body work, tools. There was really no room for an extra person in there, the crewmen were just trying to be accomodating.

At the start of the race Teo Fabi went away from the field so quickly that he was almost certain to make some mistake, if only because he was too good to be true. The level of intensity in the pits was so great that it was as if the cars made no sound at all. The crowd disappeared, and all that remained was the sun on hot concrete, the multi-colored smudges of the defocused cars, the motion of men in blue fire suits, yellow fire suits, helmets, balaclavas, and the choking smell of oxidized methanol. Time meant nothing. Roger Mears hit the wall in lap forty-five, and I wrote down "approximately lap three."

Under the yellow, several drivers, including Fabi, made pit stops for the second time. When his refueler pulled the hose from the port, methanol spewed back out at him. Fabi sat, ignorant of the problem, as crew members first poured water on the car, then stuck their hands into the fuel port to try to get it to shut, but more and more alcohol came gushing out. A few yards from where we were standing in our fire suits, fuel was flowing all over the track, up the wall, over the Skoal Bandit. Probably the only reason the fuel didn't ignite instantly was that the car was up on jacks. The fuel ran underneath, clear of the hot headers.

Fabi was so excited he didn't even bother to turn the engine off, he was out, drenched with fuel, standing right in front of the car. If a nervous mechanic had let the car down at that moment, not only would Fabi have been run over by his own device, he would have been incinerated, too. Then his flaming car would have rushed down the pit lane toward us, spreading fire and running people over. One of the great fears in the Indy pits—the unspoken fear—is that a chain reaction might occur among the tall tanks from which the cars are fueled. Quick action by crew and firemen averted a disaster. I put my balaclava on and left it on for the rest of the race.

Out on the track it was evident that Mears's car was not working. He was not going very quickly, and even at that his car was sliding high up in the turns, coming perilously close to the wall.

During one of Sneva's pit stops, his crew dropped his car from its jacks while the right side wheels were off. They just let it down, realized what they'd done, and then popped it back up. It's a miracle they didn't put him out of the race. For that is the way the sport goes, like Penske's cars eating themselves alive during the ride from Reading. Irony always attended these events. No one was sure where the blessing had come from, but suddenly Sneva's Texaco Star was the fastest car on the track. Sneva, whom Penske had fired in 1978 for coming in second too many times, was having his day. And the March car he drove appeared to be perfectly dialed in.

Once before the end of the race Unser took the lead during a fast pit stop. Al, Jr., passing illegally under the yellow, put his car between Al, Sr., and Sneva. From that position, driving with scarcely believable skill, the twenty-one-year-old rookie blocked so that his father could have his fourth Indy win on his forty-fourth birthday. As popular as Sneva has been during his ten years at Indy, the bond between father and son, demonstrated in such a breathtaking fashion before half a million people, proved a more powerful cause for celebration. The crowd outshouted the howling turbochargers lap after lap as officials waved the blue and yellow flag, the signal for Al, Jr., to move over.

Sneva was clearly faster, and in lap 187 made his move to pass. But little Al Unser slammed it shut on him with a move that brought the crowd to its feet. Throughout the entire performance, Al, Sr., had no idea what was happening, because his right mirror was broken. If his car had been working, he could have pulled away and kept the lead, but there was no more speed left in that PC-11. The three cars lapped the field, got into traffic, and Sneva was able to dart around Al, Jr.

Then he was gone so fast that he was running all alone with five laps to go. The race ended with Al, Sr., in second place and Mears in third. Fourth was Geoff Brabham, driving a Penske PC-10. Kevin Kogan, who drove Penske's Norton Spirit and won $166,457 in prize money in 1982, was fifth.

Afterward Mears said, "I was having to put on the brakes just to keep from hittin' the fence in the turns. With full fuel it was pushin', halfway down it was neutral, then it got loose as we ran the tank dry." I had never seen Mears show anger, but he did after driving the PC-11 at the Indianapolis 500 and finding that it wanted to commit suicide with him on board.

In Penske's suite overlooking turn two where Sneva had demolished his Penske Team car in 1975, Roger Penske, with his wife Kathy, son Greg, and a few crew members, sat that evening, watching the ABC broadcast of the race. Penske gnawed on a piece of fried chicken, lively, undaunted, in a crisply ironed shirt and neatly pressed slacks.

One of his mechanics, sitting forlornly in a corner, drank a beer. "It kind of makes a mockery of all this, doesn't it?" he said. "I mean all the testing. You go off on all this space-age bullshit, and you lose sight of the basics sometimes."

"Such as?" I asked.

"Such as gettin' four wheels working on the ground at the same time instead of running off to Michigan to run a simulated five hundred-mile race." He put his nose back into his beer.

Penske, on the other hand, seemed to be enjoying the show on the television. Observing that he had personally had a hand in the top five places in the 1983 Indianapolis 500, he said, "Well, they didn't blow our doors off."

The Pit

NO ESCAPE:
THE ENDLESS DREAMS OF ELGIN

One morning I was sitting in the dayroom at Kilbourne I, a long-term unit at Elgin Mental Health Center in Elgin, Illinois, when a frail blond girl knelt before me on the terrazzo floor and began praying. Her face was plain and round and pale, like that of a saint in a prayer book. She appeared to be in pain. She wore a faded yellow blouse, slacks of a flimsy dark blue material, and cloth hospital slippers. She knelt about five feet in front of me, clutched her hands together in a beatific attitude, tilted her head, and cast her eyes heavenward. "Holy Mary, mother of God," she muttered, "pray for us sinners, now and at the hour of our death, Amen. Hail Mary, full of grace, the Lord is with thee. . . ." The room was hot and close with the smell of bodies. It was an all-female unit with thirty-eight beds. I saw perhaps two dozen women, wandering this way and that or sleeping in chairs or standing, simply, in a daze. I could hear the television set in the next room. "Big Valley" was playing loud as some of the women put on make-up with the help of a staff member.

The praying girl got up and came over to my chair to look at me. She stood close enough so that I could see the dried saliva at the corners of her mouth. Her lips were cracked and caked with spots of blood. "I'm sorry, Pontius Pilate Jim Wolf," she said. She bent down and kissed me on the forehead. "I'm sorry." She bent again and kissed me full on the mouth. "I hate schizophrenia," she said.

"How do you feel?" I asked.

"Tired. And it hurts right here." She drew her fingernail

across her forehead from left to right, as if she would cut the top off to show me what was inside that caused the problem.

A black woman with a moon face came up to me and said, "I think I'm God but I might be Eve." She smiled and disappeared.

A burly woman with tight blue jeans and a 1950s haircut stood by my chair, leaning in close, staring at me intently. Her face was six inches from mine. She had been in the other room where the make-up was being applied. Her cheeks were painted bright purple, like melanoma, and her lips were a deep wine red. She looked apparitional, holy, lesbian. She looked angry, as if she were about to challenge me, but she only stared, her brown eyes clear and wet with fluorescent reflections, and we stayed like that until a scream broke our contact.

I went over to Kilbourne II, the men's side, and sat in the nurses' station, a glassed-in booth from which we could watch the patients circling like fish in a tank. Most of them were schizophrenic, though some were bipolar and others were simply so depressed that they were dangerous. About seventy percent of the 821 patients at the Elgin Mental Health Center were there involuntarily.

At 11:05 an aide wheeled out a stainless steel cart with a black plastic garbage bag tied to the side. On the tray were stacks of little paper cups, a white towel, a green plastic pitcher of red fruit punch, and a white plastic cassette of medications. The cassette looked like an oversized ice tray. Each cube contained a small white paper cup with pills in it. The orange ones were Thorazine, the green or white or yellow ones were Haldol, and the funny pastel fuchsia ones were big bombers, two hundred milligrams of Mellaril.

Most of the patients lined up to take their medications, rolling the pills like dice from a cup, then washing them down with a paper jigger of punch. It was a chemical crap shoot: If they rolled the right numbers, they got to go home. That was the idea, anyway. Even though they were long-term patients, the chronic cases, the program called for rehabilitation through chemistry and behavior modification. The days of warehousing mental patients are—theoretically at least—over.

The ward was operated on a system called the token economy. Put in simple terms, that behavior modification system allows patients to earn points for acting normal. For example, if the Kilbourne patients participated in a game of bingo, they got points. If they groomed themselves, they got points. The more things they did that looked normal, the more points they accumulated. Then, at certain times each day, during commissary period, they were given the opportunity to exchange points for candy, cigarettes, coffee, pop. The object (in case it is not obvious) was to get the patients out of the mental institution and into the world, where they could do what we all do without thinking about it: act normal and spend our tokens on those things that gratify us.

A man in his thirties circled the room, waving his hands over his head as if he were trying to take off. Suddenly his hands stopped flapping and hit him in the stomach. He recoiled from the blows as if he'd become used to attacks by invisible enemies. His behavior was odd, but it was an improvement. His ears were blown up with scar tissue—true cauliflower ears—from a time when he used to box himself in the head all day long. Behavior modification (the token economy) had changed all that. Now his hands flapped beside his head, wanting to hit his ears but stopping just short, until something snapped and they hit him in the stomach instead.

A patient with a lot of teeth missing, his head shaved and his face unshaved, about forty years old, rolled a cup of pills into his mouth, washed them down with punch, dropped the cup into the black garbage bag tied to the cart, and then knocked on the nurses' station window to get my attention. "Am I going to be discharged?" he asked in a voice so loud that I could hear him through the glass.

"Probably," I shouted through the glass. I didn't know what to say. But in the current mental health system, his chances were good if he just kept rolling those pills and playing bingo. He smiled.

I let myself out of the locked nurses' station and went onto the unit to see him. He had a big brown-toothed smile. "I plan to join the Orange Force," he said. "Air Force. It's in Mexico. Is your name Dave?"

I told him it wasn't.

"Were you born in France? Second War?"

I asked him if he had been in the war.

"Vietnam," he said. "Nineteen sixty-nine."

"What did you do?" I asked him.

"Carried bodies. Chu Lai."

"What else happened?" I asked.

"Napalm," he said.

He had deep burns between the fingers of his right hand. It was from forgetting that he was holding a cigarette and then not noticing the smell of smoking flesh or the pain. Some of the burns were fresh; others were old and crusted over with scar tissue and scabs. "Are you an MP?" he asked. I could smell his breath, like opening a bad oyster. I had a moment to reflect on whether he was going to kiss me or kill me and then the unit director took my arm and gently led me away.

Back in the nurses' station the unit director said, "I could see some things that you probably don't notice. He was becoming very agitated, and I was worried that he'd, you know . . ."

"Get violent?" I asked.

She nodded.

❖   ❖   ❖

When I first went to the Elgin Mental Health Center, I went as a reporter, looking for issues to land like big fish. But this wasn't one of those stories. After ten days there, I found myself standing in the dayroom one morning, looking at myself in a full-length mirror—that wavy, unreal funhouse reflection caused by the fact that the mirror was made out of stainless steel (the patients would smash a glass one)—and I asked the unit director why the mirror was there. "So the patients can check their appearance before they go outside," she said. "Just like normal people." I checked my appearance. I was melting. When I moved, my flesh oozed this way and that. I tried to imagine what it would do to a schizophrenic's confidence, just before going outside to greet the world, to find that he was melting.

I went to Elgin to learn about the mental health system, and instead I found one of the deepest human mysteries—madness itself. Medical science has been unable to learn what causes it or how it works. Insane people are given drugs, but next to nothing is known about when they'll work or why they have the effects they do, and everyone agrees that the side effects are devastating, perhaps terminal. The method of treating mentally ill people is not a system; it is a collection of a few dedicated and ill-equipped people throwing their lives against a hopelessness that is scarcely believable. There is too little money, too little time, and too little knowledge.

If you go insane, is it better to be in or to get out? That is the central paradox—the koan, as it were—of the mental health system. If reality has dissolved, is it better to face reality or to seek escape? There are groups of well-meaning citizens advocating change in the mental health system. Some advocate keeping patients in the hospital longer because they need treatment. Others advocate releasing patients because the hospitals are inhumane and poorly run.

"There are no answers," said Ed Throw, unit director of Souster, one of the old units on "the hill." When I visited, Souster was home to forty-seven chronically ill patients who had very little chance of improving. Some would never see the street again. Others would go out and be back too soon to know what had hit them.

Throw, with thirteen years at Elgin, is typical of the staff. He has dedicated his life to working with the impossible cases. Everyone there will tell you: If a staff member makes it beyond the first year, he'll probably be there until they close the facility. Throw's life revolves around trying to get one man to learn to keep his pants on, another to wash his hands, another to participate in a game of catch. "We are the end of the line," he said.

"You learn to take your rewards in exceedingly small increments. Any improvement is cause for celebration." Behind
him, on the couch, a young man displayed the erection emerg-
ing from his unbuttoned pants, while a dozen other patients
wandered aimlessly this way and that, circling chairs, sliding
along the walls of the barn-like room.

Souster was among the last of the unrehabilitated brick and
terrazzo barns that set sounds free to roam at will—coughing,
muttering, laughter; the whispering of slippers on tile; the occasional ultrahuman bark or scream. The smell was like in-
sects kept too long in a jar, formic acid and dried grass and the
penetrating sharpness of raw milk. The yellowing acoustical
tile ceiling looked as if it would fall at any moment. Hygiene
was a constant problem. Two patients on the ward had recently
been taken to the medical building for amoebic dysentery.
"We've got a lot of hand washing going on," Throw said with a
thin and bearded grin. I asked how the disease was transmitted.
"Fecal matter," he said. "So as long as you don't get into any of
those kinds of activities, you're all right."

One slack-jawed, soft-looking man stalked me with his hand
outstretched, waiting for some signal of recognition. I figured:
How many people will shake hands with him in an average
month here? I'd been warned, but I shook his hand anyway and
was promptly taken away to have my hands washed.

Behavior modification on Ed Throw's ward was even more
difficult than on many other wards. He used not only candy
and cigarettes as rewards but also the old "time out" room, also
known as "withdrawal of positive reinforcement," a brick cell
about five-by-six feet with a high ceiling and a small window
for observation. It gives a "recipient" (as the state calls mental
patients) a chance to reflect and to reconsider acting out (as the
state calls it when they go berserk).

I stopped to read some of the graffiti: YOU ARE GOING TO
DEATH OR HELL WE BE 7734 OR DR. DEATH WILL KILL YOU FOR
THE BLOODY KILL YOU ARE IN PAD. The messages were like in-
structions from outer space. Like the madmen themselves they

seemed cognate with order, meaning, context—they cried out with purpose—and yet they remained just out of reach of cognition.

❖   ❖   ❖

Waves of smoke, loud rock and roll music, human and TV voices, and mechanical noise greeted me as I entered ATC-1, the acute ward, where people come in desperate crisis, hearing voices, suicidal, terrified, hallucinating, catatonic. This was the other end of the line, and many of these people would be back on the street within a few weeks, though some could eventually wind up in long-term wards like Ed Throw's. Men and women moved up the long pastel corridor lit by banks of bright fluorescent light. The patients came at me, trailing plumes of smoke like the visible auras of their mingling souls, shuffling, lurching, passing, turning, retreating.

A man approached. "Are you a new patient?" he asked. I was walking the corridor, bent over, writing in a little black notebook cupped in my hand, and before I could answer, he was gone in a whirling cloud of incandescent smoke. By the nurses' station there was a security mirror, and hanging on the tile wall were silk ferns and silk ivy in plastic pots. A young man in blue jeans and a blue T-shirt walked up and down the hall, clinging close to the wall. Hammered into the back of his hand-tooled leather belt were the words BAD BOB.

I was brought in by Rick Nelson, director of Adult Services, a slim and dapper administrator with a thin smile and a guarded manner. Standing in the scalding light, wearing a silver-gray suit, he was trying to explain the system. "A sense of optimism which turned out to be bloated," he said, and I think he meant that everybody thought somebody else was going to take responsibility for insane people, but no one did. In fact, when no one else wanted them, when they'd fallen through all the cracks in all the social systems, then they finally came to Elgin. When Elgin was through with them, many would be sent back into the world. Three-fourths of them would fall through the cracks once more and would return to Elgin.

Some of them had been circling us ever since we arrived on the ward, and now a young, heavyset woman named Joanne came up to Rick Nelson, examined his name tag, and began talking. At first he tried to pretend that she wasn't there, but she really was, she was terribly and irrefutably there, and like so many mental patients, she moved in especially close to engage. She had reddish-blond hair cut short, and her skin was yellow and puffy. She had applied orange lipstick in a haphazard way to the area around her mouth. She bounced very slightly on the balls of her feet, twitching, glaring, grimacing, as if she might cry. The muscles of her mouth were out of control. Her hands made little rhythmic motions as if she were rolling something between her fingers.

"I need to keep moving and doing things," Joanne said. "I think I'd be a good candidate for employment here. If I had a key, I could take people on field trips."

"We don't hire patients," Rick Nelson said flatly.

"I've had experience," she told him. "I've been in these places five times. I can cut hair." She wore a green jacket with a yellow jacket beneath it and shoes the color of her hair.

Nelson suggested that she hold down a job for a while to prove herself. Bad Bob came out of a cloud of smoke, sliding along the wall, and scowled at us. He had dark hair and deep-set, angry eyes.

"You teach vocation here?" Joanne asked Nelson. "I know lots of secretaries. The best in the West."

A small group of patients had begun to close around us, and it was becoming clear that our theoretical discussion of the mental health system was in immediate danger of being overwhelmed by the very people it was meant to serve. Mrs. Trenton, a thin and ragged woman with holes in her shoes, shuffled up to Nelson and asked, "Can a fifty-year-old woman with low blood pressure do aerobics?" He told her that it was probably all right if she asked her physician. She had a drawn, animal look about her, hollow blue eyes, and shattered ceramic skin.

We were standing in the corridor between the nurses' station and the dayroom. A man approached with an unlit cigarette held just before his pursed lips. He picked up a Bic lighter, which was anchored to the counter of the nurses' station by a shoelace, and lit his cigarette. He didn't smoke it; he consumed it, sucking powerfully, pulling a lungful, then pulling again and again until he was lost in a cloud of smoke, his eyes wide, a puzzled look on his face as if he couldn't understand how he'd come to dissolve in that toxic cloud. The state provided tobacco, and cigarettes were rolled for the patients who couldn't afford to buy their own. For safety reasons they weren't allowed to have matches, so they had to light their cigarettes from others or from the Bic at the nurses' station.

A few years ago, there was an incident in which a man came walking out of his room in flames. No one knows how it happened. The staff had to get a helicopter to take him to the burn unit in Rockford. There's a great fear of open flames at Elgin; it seems that in spite of precautions, people sometimes just catch fire.

Joanne and Mrs. Trenton followed us as we wandered into the dayroom, where a number of people were sleeping on the brightly colored leatherette couches and chairs, while others watched the television mounted high in the wall. Throughout the hospital I saw the same box-like chairs. The frames were wood and so heavy that it would be virtually impossible to pick up and throw one. Patients liked to curl up and sleep in the chairs. They looked like people in pretty boxes with no lids.

Joanne said, "If you're familiar with a surgical procedure, what about lobotomy?"

Rick Nelson was quick to respond: "We haven't done one in thirty years."

Mrs. Trenton said, "I did a term paper on lobotomies in college, because I thought it was very cruel."

"I had my tonsils out," Joanne said.

Through the windows I could see a rusting silver water tower amid trees and prairie scrub brush and the medical building, which was designed by the architect of Marina Towers. Sit-

ting in the middle of the Midwestern prairie, the five-story louvered cylinder looked as if it had come from outer space in the
middle of the night and disgorged all those automobiles parked
around it, like so many little cocoons.

But no one was looking out the window. The patients watched
TV or stared at the walls or slept off the first devastating blasts
of Thorazine, Haldol, Mellaril, the major tranquilizers that had
triggered the mass exodus from insane asylums that began
about thirty years ago, when Elgin did its last lobotomies. There
was no point in performing expensive and time-consuming surgery once psychotropic drugs were discovered.

Having worked against mental illness for centuries with no
hint of progress, doctors embraced the new drugs as a miracle.
They prescribed them by the truckload and began turning patients loose. The sad outcome has been that mental illness has
not disappeared. (In fact, it has increased drastically.) The drugs,
far from curing insanity, have in many ways shaped the behavior I saw: the pill-rolling finger motion, the yellow skin, uncon-
trollable grimacing, puffing cheeks, puckering mouths, lolling
tongues, shuffling gait, tremors, cogwheel rigidity, and gener-
alized rhythmic movements of the body. Mrs. Trenton's low
blood pressure was probably a side effect of her medication.
Nevertheless, in many cases, psychotropic drugs are the only
means of allowing certain patients to hold psychosis at bay.

Joanne disappeared during a Sprint telephone commercial,
which came roaring out of the television, then suddenly
stopped. "Hear a pin drop," the voice said, and an actual pin
dropped in dazzling, crack-of-doom, hyperrealistic colors. A
young black man with heavy eyelids slumped across two chairs,
dreaming in and out of consciousness. Joanne returned, smoking the stub of a cigar. Mrs. Trenton admonished Rick Nelson,
"Don't allow these people to sleep so much."

"They may be getting used to their meds," he said. The first
two or three weeks on Thorazine or Haldol can be like that.
They're not sleeping; there's a lot going on behind those catatonic eyes. I talked to one schizophrenic who described her ini-

tial stay in a mental hospital: "I spent six weeks lying on my bed on Thorazine, hallucinating that my friends were being assassinated and crucified and that there was a war going on between the fascists and the angels."

Mrs. Trenton complained to Rick Nelson, "I can't get people interested in physical fitness. How much water should I drink?" Nelson looked at her as if she were crazy. It did sound like the kind of question a mental patient would ask, except that one Ph.D. candidate at the hospital was doing her dissertation on patients who compulsively drink water. Maybe Mrs. Trenton was the object of such research and had been made self-conscious about drinking water. On the other hand, maybe she was just crazy.

We fought our way through clouds of smoke to the other side of the acute ward, ATC-2, where we found a young man named Dan dancing by himself in the activities room in front of high-tech stereo speakers, radio rock and roll. He had homemade tattoos all over his hands, thin brown hair, a spotty moustache; he wore a black T-shirt, corduroy pants, shoes from which the laces had been removed, and a new, clear plastic ID bracelet. He was obviously coming off a major manic episode, and he couldn't stop moving.

"How are you feeling?" Nelson asked, looking around the room as if to say, *Why has a boy in this condition been left alone?*

"I'm feeling great," Dan said with a steely grin. "I feel great every day. Every day I feel great." Dan whirled around us, dancing and dancing. He could not stop. He sang along with the song; and when a commercial came on, he mouthed the announcer's words and even imitated the sound effects, vroom, vroom, brrrrrddht! He was at one with his radio and his meds, "probably lithium," Rick Nelson said as we left Dan there to dance.

It can take up to three weeks for lithium carbonate to stop a bad manic episode, so Dan had a lot of dancing to do before he was through. Like all medications given for insanity, next to nothing is known about why lithium works. And if it didn't work well enough, Dan might end up in the room we visited next, a plain cinder block enclosure with a view of a dead tree and an abandoned red-brick building. The single bed in that room has leather shackles with chrome latches.

❖   ❖   ❖

We assume that we are protected somehow by an invisible shield. For one thing, we'll never go crazy. For another, we're insured, so even if we do, we'll be put in a cozy private institution, where it's not so bad. But our delusions, while comforting, will do us no good. Most people don't realize that twenty-five percent of all hospital stays are for mental disorders. People also don't read their insurance policies. A typical policy will cover a few weeks of hospitalization and even less outpatient care. I spoke with more than one parent who had watched a son or daughter go from a six-hundred-dollar-a-day private institution to Elgin as the money ran out and the disease, rather than being cured, progressed from one nightmare stage to the next. Some parents have been invited by their private hospital to keep their children in at a rate of twelve thousand to twenty thousand dollars a month. Some do, and then the whole family goes down with the mental patient. Divorce, depression, addiction, and suicide can all grow out of a case of mental illness. If there is a villain in this story, it is the insurance industry.

Research done by the American Psychiatric Association in 1983 showed that only forty-nine percent of insurance policies paid for psychiatric hospitalization at the same rate as for any other medical condition. Only ten percent covered outpatient mental health care at the same rate. Since most mental hospitals today push patients out the door as quickly as possible, the outcome is obvious. "This discrimination," wrote the APA, "is bad for patients, for business, for mental health providers, and, ultimately, for the community and taxpayers." A study by the League of Women Voters concluded that "insurance discriminates against people with mental illness."

Sandy (not her real name) is a schizophrenic who started out as middle class and normal as anyone. She was twenty-six when she began hearing voices. "If you can imagine what it would be like if there were really fairies and gnomes," she said, "that's what it was like. I was literally hearing voices. And sometimes I'd also hear the voices of the people I lived with, talking about me behind my back." Of course, after they found out that she was hearing voices, they did talk about her behind her back, and then she couldn't tell when she was hallucinating and when she was eavesdropping.

The next step was the mental hospital. One of her first experiences was a private institution, "where they charged me eighteen hundred dollars for six weeks of Thorazine without ever realizing that the medication was making me worse, not better." Her family had her transferred to another private hospital in Milwaukee, where doctors changed her medication to Stelazine, and she began to calm down. (Medicating mental illness is a procedure of trial and error.) By the time they got her on the right medication, her insurance money was just about gone, and the nightmare started all over. She spent the next fifteen years in and out of state mental institutions, in and out of her mother's house, in and out of outpatient facilities.

If you met Sandy on the street today, you'd see a blond woman with pleasant features who seems a little quiet but is perfectly articulate. She takes fifty dollars a month worth of lithium, Stelazine, and Cogentin, one pill to take her up, another to take her down, and the last to put out the fires set by that treacherous chemical rocket ride. Now, at the age of forty, she has finally gotten Medicaid and can check herself into Ravenswood hospital when she loses control. "Ravenswood is nice," she said. She spends a few weeks there about twice a year, usually because she stops taking her medications. It is the central paradox for many mental patients: Do you want to be insane, or do you want to take this toxic substance? The choice is yours. (And then sometimes it's not yours.) Put it another way: Are you more rational if you choose the poison or if you choose the insanity?

I asked Sandy to describe what it was like when she was at Elgin (which was about a year before I went there) and she wrote this:

> Day after day with absolutely nothing to do, no one to talk to truthfully, no privacy, no control over anything that happens— that's what it's like. Plus an imposed hidden structure that can provide interminable punishment at any infraction of the buried testament. Either out in the cold or strapped to a bed exposed to any harm.
>
> The infractions of legal protections are numerous. Medications are given without identification. You can imagine how frightened you would be, given a pill without any knowledge of its content or effect from a stranger in a bleak, vacant chamber you've been locked into.
>
> There are laws which state medication can be refused— however, the psychiatrist can override this. The nurse will inform you of this. If you still refuse, big burly security guards will surround, possibly assault, you; and you will be strapped down to a bed by the wrists and ankles and given a shot of an, again, undefined substance.
>
> One of the techniques to control a fighting patient is to cover his mouth and nose with a hand or pillow. With the patient fighting for breath, the other staff can strap down his wrists and ankles. Twice I thought I was at the point of death by suffocation. Once, because I was in a strange place, I believed they'd be back to finish the job and I would be absolutely defenseless.
>
> The mental health community will argue that such treatment is necessary to control the uncontrolled client. I argue that such treatment can do little to stabilize an individual. On the contrary, it creates an intense hostility, hatred, and anger, which erupts over and over again, until you learn to be docile and compliant, usually by going in and out of restraints. Any confrontation between staff and patient usually ends in restraints.
>
> The traumatic and redundant restraint scene can be avoided. It is easy to identify someone who is losing control to the point of needing restraint. These people can be talked down. The staff even knows when it's going to happen: They set up the bed and the straps instead of talking to the person. They get the order for

the action, draw the shot, et cetera. All this could be avoided, but it's not.

I showed her the pages a few weeks after she'd written them and asked if she wanted to change anything. She said, "It's not Kafkaesque enough."

❖　　❖　　❖

The overall effect of the dayroom at Burr, a long-term unit at Elgin, was that of a large, surreal grade school classroom. The sixty-foot-long room was plain painted brick with a terrazzo floor. In one corner there was a stainless steel cafeteria counter about eight feet long; and behind it was the largest institutional coffee urn I've ever seen, with pipes and tubes and spigots going every which way. The stainless steel refrigerator and ice machine were both secured with padlocks. There were a few colored metal lockers against one wall and a white cafeteria garbage can near the exit. Some light came through the six tall windows with blue flowered curtains. Three out of the fifteen fluorescent lights were turned on, producing a pseudo-electric twilight. The background noise was insistent pop music from a local radio station.

I'd just come onto Burr after many days of visiting other units, and by that time, when people asked if I was a new patient, I no longer knew what to tell them. Sometimes I was taking notes so fast that I couldn't stop to answer, and they'd go away, making their own assumptions. At one point, a woman cornered me in the yard. She said she was a social worker and tried to talk me into coming back onto the unit. She couldn't figure out how the unit had received a new admission without her knowing about it. When she found out that I was a reporter, she went into a protracted fit of embarrassed apology, but I assured her it was all right, that it didn't matter at all. Then I found out that she was a patient, and I knew I'd come full circle—one flew east, one flew west.

One afternoon on Burr, a nice looking young man named

Tommy, with a Sony Walkman in his pocket, the headphones around his neck, came in and sat down at a table to play Simon, an electronic game that looked like a black plastic flying saucer with four large lights on top, red, blue, yellow, green. The idea was this: The computer inside played a tune with the lights. Then Tommy was supposed to press the lights in order to repeat the tune. As the game progressed, the tunes became more and more complicated until either Tommy or the machine went insane. Whoever went insane first lost. Or won, depending upon your point of view.

Theresa caught my attention. She was a dark-eyed, dark-haired twenty-four-year-old, with a plump, pretty face. She looked Latin or Italian. She'd been staring at me from across the room, leaning over the back of a couch, resting her chin on her arm, when I decided to go over and see what was up.

"Welcome to Fantasy Island," she said with a signifying smile. "Kukla Fran and Ollie."

Tommy had defeated Simon, which now sat on the table, blinking catatonically. With a smug smile, Tommy went to the table to paint. Rich, one of the aides, was trying to redirect his creative energy to a blank piece of paper. "You silly boy, you're painting over someone else's picture."

"You and I ought to get a six-pack each and go to a Sox game or something," Tommy told Rich. It sounded like such a reasonable suggestion, but of course, under the circumstances, it was insane; the Sox weren't playing that day.

A black woman appeared out of nowhere, dressed as if she were on her way to church, with a freshly pressed pink dress, a yellow band around her waist-length hair, a yellow bracelet to match. The patients sometimes materialized like that, out of the clouds of smoke that constantly circled the room like spirits looking for someone to become. That was how I first saw Molly, coming out of a cloud.

I felt as if I'd seen her before: classic and fair, with high pink cheeks and pale eyebrows over pale sky-blue eyes, she looked like a young woman in a Vermeer painting, a misty countenance in smoky light falling through a glass. Her manner was outgoing, energetic, accommodating; and she liked to get in close, staring eye-to-eye, until it seemed that so much electricity was going back and forth that she could no longer stand it; then she would break down and laugh and cry at the same time.

She was tall and athletic looking with curly blond hair cut in a short and stylish way. She had on a pink sweat shirt, gray sweat pants, and athletic socks. She came right up to the program director, who was sitting next to me.

"Hi, what's your name?" Molly asked.

"Fran."

"Hi, Fran. How ya doin', Fran?"

"I'm fine."

"Beautiful," Molly said, and she got down to business at the art table. She started with what appeared to be a completely random scribble with pencil on a piece of gray construction paper. At first it looked like a child's scrawl. But then she began painting red circles with water color over the pencil marks. "That's Saturn," she said to no one in particular. "Jupiter, Neptune . . ." Then she switched to brown paint.

Meanwhile, the room was filled with activity. Across the room a black girl was dancing to Elton John, and the staff shouted encouragement at her. A muttonchopped man paced back and forth, his hands trembling in his back pockets. Tommy and Rich were playing checkers. Tommy was jumping pieces, laughing, so clean-cut with his black hair shining. It almost seemed as if he was making fun of what he was doing. He seemed to know that he was young and vital and intelligent. There was a cockiness about him. Somehow playing those games and coloring with crayons like a child was robbing him of his real life, and he could see it going, but he could do nothing about it.

I noticed the faintest hint of crow's feet appear at the corners of his eyes when he laughed. It was difficult to remember that Burr was a long-term unit. Tommy was just a boy, but he was growing old in mental institutions.

Molly's universe had developed into a brown and maroon chaos with a dark green mechanical-looking area at the bottom, feeding up into swirling clouds of brown haloed in an orange mist and surrounded by glowing heavenly bodies. Molly showed the picture to Rich. "Hey, great," he said.

Molly said, "This is your green pea toilet paper," and she began laughing and crying at the same time. Then Molly tore her picture into strips and reassembled it with tape.

At 2:30 an aide named Tim hollered, "Commissary!" and everybody who could lined up for Jolly Good soft drinks and Nestle's Crunch and Almond Joy and foil packets of instant coffee. (The urn contained hot water.)

Theresa came up to me flashing her Latin eyes and said, "Fran was on 'General Hospital.' Or her twin. I feel pretty drunk, don't you?"

While Molly waited in line, I asked what her painting was called. "Pea green factory bubble squirt-outs," she said. "Would you like to have it?" I said I would. "Can I get you something?" she asked, gesturing to the commissary. I told her I was fine.

Theresa told Fran, "You'll be a legend in your time. I know why you're here. Because you're going to be a woman some day. I really do love you all, but I'm not Jesus Christ. I've only got two arms and two legs. We're family. I've got all your sisters in me."

Molly poured her coffee from one styrofoam cup to another to cool it, then drank it in one continuous swallow and sat down expectantly. But whatever she had expected did not occur, and she turned her attention to her cigarette, working it into a growing blue cloud that wrapped her like a shroud. A gracious smile came to her face. "Can I get you something? Pop? Coffee? Something cold? Anything? How about some ice water?" She took a long drag from her cigarette and blew smoke rings, watching them crash on the table top in front of her. She laughed and cried.

Theresa told Fran, "You can stay overnight if you want to."

"She can. She can," Molly said, stubbing out her cigarette

and rubbing her hands together as if she were cold. She opened a Three Musketeers bar, breaking it to share with Theresa.

Theresa accepted the candy without comment and began eating it. "And I still hear a baby crying," she said.

"Well, I'm glad you got a painting," Molly told me.

Theresa said, "I hear this noise. A radio." I told her there was a radio playing over in the corner, but she said she heard another one as well. "I write songs in my sleep," she said. "I sing better in my sleep."

"You sure you don't want something?" Molly asked.

Thinking about those young people going home to their parents, which they eventually would (at least for a while before being readmitted), I remembered Sandy telling me about returning from her first stay in a mental institution. "My mother's house was just beautiful, and I was thinking it should be an ashram, a spiritual center. I was lying on the floor and I looked out the window and I saw grapes and apples on my mother's apple tree. David and I, the man I was attached to, were going to have a heaven on earth, a garden of Eden. This, of course, was just in my imagination. I was just in torment because I knew I was supposed to be getting married; I thought I was pregnant with the Messiah, the Christ child, and I thought I was in jeopardy. I had a hallucination that my mother's walls were going to be spattered with blood. I was just really traumatized."

❖   ❖   ❖

I stood in a sunny room listening to a woman, a white suburban volunteer, strum a guitar and sing "He's Got the Whole World in His Hands" with a black man who was criminally insane and looked like a football player. The mental health professionals don't say "criminally insane" anymore. They say UST (unfit to stand trial) or NGRI (not guilty by reason of insanity).

A thin, fit, handsome man came up to me. I knew in the most general way what his problem was, because everyone

where I was, on the Forensic Unit, was either UST or NGRI
(i.e., criminally insane). But he was hard to figure—young,
with fine, curly red hair and green cat eyes. His skin was the
color of coffee with milk. He seemed luminous, like an angel. I
couldn't tell if it was the late sunlight or just my imagination.
He said, "I done five and a half solid in Manteno before it
closed and I came here to Elgin." Manteno was a state mental
hospital. I asked him what he did to get sent there. "I caught a
case," he said.

"Isn't this better than jail?"

"Oh, yeah, it's better than jail," he admitted. "But at least in
jail you know you're getting out." His case would be reviewed
in 1990. He said that, except for four months, he'd been on
Haldol for six years. As I said goodbye, I touched him on the
arm. Under his new tennis shirt his tricep was as hard as wood.

Leaving the unit, I asked the administrator what the man
had done.

"Murder," he said. "NGRI."

"Oh, then he'll never get out," I suggested.

"No, he may get out. The average length of stay is seven
years."

❖   ❖   ❖

The second time I saw Molly she was at Elgin's social center on
a Saturday morning. Any patient with a grounds pass can go
there to spend money, eat, drink, listen to music, and circle the
room cadging cigarettes and lights from others. Ashes and cigarettes and paper littered the white round tables and the terrazzo floor. Flies landed on the people and their plates of french
fries. There were movie posters on the walls behind sheets of
plexiglass. The dirty windows were heavily screened and overlooked an old horse barn and concrete block shed from the days
when the patients at Elgin ran a farm. The day was overcast,
and the dirt on the windows or some imperfection in the glass
was turning the outside into a shimmering hallucination like

that stainless steel mirror I'd seen. I moved my head and the world rippled like wind-blown water. A couple went by arm in arm.

There was an electric cigarette lighter built into the wall by the snack bar. The patients had to hold down a button and put the tip of the cigarette against the little filament in the wall, then suck. It required getting into such a peculiar posture that it looked crazy, so most people lit their cigarettes from others that were already lit, which resulted in a continuous dance of kissing flames going around and around the room, whipping the smoke clouds into whirling dust devils.

Molly flew around the room, greeting people she knew from other wards, smoking, exchanging lights and laughs. It was like a convention of intergalactic travelers. Haldol of Burr meets Prolixin of Souster. Mellaril of Kilbourne I meets Dilantin of Pinel.

Molly came up to me looking like a college student. She had put on a little make-up and wore a short denim skirt, white socks, and sandals. We made small talk.

"Hi," I said.

"How are you?"

"Fine. What have you been up to?" I asked.

She told me about Brown School near San Marcos, Texas, where she went when she was little. She said she had liked it a lot. Brown is one of the more famous mental hospitals for children, noted for dealing with really difficult cases. She remembered that the school smelled very good, "like earth and the laundry smelled good like outdoors and medium." She said she'd been in institutions since she was fourteen. She loved San Marcos. She smiled a lot, her eyes shining with excitement. She said she was going to order a seltzer, but she was so excited that she forgot and just kept on smoking, as her cloud merged with the next and the next, as people passed around us in aimless circles. Molly was so sweet, it was almost as if she worked too hard at it, doing battle with a demon inside, and fire was coming off her in the friction.

"Listen," Molly told me in her breathless, eager, attentive way, "if you want to take a plane to either Egypt to see the ruins or to San Marcos—hey, first-class flight would be fine with me."

"OK," I said. I was caught in the classic dilemma of dealing with those who are mad, and I think it forms the basic paradox of treatment. I didn't want to lead Molly too far along in her delusion. On the other hand, her delusion was as real to her as my reality was to me. And so, when my drab reality encountered Molly's dazzling universe, I was left to respond with a noncommittal answer until the whirlwind passed and she anchored herself once more in my world.

As I was leaving the social center, Molly invited me to a picnic at Burr. She said that her parents were coming and I should drop by, share a sandwich, join in the fun. I said I'd like that. Fran, my escort, called Burr to ask if it was all right for me to come. I thought that if Molly's parents were coming a long way to see her, they might want to see her alone. I didn't want to be in the way. Fran came back from the phone with an odd look on her face. There was no picnic, no parents, no plan. It was all a flight of fancy.

❖   ❖   ❖

By my last day at Elgin, I had stopped interviewing administrators and psychiatrists. I had even stopped carrying my tape recorder. All the issues and the politics of insanity, all the rhetoric and syllogism of the system, had fallen away, leaving nothing but the people who'd baffled and thwarted us all by going mad. By then they had taken me in, and I felt that it was all I could do just to be there. I had begun to understand why some will stand in mute amazement without moving, sometimes for hours on end, the way fish stay still where the water is whitest.

Molly came out into the Burr courtyard, which was formed by the two wings of the red-brick building and by a high chain link fence topped with small, brightly colored, triangular flags. I could tell that something had happened. Her aura of energy seemed to have collapsed. She came out wearing pink jogging pants pulled up to expose her calves, but she wore no shoes, which was against the rules and unlike her—she was neither defiant nor sloppy. Yet her hair was in disarray and her gaze was turned inward. She looked angry, or perhaps she had been crying. Her hair was wet, which made it look brown instead of blond. It hung in tight ringlets around her ears and on her neck. The unit director chased her back inside to get her shoes, and after a few minutes Molly emerged again wearing a man's black suede shoes from which the laces had been removed. The tongues lolled out as she walked unsteadily into the sunlight and sat at a picnic table under a tree.

Someone she knew walked by outside the gate and said hello. "Hi. I can't come out today," Molly called. "The staff won't let me." Then she called through the fence. "Have a nice day!"

Theresa sat at a picnic table with me. "Hi, Kukla Fran and Ollie." I turned over a magazine that was on the picnic table between me and Theresa: *Esquire* had a cover story called "How to Buy Clothes."

Tommy was lying curled up on his side beneath a tree, wearing a crucifix around his neck. He was pressing the unit director to call his social worker, but she said she wouldn't know where to find him at this hour. Tommy said he was in his office. "That's where he was," Tommy said, "at least before they arranged to kill my mother. My alleged mother," he added with a hint of sarcasm, and I had the same sense I had gotten before that he was suddenly going to get up and laugh, dusting off his pants, and say, "I had you fooled, didn't I? You thought I was really crazy." But he just curled himself into a tighter ball under the tree.

A nurse came out to make sure that the people on Thorazine used sun screen. "It blisters them if they're out for more than ten or fifteen minutes. Tommy's OK, he's in the shade."

Molly stood beside a steel pole where a red ball was tied on a length of cord. She listlessly batted the ball around the pole, looking abstracted. The courtyard was beginning to fill with people, and now out in the bright clear sunlight, without their protective auras of smoke, they looked larval and delicate.

Kim, a pretty technician with curly red hair, was trying to coax a patient out into the yard for some exercise. "Dan, you want to think about coming out now? You're so close. You want me to help you over the step? You're smiling; you're teasing me." I could see Kim standing in the sunlight talking, but I couldn't see Dan, who was in a shadow inside the building. Was Kim having hallucinations there, talking to an invisible man? "Come on, Dan, you can do it."

After twenty minutes of coaxing the darkness, Kim succeeded in getting Dan out into the light. He looked gray and shaken, a man in his early thirties, unshaven, six feet tall, with short brown hair. He wore gray woolen bell-bottom slacks and a blue plaid, long-sleeve shirt, and brand new white tennis shoes. He had a kind of defiant, gleeful, petrified look on his face, as if—for reasons he couldn't fathom—he had decided to walk a tightrope across Niagara Falls. Kim put a Frisbee into his hand, and suddenly a change came over Dan. With a graceful fluid movement, he crouched a little, tucked his wrist in close to his body, and fired the blue disc into the sunlight. The courtyard went wild. Dan had a talent. He must have been a Frisbee player in his home galaxy, because he had the moves.

"Hey, you've found your calling!" Kim shouted as she nabbed the Frisbee out of the air and sent it back. All at once a group of patients became involved in the game, and everyone's technique, as if by the power of suggestion, improved. The game went on for ten minutes or so, and the Frisbee went over the fence only once. But then Dan froze with the Frisbee in his arms, as if he had suddenly remembered how thin the rope was, how far the drop. Everyone gathered around and talked to him, but he just looked and looked, first at the sky, then at the people, then at the roaring cataract down between his feet.

Tommy uncurled beneath the tree and got up to sit at the picnic table with me. He smiled and squinted in the light, like a man who has just taken a good summer's nap. I thought: Now he will return to normal. Now he will finally make sense. "I didn't play post office when I was a kid," Tommy said. "They wanted me to, but I wouldn't let them. I told them I was going to play it when I grew up." His eyes were slits, and he talked with his mouth almost closed. He yawned and got up to lie down again. I wondered if they'd changed his meds. "Zenith, Magnavox, Buster Brown," he said. Across the courtyard Kim was not about to give up on Dan. She talked and talked, coaxing him gradually out of his panic until, just before I went inside, I saw him wearing the Frisbee on his head, laughing, putting everybody on.

I found Molly stacking books, straightening up in the dayroom. "I was thinking about buying that school there in San Marcos," she said. Our voices echoed as if we were in a church.

I asked her what had happened over the weekend that took away her grounds pass.

"I went swimming at the water hole and security caught me," she said. "The river by the trees where the trees are. Security said, 'Don't do it again; people have drowned in there.' I want to have a swimming pool put back there. Hey, it's summer," she said defensively. "I thought I'd go down and take a dip." She said a group of patients went U/A, as it is called, unauthorized absence, in order to go swimming. "Hey, I've got a picture for you; I'll get it; wait right here." She flew out of the dayroom and went to the dorm, returning in a moment with a large sheet of pale purple construction paper with multicolored crayon words on it. I asked her what she called it. She said, "Once three times a lady she is the lady."

She brought out construction paper and crayons and made a picture of the earth, which she labeled with the cardinal directions, N, E, W, S. She titled the picture, "Through the earth I see them shine, I see the earth as a bottle of wine."

She drew clouds and they reminded her of the time she took an airplane home from the Brown School in San Marcos, Texas. "I had a steak and a glass of wine served to me. It was absolutely beautiful. I was alone. It was the best adventure in my life. My mom and dad met me at the airport: 'Are you bad! Come on, let's get some lunch,' they said." As she spoke, she cut up her earth and clouds with scissors. "Whenever you want to find the north-south-east-west," she said, "you mark north-south-east-west, move them around and transfer them around. Here." She moved the clouds to the top of the earth. "Now it's raining in the north. I want to buy Brown School, do you know if it's for sale? How much do they want for it?"

I said I didn't know, but that I was sure it would cost a great deal even if it were for sale. Millions.

"That's OK, I'll find some money."

"How?"

"I'll just find it."

People were beginning to come in for 2:30 commissary. Tommy came in yawning. Theresa asked a woman, "What is algebra?" The unit director, whose name was Diane, turned the television on loud. It was "General Hospital."

I asked Molly how she liked television. "It's terrible," she said. "It's horrible. Some people staring at you. Soap operas are especially terrible, all this weird stuff between men and women—paranoia and depression and schizophrenia. They're terrible."

I remembered Sandy telling me that when she was at Elgin she used to have to skip dinner just to get away from the television.

Molly turned to Diane. "Can you put on something besides this sad stuff?"

"Well," Diane said, as if speaking to a child, "Linda asked for it, so when it's done, what do you want to watch?"

"A ball game or something," Molly said. "Diane, really, this is horrible."

People lined the walls, smoking and staring, waiting for the clock to say 2:30 so that they could get coffee or a candy bar. A man who looked like a truck driver, in new blue jeans and a neatly pressed plaid shirt, sat down at the table with me and Molly. Bob looked about forty. He was well-groomed, big-boned, with a recently-trimmed flattop and an open, friendly face. I hadn't seen him before, so I asked him how long he'd been there, and then remembered when I'd first arrived, being asked if I were a new patient. Maybe Bob was on the staff.

"Since this morning," he said.

Maybe Bob was another reporter, I thought. "Where did you come from?"

"I came from Wyoming at 9:00 a.m." He had an even smile, a steady gaze, and clean fingernails.

"How did you get here?" I asked.

"Astrally," he said. "Through the air. I go about two million miles above the earth at night by levitation. Then I usually have gravitational pull and come back in. I travel astrally about a million times a day. I used to travel astrally in yoga position, but since I've become bigger and gained weight, since I've been farming and ranching and—being an astronaut—I travel by teleportation."

Tommy sat at the next table over and picked up a book. "Ah, *The Cat in the Hat*," he said with a hint of sarcasm. "I remember *The Cat in the Hat*." He began to read aloud, as if to point out the kindergarten atmosphere of the place and hold it up to ridicule.

"I'm going to get in line now," Molly said. The commissary had opened, and people were getting little packets of instant coffee and Reese's peanut butter cups and pop. Molly brought coffee and cranberry juice for us, and now, as she sat drinking, she began to turn inward, her shoulders rocking gently.

"Did you get a chance to attend the Olympics?" Bob asked. I said I hadn't, but that I had seen some events on television. "I was a gold medalist in every event at the Los Angeles Olympics," he said. "Five thousand two hundred twenty-four, three million nine hundred thousand eight hundred and thirty-eight . . ."

Molly withdrew into her cigarette, laughing and crying softly. A loud Kraft mayonnaise commercial was blasting us as the screen filled with cumulo-nimbus whorls of creamy white. A giant came up and muttered at me incoherently, taking my hand in his great, soft paw. Bob rattled off numbers, while

Tommy read *The Cat in the Hat* and Molly cried. A girl on the couch shouted, "Goddamnit! That's it!" Checkers went rolling across the tile floor as people wandered up and down, eating, smoking, drinking. I don't know whether it was the sugar or the time of day or the excitement of interacting at the commissary, but the room seemed to be reaching a symphonic climax.

Molly pulled herself together and tried to explain her predicament. "These aren't my real teeth," she said, placing her right hand flat on the table, fingers splayed. "They had to put on lots of lotion to get the pin taken out of this finger. They'll straighten up all right."

Tommy shouted, "Electron bombardment!" then resumed reading:

> He picked up the cake,
> and the rake, and the gown
> and the milk, and the strings,
> and the books, and the dish.
> And the fan, and the cup,
> and the ship, and the fish,
> and he put them away.
> Then he said, 'That's that.'
> And then he was gone
> with a tip of his hat.

I asked Molly what she did when she was little.

She said, "Played volleyball, smoked pot, drank Southern Comfort and fruit punch. Say, I know a writer. He wrote diographies. He had a good tact. Do you want me to sing for you? Let me get my radio, and I'll sing for you." When she headed for the dorm, Tommy came over with a coloring book and flipped the pages for the unit director, narrating each drawing. The unit director was clearly made uncomfortable by Tommy's closeness and perhaps by the sense that he was mocking her, mocking the coloring book, mocking the insanity of their circumstances. "These are ICBMs," he said, pushing the drawings close to her face. "Save the last dance for me. They say the world's been destroyed before. It was a hell of a car, a Nash, you could find it in any Bible." But as before, his speech seemed to have a subtext: *OK, you want me to be insane? How's this? Is this insane enough for you?*

Molly came back quickly, saying, "There's people in my home now holding me at gunpoint telling me I can't get my radio, so I can't sing for you. I'm sorry." Then she broke into song anyway: "*Mine eyes have seen the glory of the coming of the Lord, he was peeling down the alley in a green and yellow Ford, he had one hand on the throttle and the other on a bottle of Pabst Blue Ribbon beer!*"

The unit director informed me that someone from the administration building was coming to take me away.

"I've got to go," I told Molly.

"I'm sorry I couldn't get my radio and sing for you," she said.

"It's OK," I said. "Maybe some other time."

Tommy said, "Sorry. Sorry for spoiling your visit."

"You didn't drink your cranberry juice," Molly said.

"You drink it," I told her.

"OK. Bye-bye."

❖   ❖   ❖

One day I was walking the grounds, meditating on what I'd seen. Elgin is a beautiful place set on two hundred acres in the Fox River Valley, with lines of trees in hollows and hills, red tile roofs on yellow brick dorms, and throughout the area I could see patients taking walks, singly or in groups of two or three. Without warning, a storm broke, and when the rain started, it was as if they didn't know what to make of it. Instead of running for shelter, they froze in mid-stride with the rain pouring around them. I stopped, too, fascinated by what I was seeing; and suddenly I couldn't seem to remember which made more sense, stopping to feel the rain or running to avoid it. Then I started laughing: There we all were, standing in the rain, trying to figure out the right thing to do.

ANATOMY OF A DRUG BUST

One: The Playground

One day last summer I went down to the new Criminal Courts Building to meet a special investigator from Richard M. Daley's Office of the State's Attorney. Call him Tony Guido. (I won't use real names; someone might get hurt.) He was going out to buy some cocaine, so he xeroxed about four hundred dollars in fives and tens and twenties. It was an easy way to make a record of the serial numbers. Guido put the bills in his pocket, the Xerox copies in his brief case, then he shrugged into a white leather jackass rig with a chrome .38 in a shoulder holster. A heavy-set man in his forties, with curly black hair and thick features under a full beard that had just started to show gray, Guido had a big laugh always at the ready. It was hard to judge him from his looks; he was proud of that. He liked to brag that he could pass for anything from a hit man to a stock broker. In his fifteen years on the street he had done both.

We went out into the city. It looked like the buildings were dissolving in the hot, acid wind. Guido's maroon Chevy sedan had not been washed in a very long time. Guido had removed the hubcaps because they tend to come off in high speed turns. It looked like a working man's beater, but it had an overhead cam racing engine beneath the dented hood; I could hear the carburetor throats sucking down fuel as we proceeded north from the Criminal Courts Building and Cook County Jail.

We cruised up California, past Mount Sinai Hospital. It was more like going up a river than a street. Ahead there was only the long reach, deeper and deeper into the heart of Chicago's gang territory. Destroyed buildings rose like cliffs on either side, and every time we turned a corner it seemed as if another dark stone door had closed behind us.

"You're in the heart of Indian country now," he said. "This is Disciples territory." We were moving slowly up the east side of Garfield Park. After a few more blocks, he said, "Now we're on Latin Kings turf. We call this neighborhood the playground."

The light became weaker, the people on the street fewer, and the devastation more wholesale and more unbelievable, until at last it looked as if we drove through a city that had been hit by the hydrogen bomb. Those people who moved in the gray misty light looked like black cadavers in cosmoline.

Guido turned west around the north end of the park on Roosevelt, then north on Whipple. A vacant lot on the right hand side, a scene of rubble and truck tires and gutted cars. Another building, blown inexplicably across an alley, poured bricks and mortar into the lot, where half a dozen bare-chested blacks lounged in the heat. Their chests were intricately muscled, the abdominals shining with sweat. They were at once watchful and serene, as if they slept on full alert.

"These are the PCP dealers," Guido said. "They're selling Happy Sticks, marijuana dipped in PCP. They know we're The Man, but for anybody else, they'll come right up to the car and sell to you. We sit back there in the park with high-powered binoculars and watch them do it all day long. We've had our buying agents, black undercover cops, buying from them for weeks. These motherfuckers'd kill you for a dime. I mean a fucking dime," Guido said. "Lookit how they start to move as we come by." He grinned maniacally and shouted, "Hey, motherfucker! It's The Man!" But we had the windows rolled up and the air conditioning on, and they couldn't hear him. We might as well have been in a time machine, traveling back to the day when the first black biped stepped out into the first pale light of dawn. "Lookit that son of a bitch move." There was a note of awe, even respect, in Guido's voice.

While the others stared with suddenly heightened intensity at us through sleepy eyes, one of the creatures stirred from where he leaned against a blown-up car and started walking slowly to one side of the vacant lot. His movement conveyed so much. It was no accident that the police called themselves The Man and referred to him and his comrades as The Animals. His slack-limbed and sullen gait was that of a lion disturbed from an afternoon nap.

Certainly jail held no threat for him.

It was not hard to believe that he would kill me for a dime—even gratis with the proper provocation. And yet he looked as beautiful as he looked deadly.

As we drifted up the block, the same scene was repeated four more times: A brood of black bodies, glistening with heat, in postures of lassitude, stirred at our approach, then resettled around a collection of destroyed vehicles, in between blown-up buildings. Guido had opened up the glove box to reveal a Motorola Citywide police radio, and now it spoke up: "Citywide, man shot thirty-sixteen West Lexington, man shot."

"The 'b'hood is waking up," Guido said, navigating over toward Kedzie for the nine-block ride to Fort Harrison.

Two: Fort Harrison

On the back side of the police station at Harrison and Kedzie was a two-level concrete parking structure that produced the effect of entombment without actually being underground: concrete, cold and thick, with nothing coming in or going out, noise, radiation, weather—nothing. In the far corner of the garage was a thirty-gallon oil drum with the lid welded on and a five-inch hole cut in the top. It had been mounted on a stout steel stand so that it faced us at an angle. It was painted policeman blue, and around the top the word SHOTGUN had been stenciled in black letters.

"That's so these assholes don't blow their fuckin' heads off unloading their shotguns after a raid," Guido said. "You get pretty hyped up going in, and a few guys have put a load of shot into the ceiling of this garage jacking rounds out of the chamber. So they put some sand in the bottom of this oil drum and hope somebody uses it."

We went through double glass doors to Gangs West headquarters. Men with guns hurried back and forth. Here a mild-looking young man with blond hair, a faint moustache, and spectacles glided by with a cannon strapped to his waist, another beneath his armpit, another to his leg. He looked like a graduate student in sociology on his way to visit El Salvador. He didn't have to go to Latin America to find trouble; he was just going out the door. In the space of a few minutes, twenty men moved past with their artillery showing and looking for all the world like pharmacists, gas station attendants, professors, short-order cooks, lawyers, gang members. Their guns—the size and shape and color of each—were as diverse as the features of male anatomy.

Guido had borrowed a buying agent from Gangs North, Billy Poole, a young, handsome black cop with just the right flair and flash to go in and make drug buys without putting the dealers uptight. We went into an interrogation room, Guido, Poole, and I, to wait for John Cudahy, a Chicago Police Department gang specialist. Although we would only cruise around in the area while Poole made the buy, he had to have backup in case someone decided to kill him or rob him.

Poole wore a short-sleeved khaki jumpsuit and light brown patent leather slip-on shoes that had cut out patterns like sandals. His socks were sheer and brown, almost like a woman's stockings. He had a goatee started and looked to be in his mid-twenties, ten years younger than he was. He stood against the jaundiced wall of the close room. Guido and I sat in red plastic chairs at a formica table that seemed too large for the room. A heavy steel ring was fixed to the wall so The Animals could be chained when they were brought in. A hubcap served as our ashtray.

Poole's body undulated as he spoke. His thin cotton jump-suit showed no signs of sweat. He was hyped up, but he wasn't going to sweat; it would mess up the image. It was one of the reasons Poole was so good. He had a superhuman control over himself. Still, he panted when he talked. I once interviewed a man who jumped his motorcycle over twenty-one cars as a stunt. People paid nineteen dollars to see it. He always panted like that before he jumped.

"It's a pee-heese of cay-hake," Poole told Guido, breathing on every word. A phrase such as *you dig* came out as *You-hoo dih-hig*. His thin black fingers, like those of a pianist, played in the air as he spoke. "This place is wide open. They've got these runners. Just kids on the stree-heet. You drive by there, you'll see five or six people on the street across from this building all the tie-hime. Now, there's one guy flipped me in yesterday, and I want him. We've got to get him."

The previous day Poole had bought a gram of coke for ninety dollars of state money, Richie Daley money. The cocaine sell-ing was wide open at Augusta and Campbell. Poole simply drove up to the corner (in a big yellow Lincoln that had been impounded during a drug bust in Joliet, Illinois) and kids came right up to the car to ask if he wanted drugs. One kid rang the building's doorbell, and he and Poole were buzzed inside. In the dark and narrow stairwell, Poole slipped forty-five dollars through the door and was made to wait. Then someone slipped half a gram out to him. That's one good search warrant a judge would buy.

He went back half an hour later, saying the cocaine was not good enough. He was sent to the next entrance to the same building on Campbell, where he bought another half gram. That's two good search warrants. Today, like a gambler who's won a few hands of ten-cent poker, he was going back with his bankroll, the buy money Guido had gotten from the state's at-torney's office. Poole would try to get a quarter ounce for $390, which would qualify this as a major drug operation. If you busted a place that sold grams, you might get an ounce. If you busted a place that sold ounces, you might get a kilo. Poole also hoped to see a third apartment, upstairs, which he suspected was involved.

Guido handed him the marked money, $390 in tens and twenties and fives that had been xeroxed for the serial numbers. Poole began counting.

"We've got the search warrants all typed up," Guido said. "And I've got two guys standing by to line up a judge to sign them. If we can make the buy around one o'clock, we should be able to go through the doors by two, maybe two-thirty, be wrapped up by five."

"Yeah," Poole said with a slow, sad smile. "Everybody wants to go home on tie-hime on Fridays." He fed the buy money back into its rubber band and slipped it into the pocket of his jumpsuit.

Cudahy showed up with a temporary partner, Roland, a short, round, black man in his mid-thirties who wore a blue fishing hat, a golf shirt, and blue jeans. Roland looked like a jazz musician from the be-bop era. Another fifteen years, and he'd look like Coleman Hawkins. Unlike most of these men, his weapon, though in his belt, was not visible. Cudahy, who was probably thirty-three, had the bright red hair and pale complexion of an Irishman. A beer gut filled out a dirty-looking gray T-shirt that said 10TH INNING on it. His green corduroy pants were torn and greasy, as if he'd been working on his car. Nike track shoes, an immense revolver in a very worn holster on his belt, another revolver, a snub-nosed .38, strapped to his ankle: Cudahy looked like a practical man going into the woods where the animals were known to be very big and very bad. He looked like a man who had been meanly athletic back in his school days, and today he looked sweaty and irritable in addition. He was well known throughout the Chicago Police Department as a good cop and an expert in gang operations.

"How many men we got?" he asked.

"I can get two more guys from my office," Guido offered. This was a strange hybrid operation of the state's attorney's office and the Chicago police, one of many that would grow and build in the summer and fall of 1984 as the powers that be in

Chicago fought to control wave after wave of gang crime. (Any Chicago drug bust in the Humboldt Park area was presumed to be gang crime.) Guido's purview was not, strictly speaking, manpower. He was supplying the money, the clout, the car. ("I had to kiss a lot of ass to get that Continental.") He was also known as a highly professional street operator with a fifteen-year track record of successful operations in the underworld of Chicago crime.

The Chicago Police Department was supposed to supply the men. But there was a Puerto Rican celebration going on all weekend in Humboldt Park, and every available body from Gang Crimes had been dispatched to help keep the delicate peace.

"We're gonna need at least three men outside," Cudahy said. "At least. Then if we've got three apartments inside, we'll have to have a minimum of two guys on each apartment door in front going in." Counting Guido and Poole, that would mean a minimum of eleven men. Since regulations called for taking along at least one and usually two uniformed policemen on raids, the count would have to be a dozen or more. The way Fort Harrison was buzzing with activity, there wouldn't be a soul left to choose from in another half an hour.

"What did the Chief say?" Roland asked.

"Well, it's up to him whether we go or not," Cudahy said. He turned to Guido. "If you want, we could go in and make the buy, then bust 'em Sunday. Even Monday or Tuesday, for that matter."

"I don't want to let the money float for that long," Guido said. "We'd really like to get that money back. No sense in feeding them for forty-eight or ninety-six hours."

"Well, if you're really concerned about getting the money back, we'll have to bust 'em right away," Cudahy said. "We'll just have to see what the Chief says." He turned to Poole, who was floating there beside him like a khaki paratrooper. Cudahy touched the black Papermate in Poole's breast pocket. "Get rid of that pen," he said.

Poole grinned, and his closely-cropped head bobbed and weaved like a fighter's. "I *all*-ways get rid of mah pe-hen," he said.

❖   ❖   ❖

Guido and I went for coffee in the electro-mechanical canteen in the basement next to the pistol range. On one wall was a pay telephone. Several cops in a row tried to use it. It ate their quarters and gave back not so much as a dial tone. A candy machine gave no change. It would spit out a pack of gum for any amount from thirty cents to a dollar. It wasn't broken; it was designed that way. Guido, whose office had Krupp coffee makers to brew state-supplied coffee, said, "They don't give these guys anything, do they?" Tins of soup and chili con carne and even lasagna were lined up in the display window of another machine like C-rations, C for Campbell's, C for Combat, C for Cop, C for Calm down.

"This is called hurry up and wait," Guido said. And a few minutes later: "You go in there without enough men, you're liable to end up takin' a dirt nap." Normally Guido liked to brag about the bad old days, busting gangsters on the street. He was renowned for dressing up like one of them, going out into their world, getting their confidence, and having them drive a semi full of stolen Panasonics right into the police parking lot. He had a foot locker full of news clippings. But now he was quiet; he was thinking a mile a minute, and he wasn't his usual cheerful self.

It was nearly one o'clock when word came from the Chief: Today was the only day this buy could be made, men or no men. No explanation given and none requested.

We stood around in the cool cinder block hallway upstairs just outside Gangs West headquarters, talking, then waiting, then talking again, then, finally, looking at each other. While we were talking, two cops had come in and exchanged pleasantries with Guido and Cudahy.

"Hey," Guido said, "we're going on a little raid; wanna come?" The more nervous he got, the more he sounded like a TV cop show. And why not? What's a cop supposed to do when he goes to a bar after work and sees somebody on the tube who makes half a million dollars a year for acting like a cop?

"What time?"

"Maybe two, two-thirty."

"Sure, how many guys you need?"

"As many as you can get, we're gonna hit three apartments at once." Maybe that's the way cops are supposed to act. Maybe if you act that way somebody will give you half a million bucks.

"You'll need twenty." Anyway, all the other cops do it too now. It was no longer possible to tell if the cops were imitating the TV or the TV was imitating the cops.

Outside the double glass doors, intermittent patches of sun had begun to appear now and then on the breezeway; the overcast was breaking up. With the new recruits, it now looked as if there were enough men to make the raid, but everyone knew that whether we went or not was up to Poole in a more fundamental sense that transcended politics, manpower, even the Chief's orders, for he was the only one of this small group who had volunteered to put his head in the lion's mouth. He finally spoke up, breathing out the words in five and seven syllables, his hands playing piano in the air. "I think we ought to ju-hust go over the-hair and do it."

Cudahy said, "Let's do it."

Three: The Buy

We were issued walkie-talkies—man-to-man radios with a range of only four or five blocks—and going out the door, Cudahy did a radio check, "Cudahy to Poole."

"Poole."

"Cudahy to Guido."

"Guido."

We were walking within a dozen feet of one another, but we looked around and heard the voices coming through the walkie-talkies: Those voices, thin, drawn tight by the tiny speakers and wires, were the phantoms of men, the only sign of life among this group that we'd have for the next hour or so.

Roland and Cudahy rode in one car, a black sedan so nondescript that we lost visual contact before it left the parking lot. Poole pulled out in the yellow Lincoln, which showed up in traffic as clearly as the sun now glaring through the clouds. And Guido and I went in the maroon sleeper. Before he got in, he took a pair of high-powered binoculars from the trunk and laid them on the seat. And just before he pulled away from Fort Harrison, he flipped out his revolver, snapped open the chamber, and checked to make sure he had put bullets in it. He gave me a look like, Ha-ha, don't want to walk in with my fly open.

With Cudahy ahead and Poole behind, we lost both of them two minutes out, and several calls on the walkie-talkies failed to raise any response. We drove up Kedzie to Humboldt Park, whose southern border is Augusta. Our target was at the intersection of Augusta and a narrow residential one-way street called Campbell. (Like so many Chicago streets, Campbell, though seemingly insignificant, runs the entire length of the city, from Howard to Blue Island.) We turned east on Augusta, still out of contact with the others.

"Check it out," Guido said as we approached. "Augusta side, west, second floor." We rolled past the building. "Look at all those motherfuckers out on the street. Woofers and tweeters. They're lookouts. These guys have an amazing communications network. Sometimes they use CB radios, walkie-talkies. You never know when you're on the street who you're looking at. Some mother with a little baby could be tipping 'em off that you're coming in, and that could mean bad news when you get there."

They weren't lions; they were cubs, Puerto Rican kids playing across from the apartment building. The neighborhood was not like the one we had seen before, where the PCP dealers were providing curb service. This was a newly renovated building. The cars on the street were average, not too flashy, not stripped down for parts or burned out where they lay. The street was remarkably clean. The kids looked just like any kids playing on a hot day.

Guido said, "They know you're coming, and they know when you're gone. If we just cruise by, they'll just suppose its the Gang Unit doing its thing."

The street was one-way heading south. We went around to approach from the north, where, with the binoculars, we could get a good view of Poole going in, but the street had been cut off with saw horses for a block party. It was all connected with Puerto Rican independence.

"Fucking Pork Chops," Guido said, meaning Puerto Ricans. He picked up the walkie-talkie. "Guido to Poole."

"Hey, Tony. Cudahy. Where's Billy?"

"I don't know, maybe he had car trouble back there. Let's hang here for a minute. Where are you?"

"I'm just north of the target," Cudahy said.

"Campbell's blocked off north of Augusta. I'm going around to the south."

"Ten-four."

We criss-crossed the neighborhood without drawing stares from anyone. There were a lot of people out now, and the only way we could tell if they were people or animals was if they stared at us too much. An old man out for a walk with a three-year-old. A woman and her baby. There were white people who looked like college students. It was a mixed neighborhood that had not yet been blasted back to prehistory. Perhaps this operation would help postpone that time a little longer. Perhaps not.

On the far side of the target we stopped again and radioed. Suddenly Poole's voice burst in over the static: "Poole to Cudahy, I'm going in now."

"Hey," Cudahy said, "your ankle holster's showing pretty clearly."

"I got rid of that," Poole said. "And the pen, too. I'm going in now, I'm shuttin' off my ra-hay-dee-o."

"Ten-four."

And then the silence closed around us as real as if the sun had been blotted out by the shadow of the moon. The Chevy growled up alongside Chopin Elementary School two blocks south of the apartment into which (we knew, though we could not see) Poole was taking his thin and lanky and handsomely athletic body, sheathed in the scant khaki material of his jumpsuit, naked to whatever might come roaring out of that door when he rang the bell and asked for drugs. Poole was not wired. Now we had no way of knowing, other than by pure chance or instinct, whether he was in trouble or not. His walkie-talkie was down under the seat of that yellow Lincoln. Worst of all, he had taken off his gun. Now he had no bark and no bite either. And we were sitting there in the hissing air conditioning, watching fifth graders play basketball on the asphalt.

The Citywide police radio crackled. "Northside Gang Unit, Northside Gang Unit, man shot . . ." My heart went down into the deepest reaches of my abdomen, seeking the darkness there. Guido adjusted the squelch on the police radio and chuckled. He put the car in gear and we moved out.

At first I thought he was responding to the call, but he just idled around the school and back toward Campbell again. From the other side of the school yard, looking down Campbell, we could see the area of the street in front of the apartment where Poole was. Guido picked up the binoculars and peered down the barrels for a moment.

"I can see a yellow car, but it's not his."

We sat back and waited. People came and went, white, black, Latino. I looked into each face, but saw no awareness there, only the blank, detached looks of people walking in the heat, going somewhere, coming back, passing through the events taking place all about them without seeing, without the slightest suspicion. It was after one in the afternoon. Noise from the school reached us periodically, the occasional piercing scream of children at play. And yet the whole environment, the locale itself—houses, trees, fencelines, sky—seemed poised, mute and implacable, ready to swallow us the moment we lost our concentration, as if by an act of mental power alone we were keeping one reality in place and another at bay.

"There. Look." Guido slowly, carefully moved his hands to the steering wheel—no sudden reflexes. Across the street were two boys, one about eleven, the other no more than eight or nine. The little one had the ghetto blaster, a silver radio the size of an American Tourister suitcase, and they were both laughing and pointing at us. They were woofers and tweeters. "Hey, that's right, motherfuckers!" Guido shouted in the sound-proof car. "It's The Man, yeah!" Putting the car in gear, he said, "We'd better move in case they're on their way up the street to tell The Animals that The Man's here."

We pulled out, went around the block, and settled once again south of the target. We parked on the right hand side of the street. The apartment was now directly behind us and on the same side as we were. Ten minutes had passed, more than enough by far for Poole to slip his money through the door and get some coke. I mentioned that it had been a long time.

"Yeah, too long," Guido said. He picked up the binoculars and trained them on the side-view mirror. "Hey, this really works," he said. "I can see right down their throats."

The police radio sizzled again. "Eleventh District, man shot, man shot . . ."

Who were all these people being shot? I wondered. No one seemed the least bit alarmed by it either. And they certainly didn't show up on the news. Maybe they were just false alarms.

"Come on, Poole, come on, get the fuck outa there."

It was so quiet then. The sun blazed away all shadow from the neighborhood. A tiny two-year-old Latino walked by with her mother. The air conditioner or something was causing the hair on my arms to stand up, and yet I felt almost as if I could fall asleep there, sitting in the cushions of that Chevrolet. Except that the door post was blocking my rear and peripheral vision, and people kept sneaking up on me, startling me out of my reverie.

"I hope he's in one piece," Guido said. He crushed out a cigarette he'd just lit. "And people wonder why I smoke three packs a day."

Softly now, the walkie-talkie came to life—Cudahy to Guido—and Guido grabbed it as if it were a grenade with the pin pulled. "Yeah, John, what's up?"

"I just made a pass. His car's there, parked on the east side of Campbell right near Augusta. There's a bunch of kids sitting on it."

"Where the fuck is he? I'm going around for a look." So much for the eternal patience portrayed by TV cops on the stakeout. In real life you can't lap dissolve past the parts you don't like.

"Ten-four."

Guido made the circuit around the school once again, and we approached the apartment building, heading west, going at a fair clip to avoid giving the impression that we were spying, which we were. Just as we went by, I saw the big yellow Lincoln, parked illegally blocking the crosswalk. A split second later, I noticed that Poole was inside, leaning over the seat doing something. I told Guido.

"Well, get on the fuckin' walkie-talkie, Billy."

Racing west, Guido slammed on the brakes. We turned up an alley, then a side street, and were back around almost behind the apartment when Poole came on, panting, barely able to speak.

"Poole to Cudahy, Poole to Cudahy, it's one dude, male, Latino, black hair, name of Alvarez, first floor . . ." the signal began to break up as Poole gave complete descriptions of the people and actions he had just seen, laying it all out even as he sped away from the scene so that the others could have as close to a first-hand impression as they could get without actually having been there in person. Like the professional he was, Poole was thinking about the day he and the others would be in a courtroom facing a hostile defense attorney who wanted to know for sure, beyond the shadow of a doubt, if he really saw what he thought he saw.

For the next four or five blocks Poole's grip was tight upon the talk button as he breathed out the words. All we got was that there were two, this Alvarez fellow and the main man, someone named Nito (pronounced Neat-O, short for Benito) Guzman.

When Poole finally let up the button so someone else could talk, Cudahy asked, "But did you score?"

"Yeah, I scored."

Guido gave a war cry. "Then let's go!" He put his foot to the floor, and the Chevy howled down the boulevard. He ran a few red lights, saying, "Fuck these." Then he picked up the Motorola microphone and called, "Three-oh-Six to Twenty-Sixth Street." No answer came from the Criminal Courts Building. "Twenty-Sixth Street, come in." And to me: "Fuckin' cunt's probably in the ladies' room." Nobody's going to give him half a million dollars for saying that on TV.

A woman's voice came on. "Yeah, Tony."

"Hey, uh, Angie, get a hold of Burger and tell him to get a judge lined up. We're gonna be going through some doors in a couple of hours."

"OK, Tony."

Four: The Judge

Making a drug bust is like running a complicated and dangerous obstacle course. There are snake pits and fire-breathing dragons, there are infuriating and torturous, twisty pathways that must be followed, and there are arcane rules and regulations to which the participants must adhere, or the whole game is declared void. So far, the running of the course had been smooth, and no one had been killed or injured. Now the only matter standing in the way of going "through the doors with guns blazing" (Guido's phrase) was the matter of search warrants, and we returned to Fort Harrison to make plans and fill in the blanks on the warrants so that a judge could sign them.

In a small room at Gangs West headquarters Billy Poole sat at an old manual Olympia typewriter filling out the pink buy forms. There was a map on the wall that had been inked in with red and blue and yellow and green and black zones to show the different gang territories, Latin Kings, Disciples, Traveling Disciples, Rangers, Kedzie Rangers, Traveling Rangers, Ranging Travelers—it looked like a homemade patchwork quilt.

Next to the Olympia typewriter was a small clear plastic bag of white powder. Cudahy and Roland came in and stood watching with their arms folded. Cudahy picked up the cocaine, rolled open the top of the baggie, and smelled the contents.

"Fuck this raid, let's get some straws, it's Friday," he said. "Somebody close that door."

"Aw, that's not the good shit," Poole said, his thin black fingers moving nervously over the typewriter keys as if he sat at a concert grand. "We goin' back for tha-hat."

As we sat there, he explained that he had not been allowed into the third-floor apartment, the one in which everyone suspected the largest amount of cocaine might be kept. He had been "one foot inside" of an apartment that had, the day before, had the name Alvarez on the door. "Today he's removed the name plate," Poole said. The other apartment, that of Benito Guzman, was the one from which he bought the eighth of an ounce in the plastic bag in Cudahy's hand. "I saved the state a little money," Poole told Guido. "Two-seventy-five for an eighth."

"Great, gimme the change," Guido said.

Poole handed over the remaining bills in their rubber band.

"So we can't bust the third floor," Cudahy said.

"No, we can't," Poole agreed. He had taken so long because

he'd had to wait outside in the hall while Nito brought the cocaine. "I waited ten minutes. He could've gone anywhere."

"Or he could've been mixing it up," Cudahy said.

"You know what I think," Roland said. He lifted his blue fisherman's hat and resettled it on his head. It was the first time he'd spoken for a long time, and he was a police detective with a lot of drug experience, so everyone listened. "I think he went upstairs and got it. I think the dope is in that third-floor apartment."

"Could be," Poole said. "I never set foot in there, though, and I never even laid eyes on Nito."

"But you did buy the drugs from that door."

"The second floor. Yes. Handed in my money, and he handed out that," Poole said, pointing to the packet of white powder.

"Any gates?" Cudahy asked, meaning reinforcing gates on the doors to the apartments.

"No gates," Poole said.

By the time the call came back from the Criminal Courts Building saying that a judge had been located, it was after two, and Poole had talked the case out, step by step. "I can just go up to the door and ring the bell. I'll take Roland back with me and say I've got another customer. They'll buzz me into the hallway, and you come in right after me."

"Can you put something there to hold the street door open for us?" Cudahy asked.

"Maybe. Then meanwhile, somebody has to jump that back fence."

"How tall is it?"

"Taller than I am. But you have to come in fast once I'm in, because these guys might think we're comin' back to rob them. They were robbed two days ago by two bla-hack dudes, and they're very nervous."

We drove south in two cars to meet a judge who'd agreed to be at the Criminal Courts Building at three o'clock for five minutes to sign the search warrants. It was only two-thirty when we arrived, but the judge had left.

"Fucking Friday," one of the assistant state's attorneys told

Guido. "I called ten judges, and only two of them were still even in town. One's sitting at a death hearing right now, and he can't be disturbed. Go down to Judge Mahaffy's, he'll sign it for you."

Cudahy, carrying a file folder with the warrants, Roland in his blue fishing hat, and Guido in his beige wind breaker rode down in a crowded elevator. Already the building was beginning to empty out for the weekend.

Another cop, this one in a suit and tie, maybe fifty-five years old, entered the elevator, popping a file folder on his arm. "Hey, Tony, how's your sex life?"

"Fantastic."

"So how is Bruce, anyway?"

We left the elevator and crossed over to the old Criminal Courts Building. The police officer in the suit went into Judge Mahaffy's office first and got his warrant signed. He came out grinning and popping the file folder on his arm. The sheriff guarding the door motioned us in. Before we'd taken two steps, Judge Mahaffy came out with his hat on, saying, "Sorry, I don't sign search warrants."

"But your Honor—" Cudahy began, but Judge Mahaffy pushed past him and was gone. I saw what fun it was to be a judge; you could push people around, even if they had guns.

"Thanks a lot, motherfucker," Guido said once Mahaffy was out of earshot. "I'll remember this." Indeed, it was completely within Judge Mahaffy's right to refuse. On the other hand, the police expected to be given some service now and then if they were going to go out and risk their lives to fight crime. And Mahaffy had just signed the other officer's warrant. He probably just wanted to get out on his boat before rush hour.

A blond woman in her twenties walked in wearing an aqua blue business-style dress. She began talking and twitching as if she'd been taking speed. "I'll get you a judge, don't worry." She dialed the phone three or four times before she got an answer, then twice more before she got a judge who was in. "Room three-oh-one," she said. "Judge Arnold will see you now."

We left with Guido grumbling, "That bitch was flying."

"Looked like she was taking the cocaine around here," Cudahy said.

"Fucking Mahaffy."

"What an asshole."

"An-and that Neat-O's probably in fucking Brazil by this time."

"Nah, he'll be dealin' all weekend long there."

Up on the third floor all the courtroom doors were closed and locked, and the lights were dimmed. The faintly yellow walls were decorated here and there with the inscrutable rococo signatures of gangs, like the trails of some species of schizophrenic snail that crawled invisibly through the night. How did they get on these walls? I wondered. I realized that I had never actually seen a gang, only reports of gangs, dead gang members on the news, Richard Daley promising to stop gang crime. Where did these gangs meet en masse? In the halls of the Criminal Courts Building?

"What'd she say, three-oh-eight?"

"No, three-oh-two."

"Shit, I thought it was three-oh-one."

"Three-oh-one."

We went from door to door, trying locks, wandering down the halls, cursing and grumbling, carrying the search warrants that, without a judge's signature, were as worthless for making a drug raid as water pistols would have been. Along one corridor were dirty floor-to-ceiling windows looking toward the lake. Pigeons had nested on a ledge outside, in spite of thousands of needle-thin spikes placed there like some kind of Laotian torture device to keep them off. Baby pigeons sat screaming in their nests, and here and there on the spikes were impaled the decomposing bodies of adult pigeons. How they came to die that way, I could not say. Roland came up beside me to look.

"Jesus Christ," he said, "lookit that. What do you suppose happened to them? Lookit those babies there." Pigeon eggs here and there had rolled out of the nests and lay about, evidently forgotten by the parents. Some of them had been punctured, and the yellow life had already oozed out of them. The entire band course, a sheltered shelf that ran the circumference of the building, was deeply encased in the solidified excreta of pigeons.

We finally found an unlocked courtroom that had a bailiff in it. He came out like a Doberman, seeing men dressed like sixties hippies, with enormous guns openly displayed, entering his domain. The shields came out and the crisis passed. Our group was ushered into the judge's chambers.

Judge Arnold was in his sixties, a large-boned man with curly white hair and droopy skin. He wore a white shirt, casual slacks, and crepe soled shoes. His desk had no modesty panel, and I could see his feet. His heels touched the floor, but his toes pointed at the ceiling the entire time we were there. His big shoes looked somehow dislocated. Behind him was a wall of *Illinois Reports*, standard law books. On another wall were the Declaration of Independence, the Bill of Rights, and cartoons of barristers in another era.

Cudahy handed the judge the documents, paper-clipped copies of the warrants, separated by carbon paper. Judge Arnold raised his right hand and a scowl overcame his deeply-lined countenance. He demanded, "Do you solemnly swear that the statements made in these documents are the truth, the whole truth, and nothing but the truth, so help you God?" It was necessary to swear in an officer in order to make a legal search warrant, then to take his testimony as to what he saw. Most judges could make this into a thirty-second affair. Judge Arnold evidently had a different approach.

Cudahy raised his hand and said, "I do."

"This'll take a minute," Judge Arnold said, and began reading the warrants as we stood before him. "Have you got proof of residency?" he snapped.

"Right there, Your Honor," Cudahy said, moving in to point it out.

"OK, take this copy," he said, handing one of the warrants to Cudahy. "Now, what I want you to do is to read me everything from here down, just like you have it printed there."

"Yes, Your Honor," Cudahy said, and he began reading the

warrant to enter the dwelling at such-and-such a number on
Campbell in the municipality of Chicago in the County of
Cook in the State of Illinois for the purpose of recovering U.S.
Currency and a controlled substance, cocaine . . .

"Wait a minute," Judge Arnold said. "Read the serial numbers, too."

"Of the bills?" Cudahy asked, incredulous.

"Yes, read the numbers, too."

"G-zero-five . . ." Cudahy began with a sigh. There were a
lot of bills, and Judge Arnold interrupted Cudahy several times
because he did not understand that the officer was saying "zero"
where the judge thought he was seeing the letter O. Gradually
and at last the recitation came to an end, and Cudahy gave the
warrants back to the judge, and the judge motioned for us to
be seated, because it was going to take a while longer still.
Cudahy looked around to exchange glances with Guido. The
look seemed to say, We have a live one here, and he's probably
still here because he can't find his way out of the building.

I could see Roland's feet going nervously under his chair.
Judge Arnold's feet tipped this way and that, pointing at the
ceiling like blind animals, searching for a scent.

At length, the judge said, "Somebody give me the time."

Cudahy looked at his wrist, but there was no watch there.
He turned to Roland in the chair beside him. "Give him the
time," he said in a tense whisper.

Roland stirred as if from a sleep. "Oh, yes, it's three-sixteen."

The judge began writing, then stopped, then read again. Two
minutes passed in stillness, and then he barked, "Time!"

"Three-eighteen," Roland said.

We were in grave danger there, I thought. This was not standard operating procedure, not even by a long shot. I could feel
the tension billowing in the room like smoke from a fire that
has not yet broken out but was only just then boring through
the stuffing in some piece of furniture, making its greedy way
toward the surface, ready to explode when it hit fresh oxygen. I
expected at any moment that one of these good and gentle officers would leap to his feet and scream, Judge Arnold, you're ab-

solutely mad! Can't you see that out there the whole world is going obscenely on, and we're trying to catch criminals! Do you think criminals sit around and wait for us to come visiting? Do you think we have an appointment with these criminals? What do you think we wear these enormous guns for, Your Honor? Because criminals like to wait for Your Eternal Pleasure in signing these ungodly search warrants?

But not a leaf upon a potted plant stirred in the silence of that room. I think even the air conditioning had been turned off or was resting, because I have never heard such quiet. Not one of us had had anything in the way of sustenance that day, other than coffee, but not a stomach rumbled, not a sigh escaped our lips.

"Time!"

"Three twenty-one."

Five: The Bust

We made another brief stop at Fort Harrison. There was the matter of signing out some equipment: two eight-pound sledge hammers with three-foot handles, one pair of bolt cutters that looked as if they could cut down small trees, a three-foot-long pry bar, and an armload of walkie-talkies. The little crowd standing around outside Gangs West headquarters had grown considerably since the beginning of the day. Police were gravitating toward the operation, being drawn into its widening vortex the way scraps of paper are drawn into a whirlwind.

We all walked out of Fort Harrison and through the breezeway to the parking lot. Once again we stood in a group there, talking over the plans or lack of plans. A handsome collegiate man stood practicing his putt with an eight-pound sledge. He wore a sidearm so big it appeared that the weapon would realize its maximum stopping power when he dropped it on someone. He looked up from his putt, cocking his eye at Poole. "You want me to go in first?" he asked. He swung the hammer.

Police, going home or arriving to work the night shift, eyed us, eyed our equipment, and nodded. I heard one of them say, "Somebody's gonna sleep in Cook County Jail tonight."

We hit the street shortly before five o'clock that Friday afternoon, and by the time we were approaching the area, there were between fifteen and twenty men roaming around in cars looking for each other on Chicago's hot and windy West Side. I was deeply impressed by that time with how much was out of the control of these police officers. Who would conceive of starting a drug raid with half a dozen cars and twenty men in the middle of a Puerto Rican annual festival during a heat wave and freak wind storm at rush hour on a Friday in the heart of the Puerto Rican neighborhood when there hadn't been enough men with which to do it in the first place and were only now enough by chance?

The answer was that no one would, no one did, no one was in charge. I couldn't help making the obvious comparison to operations in Vietnam, where warfare was a Chinese fire drill; some of these guys had been there.

On the radio Cudahy said, "Let's meet at California and Sacramento," two streets that happen to run as parallel as railroad tracks from Evanston to Indiana. No one caught him on it, and the cars moved around in what might as well have been the inky blackness of outer space for all we could see of the others. Still, we were within radio range, circling and circling in a widening gyre, as it were.

"Guido direct to Morton," he said, abandoning the walkie-talkie for the Motorola police radio. A voice responded. "Yeah," Guido said, "let's uh, why don't you, uh . . ." Clearly, the business about the two parallel streets meeting had finally filtered through all his other thoughts, and the machinery had ground to a halt as it stumbled over the error in logic. Other voices were now coming in on the air.

"Roger."

"Citywide, citywide, five men with guns . . ."

"Boy, they'll be going like the Indianapolis five hundred now," Guido said, meaning the police who responded to that call. "Guido to Morton, don't go to the, uh, target area yet, ten-four?"

"OK."

"Why don't you just hang in there a minute while we meet up."

"We're just west of the area."

"Let's meet at Augusta and Sacramento," Cudahy said, evidently having perceived that nowhere on this Newtonian earth will California and Sacramento ever meet.

"Ten-four."

We rolled left, the G-forces pressed us back into our seats, and in a moment we'd pulled into what appeared to be a convention of the extremely fraternal order of plain-clothes police, right across from Humboldt Park. Guido slammed the Chevy into a no-parking space and we leapt out among the troops. Some of them had two, three, even four great holstered black revolvers strapped to their bodies. One special investigator had an automatic slung under his armpit in such a way that if I stood behind him, its naked barrel was pointing right between my eyes. I kept moving, but he kept turning so that his back was to me, and I couldn't help but wonder if he had some secret way of setting the thing off without unholstering it.

Sledge hammers, night sticks, giant flashlights, sun glasses, automobiles, radios crackling—one car even had a computer terminal mounted on the dash that could pull up arrest records, extradition files, even suspected terrorists and organized crime information. That car was left with the air conditioner running to cool the microchips while we milled around in the sun, hollering across the street at each other and sipping coffee from styrofoam Burger King cups.

"Who the hell are we going after today, the Dalton Gang?"

"Couple of dope dealers."

"Yeah?"

"They've got a lot of doors." It was like "Charlie's Angels" with guys.

Poole held roll call at curbside, and a few men at a time came by for briefing. No, there were no gates. Yes, someone would have to vault the fence in back. At least three men would be required to cover the back, even more for the front. There were two alleys, each one running parallel to Augusta and to Campbell, by which the apartment building could be boxed in.

"I don't think anybody can get out the back, but they can sure jump out those front windows," Poole said.

"Hear that? Anybody comes out the windows is a bad guy." That was a "Hill Street Blues" watcher.

"Got it."

"What about the kids in front all over the street?"

"Gra-hab them," Poole said. "They're the runners. I want that kid who flipped me in, and he's gonna be out there somewhere."

"What'd he look like?"

"Aw, they all look alike," Poole said, smiling, dropping his chin modestly: T. C. from the "Magnum P.I." cast.

A large black officer, who had been standing by his car when we arrived, had a tiny gun on his belt and wore a blue T-shirt that said CHICAGO POLICE. His baseball cap said GANGS WEST on it. He looked like a Bears fullback. A marked squad car pulled up and the Chief stepped out, a sixty-year-old man with alcohol-blown veins in his cheeks and nose and the flushed, irate look of an Irishman about him. He looked like the chief of police whom Michael Corleone assassinated in *The Godfather*. He started hollering and swearing up and down the street at anyone he could find, and the troops howled with invective laughter.

The big black Gangs West cop went over and hollered at him. Cudahy crossed the street to scream in the Chief's face at the top of his lungs, waving the warrants around in the sunlight and pointing, but it was evidently all Irish jest, for after a minute, the scene quieted down once again and the Chief was milling around with the rest of the men.

We were only eight blocks from the apartment we were going to hit, but there was no attempt at concealment and no indication that there was any longer a hurry to get there. On the contrary, the men lounged around on their cars, sitting on the curbs, hollering and laughing, as if we were going to spend the night and were just waiting for the beer and potato salad to arrive.

I don't know what finally set the operation in motion. One moment we were standing around, the next moment Poole was pointing at people, saying, "OK, you go in with John, you take the back." He turned to me. "Guido and Gonzales, go through the front door right after me." I felt my rib cage constrict around my heart. Then we were piling into cars, and engines were roaring to life.

Poole, with Roland in the front seat beside him, pulled his big yellow Lincoln to one side so that all the police cars could get around him. Then he went one way and we went the other in a great long caravan inching east on Augusta toward the target. The radios and walkie-talkies were crackling with static and voices.

"Whoa, now, wait up, Billie, don't go in too fast."

"Ten-four."

"Give us a chance to get organized here."

"OK."

"Where you at, John?"

"Heading east."

"OK, pull up there and let's wait so Billy can get into position."

"I'm ready when you are."

"Anytime."

"Here I go."

"We'll give you one minute."

"OK, now I'm parking. I'm goin' to shu-hut off my ray-hay-dee-oh now."

"Ten-four."

Augusta is not much more than a two-lane street at that

point, and cars were parked in a solid line at the curb where we had pulled over. We were double parked outside of those cars, the Friday rush hour was fully developed, and traffic was trying to get around us, the drivers angry and impatient in the heat and wind. We had more than half a dozen cars lined up there with close to twenty troops. I could see Cudahy's arm hanging out the window of his black car up ahead. We covered a residential city block there like a python on a stone, and we could see that the locals now knew.

Guido, whose normally sleepy eyes now showed white above and below the iris, said, "They just don't know where. Lookit that fat man watching us."

A black man the size of a hippopotamus sat on his brick front porch sipping a 7Up and rolling his eyes at the spectacle we made there. "Yeah," Guido told him, "it be happenin' any minute now." Anyone looking closely at the cars could see the sledge hammer handles sticking up between the seats (I had one between my legs), the men nervously fingering walkie-talkies. And a blind man walking by could have felt the tension radiating off the air conditioned vehicles, could have smelled the adrenalin.

All at once the line was in motion, but the rush-hour traffic didn't exactly part like the Red Sea. It wasn't like on TV; no cop in his right mind would speed around the city bashing into parked cars. In fact, the moment we took off, we were all stuck in a traffic jam, and people were honking at us to quit trying to cut in on their line. "Major police ops," Guido said, handing me the walkie-talkie. "Hang onto this. This is where the fun begins. This is where we come in like shock troops. It'll be like you'd taken a vacuum cleaner and vacuumed everything off the street. People will be diving into holes." He paused, rubbing the steering wheel. "If we ever get there."

The traffic broke up for a moment, and even through the air conditioning, I could hear the souped-up police engines of the other cars whining out as they made a dash for the intersection of Campbell and Augusta. I felt the sharp pressure drop as everything below my heart collapsed. All at once we were upon the place, cars parked askew up and down the street. There were guns out, Puerto Ricans flying, and cops screaming for them to get down.

"Get down!"

"Get DOWN!"

"GETDOWNMOTHERFUCKER!"

The device in my hand began speaking in a panic. "Poole to Cudahy." I could see Cudahy running on the street, carrying something—a shotgun or a hammer—but he wasn't listening. "Poole to Guido! Don't hit the house. DON'T HIT THE HOUSE! Oh, shit . . ." We were already on it, though, in the streets and pouring into the buildings.

"What'd he say?" Guido asked, but it was no use, the bust was coming down all around us, and stopping it was like trying to stop an orgasm-in-progress.

We ran through the windy sunlight and hit the stairs of the first apartment. The darkness closed on us. We were blind. There were two uniformed cops already at the door, shouting, "Police. Open up!"

A child's voice came to us in the darkness. "Nobody's home." I couldn't tell if it was a boy or a girl.

Guido handed the cop a sledge hammer.

"Open up or we're going to have to break the door down."

"Nobody's home," the little voice said.

"Holy fuck," Guido said.

We went back outside. The front window curtains of the apartment were blowing inward with the hot breeze. Someone shouted up at the building, "Come to the window."

Another: "Open the door, little girl."

We went back up the stairs and were about to hammer it open when a tiny hand turned the knob, a thin wrist appeared, and the door peeked open. Six cops went through it at once.

The small two-bedroom apartment was neatly decorated and very clean. It might have been in a middle-class Jewish or Irish or German neighborhood. A matching apple red couch, chair, and love seat were covered in heavy clear plastic to keep the dust off, but there was no dust. A girl, twelve, and a boy, nine, sat on the single red easy chair, the girl on the arm, the boy in the seat, as if they were posing for a photographer. They wore T-shirts. They were brown and thin and pretty, with wide eyes that were at once aghast and serene. They were completely still there, but the girl's left arm was twisted up into the material of her T-shirt as if she wrung her hands beneath.

The cops moved through the small apartment quickly, coming in from the back and front, and when they realized that we had busted a place with no one but two children in it, they quickly left. In a moment there was no one there except me, Guido, and one other Chicago policeman named Ahern. And they began turning the place inside out looking for cocaine, while a uniformed patrolman sat with the children.

I stood in the doorway between the parents' bedroom and the living room, and the girl fixed me with her stare and would not let go. I was dressed like the cops, jeans, running shoes. I had the walkie-talkie, the sledge hammer. To her I was a cop, and I suddenly wanted to drop the radio and hammer, to go over to her and say, Wait a minute, now, you see, I'm not actually a cop, and I don't do things like tear the linen out of the infant crib in your mother's bedroom looking for cocaine that's probably not there. No, I don't do things like that; I'm just a professional voyeur.

Behind me in the bedroom, I heard Ahern say, "Where the fuck is this shit," as he tore the clothes off the neatly-made queen-size bed where the girl's parents slept. I had the impulse to turn around and tell him to watch his language, but I didn't. I just watched as they systematically tore the place apart.

"I'll bet he's hiding upstairs right now."

Poole came in, breathing hard, his hands flying in the air like brown piano birds. "I-high try-hide to caw-hall you-all," he said with a sad smile. "Wasn't nobody home." He turned to the kids and his face fell. He was the first policeman I'd seen who seemed to recognize something tragic in the fact of their being there at all. He cast his eyes down at the floor and shook his head sadly. "Kids," he said. "Kids. You can save us a lot of trouble and save us having to mess the place up looking, if you'll just tell us where your daddy keeps his money." Poole knew that they didn't have to find cocaine if they could find the marked bills with which he'd bought cocaine earlier. It wouldn't be the big bust they'd been after, but it would at least salvage the operation and justify it.

The children looked into space. Poole shook his head sadly, as if he understood completely why they would not deign even to look at him, let alone dignify his suggestion with a response.

Of course, he was just being kind. And when they refused to help him (if, indeed, they had any idea where their father kept anything) we took it all to pieces, then took the pieces apart. After a while, when no drugs and no money turned up, the search began to take on a frantic, almost vindictive character. I found myself making suggestions and even helping out.

"Here, Gonzales, help me with this couch."

"How about those heat registers?"

"Yeah . . ."

The vents were taken out of the walls. Books were flipped off the shelves, opened, and tossed aside. Psychology, chemistry, accounting, sociology texts were thrown on the bed. Someone had gone to college. Maybe the father was putting the mother through college by selling coke. Two large soft-sided suitcases were opened and tossed aside. They contained the family's Christmas ornaments.

In the kitchen—a very clean kitchen in which someone had fried eggs and brewed strong coffee that morning—Special K and catsup and potted plants lined up neatly on shelves and window sills. There was a new washing machine in one corner, and the table had been carefully cleaned after breakfast. The floor was spotless. I couldn't get over how middle class it was. We went through every container in the cabinets—coffee, flour, sugar—then moved to the children's bedroom.

There were bunk beds and Disney character curtains,

Mickey, Goofy, Donald, sighing inward with the breeze. A lone poster showing the pre-pubescent Latino rock group Menudo hung by yellowing bits of Scotch tape from the otherwise blank wall. The room was clean but disturbingly bare. Whatever he was doing with the money, Nito wasn't buying toys.

The back door opened and police came in. One of them went into the bathroom and began rummaging in the cabinet under the sink. "Hey, old lady's on the rag," he called out after finding a box of Stayfree Maxi Pads.

I looked into the living room. The nine-year-old boy was watching us. His face was completely calm. He had not moved an inch from the chair since we'd arrived. But his eyes were like little coals burning on a dark, cold stone. I shuddered to think what he was going to do to compensate for this when he was thirteen, nineteen, twenty-five—for the indignity inflicted on him, on his mother and sister, for the procacity of our position in his house. At the very least, our presence there ensured that that nine-year-old boy and that twelve-year-old sister (whom he already felt responsible to protect) would never be normal by any white, middle-class definition of the term. At the very least, we had given them nightmares for the rest of their lives.

And yet how could we not have been there? Whose fault was it? Nito, their father, had sold Poole the cocaine right through the door. Children outside no older than the girl (they were now handcuffed together, waiting on us in the street) had enticed Poole in, acted as agents in the crime of distributing a controlled substance. Were the police, then, to ignore the crimes against which society had made its laws? For the sake of sparing these children the sight of us? Were they to spare society the turning of these children permanently against society by letting this crime go? It was an age old question: How far was society to go in protecting itself against its members?

And there were other questions, too. Was it wrong, perhaps, to outlaw cocaine? Or could we simply (as almost everyone there ultimately did) blame the damage to the children on the parents? The children weren't hurt by the bust; they were hurt by the fact that their father was a dope pusher. (Hey, listen, buddy, crooks have kids, too; there's nothing we can do about that.) Let's put it another way: These were Puerto Ricans, this was gang territory, and this was Chicago. Who are we kidding? Besides, it wasn't that big an operation. Just a small drug bust that everyone hoped would net more coke than anticipated.

But the most horrible thought of all we pushed deeper beneath the surface as the search went on: What were we to say to ourselves if we found no cocaine—if, indeed, we could not prove that a crime had been committed?

The panic produced by that last question whipped the search into a new fury of ripping and tearing at whatever might conceal. At one point I even suggested that the girl might have it in her hand beneath her T-shirt, and Ahern dutifully pried open her fingers to look. We were only following procedure.

A large police officer had come in and was attempting to lift the gas stove away from the wall when Ahern came in from the bedroom, where he had been concentrating his search. He had a small sheepskin jacket and was feeling the lining, muttering, "Probably some fucking candy bar stuck in there," but I could tell that he had homed in on a target, he was hot. His face was flushed, his find had an almost sexual thrill to it. As he spoke his voice trembled. He turned to me. "You got a knife?"

I handed him a butcher knife from the sink.

"Yeah, that'll do." Although he was holding the shell of the jacket in one hand and the lining in the other and could have pulled gently to separate the seams, he could not control himself. His shaking hand plunged the knife into the sheepskin with a trembling urgency that was embarrassing to see, as if I'd inadvertently walked in on a scene of great intimacy. Suddenly cocaine was pouring out onto the linoleum floor and blowing all over the kitchen in the breeze that came from the open back door. I grabbed the girl's eighth-grade notebook from the breakfast table and held it under the shower of cocaine with one hand while I closed the door with the other.

"Jesus Christ, there it is."

"Baggie!"

"Gentlemen. The evidence."

"Goddamned animal keeps his dope in the kid's jacket."

The sentence had been pronounced; the rationale had been put to words: The object of this search was not a man. We are The Man. He is an animal. It was a crucially important operating tenet for this kind of work. For without it, one was forced to admit that the questions surrounding what we'd done were literally overwhelming in their complexity. It was not a matter of insensitivity to pronounce the man an animal, it was just the opposite. It was to admit that we were powerless to address and resolve the myriad, deep, and intensely real philosophical and sociological questions that threatened from all sides, that were so eloquently spoken by the unwavering stares of those two children we could see through the kitchen doorway from where we stood.

Suddenly cops were moving in to form a little circle around us at the family breakfast table.

Back in the living room, the uniformed policeman had tuned in Tom and Jerry on the television to distract the children, but he alone was watching the cartoons. The girl and boy were watching us. Were they hungry? I wondered. Would they ever be hungry again?

I saw then that the "aw-shit" TV cop toughness was a barrier to block out those crippling doubts and questions the way lead blocks radiation. In a state of comprehension and compassion, actions such as these would be impossible. It was the great paradox of man's compassion to man that it necessitated such brutality as well. It was the source of the most famous quote to come out of Vietnam: We had to destroy this village to save it.

❖   ❖   ❖

The find was an ounce, more or less, and rather quickly after its discovery, probably spurred on by the knowledge of our righteous purpose, Ahern returned to the bedroom and discovered a strong box with about two thousand dollars in cash, which had been concealed behind a dresser. He brought it into the kitchen, and Guido put his foot on it while Ahern hit it with a sledge hammer. It fell open easily. Inside was an odd assortment. The thousands, of course, were in small bills, mostly twenties and tens, though there were four or five hundreds. But there were also papers—the man's green card from INS, some old bank books, light, gas, and electric bills (which we took as proof of residency), and plastic Zip-Lock bags filled with Kennedy half dollars. In the bottom of the box was small change, including buffalo nickels, as if someone had dabbled in numismatics but did not quite understand the principles. It was a little like cracking open someone's brain, and the randomness, the work-a-day unimportance of another's deepest thoughts, was startling.

Soon we had found a pharmaceutical triple-beam balance for weighing the drugs, and a special grinder for cutting cocaine with other substances.

Oh, it was a real cocaine operation, all right, albeit a very small one. This man, Guzman, evidently bought ounces and sold grams and half-grams. Whoever he bought from (perhaps someone in the off-limits third-floor apartment) sold ounces and bought kilos or half-kilos. And someone else yet one more step removed sold kilos and half-kilos and bought—what?— Bushels? Tons? Was he, then, Mr. Big? Was this insubstantial place with these two children in it the nexus of a dope ring two steps removed from Mr. Big? I found it difficult to fathom, but that was the theory by which law enforcement operated, and no one had so far stepped in to supply a better theory.

While we were busy, another team had managed to bust a little old grandmother-like Puerto Rican lady in the other apartment. She was caught running out of the building with about half a pound of marijuana and seven hundred dollars in cash. The only other arrests that could be made were a couple of the kids on the street, who had solicited Poole.

Before we left, the uniformed officer said, "Uh, may I make a suggestion? It's kind of dirty, but these kids are technically in possession of this apartment and its contents. If we took 'em in, the parents would have to come get them sooner or later . . ." He looked expectant.

There was a round of coughing and sideways glances as the officers contemplated the nine-year-old boy with his burning eyes, the twelve-year-old girl, ringing her T-shirt. The two had not moved or said a word the entire time. They had simply fixed us with their eyes and memorized us forever and ever.

I carried my radio and sledge hammer out into the sun, and Guido and I got into the old maroon Chevy. One of the people from the state's attorney's office came out, a broken-toothed grin on his face. He was the one whose automatic pistol kept pointing at my head earlier. Guido motioned for me to roll down the window. We were parked right under the window where the boy and girl were sitting with the uniformed policeman. I could hear Tom and Jerry hooting and howling.

"Hey!" Guido shouted, "I'm gonna take this evidence back and tidy up and then I'll meet you at the Candlelight for about a gallon of drinks!"

There was laughter all around. It was manic and half-mad and all out of proportion to anything that might or might not have been funny. It was relief. No one had died, and we had nabbed drugs and money. That was the job. It wasn't a great operation, but at least nobody was going to be embarrassed by it. An ounce of coke was an ounce of coke.

On the way back to Fort Harrison, I asked Guido why they didn't consider the officer's suggestion to take the kids in and wait for the parents.

"It's too complicated," he said. "You'd have to get a juvenile officer, and then it starts getting real complicated."

I asked what would happen to the kids. He said someone would take them to a foster home.

And what about Benito Guzman, the dope pusher? What would be done to catch him? What if he disappeared? What, precisely, was all this about?

"Nothin'," he said. "It's just a fucking game. I call it the Secret War. Nobody knows it goes on. But it goes on all the time. We'll go out next week and do the same thing all over again. It's just a game."

WHEN DOCTORS ARE ADDICTS

Dr. Russ Reed, now in his sixties, was the eighth generation of doctors in his family. "My father was the kind of physician who believed that doctors should try each drug before giving any to a patient," he said. The senior Reed was also the kind of doctor who took three Nembutals—heavy sedatives—to get to sleep at night. "At that time no one thought of that as addiction," said the son. "The word was hardly used in polite society, and it was certainly never applied to a respected physician."

After his father's death, Dr. Reed found a bequest: "bottles with little pills of scopolamine and morphine in them. They were the old kind that you put in a spoon with some water and heat them up until they melt and then inject the liquid." So, having a reason to medicate himself (grief over his father's death), the modern-day Dr. Reed tried his father's nineteenth-century medicine. "And I really liked that. I liked the feeling I got from those," he told me, as we sat in his north suburban office, surrounded by his collection of artifacts from the world's great religions—Buddhist prayer wheels, Christian rosaries, Islamic prayer beads. Dr. Reed used the little pills, melting and dissolving and injecting them, until his dead father's supply was all gone. Sometimes a son can try so hard to avoid being like his father that he becomes just like him.

Dr. Reed did as his father bade him and tried every new drug that came on the market—at least the psychoactive ones. Then he discovered Talwin, synthetic morphine. "It didn't exactly get me high. It had all the bad side effects of the more powerful narcotics with none of the benefits. It was just the drug for me."

In the meantime, his general surgery practice had become rather frantic. Drug addiction can take up a lot of time, he discovered, especially if one wishes to keep it a secret. "Mondays and Tuesdays I'd work my ass off," he said. "Wednesday and Thursday I'd have rounds. I was injecting myself at work, often right through my pants so that I didn't have to slow down to take my pants off." Dr. Reed would sit in his office chair and stab the needle right into his thigh muscle. "It's a miracle I didn't get some kind of infection. Sometimes the needle would go right through the money in my pocket, and money is one of the dirtiest things there is," he said with a smirk.

The more frantic Dr. Reed's schedule became, the more drugs he seemed to need. The more drugs he took, the less efficiently he performed his work, leading to more anxiety, panic, desperation. To make matters worse, he was also drinking.

Incidents began to occur in surgery that made him realize that he was teetering on the brink of something—if only he could see over the edge, perhaps he could tell what it was. But like a man in a boat, paddling madly down the Niagara River, he could not see until he was already on his way over the falls. One of the most profound characteristics of addiction is the inability of the afflicted to diagnose it. That effect, called denial, is the most formidable obstacle to treatment—when a drug becomes everything to a person, he hardly has a desire to give it up, no matter how painful his life has become. The surprising fact is that denial seems to be stronger for doctors than for other people with addictions, and addicted doctors are more difficult to treat than many other types of patients. Some of the pioneering work in that area is now being done in Chicago.

"Many health care professionals know little or nothing about the early recognition of alcoholism, and as treaters themselves they may be unusually slow to seek help or to assume the patient role," wrote a former president of the American Medical Society on Alcoholism. "When the search for help does begin, it often leads to a friend or colleague no better prepared to deal with the problem." And certainly the physician with addictive disease isn't likely to understand or admit to himself the nature of his own problem, sometimes not even after the first round of detoxification and treatment. "One of our physicians at [the] follow-up [interview] was using Librium, Quaalude, LSD, hashish, marijuana, and cocaine. He did not feel he had a drug problem."

The world has undergone an enlightenment about addiction in the past fifteen years. With that have come two new concepts: first, that drug addiction (including addiction to the drug alcohol) is a disease; and second, that the disease is one and the same, whether the patient happens to use heroin, gin, crack, or some other mood-altering chemical, such as Talwin or marijuana. With the spread of those concepts, drug abuse treatment centers have proliferated in hospital settings. We now see them advertised in the newspaper and on television. Most insurance companies now cover lengthy (and expensive) hospital stays for patients with addictive disease (up to four weeks). Similarly, groups such as Alcoholics Anonymous, which help patients care for themselves after formal treatment is completed, have multiplied across the nation. The pointed irony in this enlightenment has been the difficulty doctors themselves have in getting help when they are afflicted with what is now called primary addictive disease (PAD).

In her landmark research, LeClair Bissell studied not only doctors, but other professionals, such as lawyers. She wrote in *Alcoholism in the Professions,* "As treaters of others, professionals may be unusually slow to seek help for alcoholism. Inappropriate treatment and long delays in intervention have been the rule. We cannot know how much harm is actually done to patients or clients by the alcoholic or drug-using professional, but it must be significant." One doctor described doing surgery in a blackout. That is, he performed an operation from beginning to end and the next day he could not remember a thing about it. "Generally, professional intervention still takes place quite late in a drinking career and usually even then only when some other agency has first become involved." The head of one treatment center for doctors and other health care professionals said that seventy percent of the doctors he saw came for help only when they were finally in danger of losing their licenses. Yet more than forty percent of the doctors surveyed by Bissell had never had a colleague or superior mention the problem, even when they were drinking on the job, indicating a high degree of denial among doctors and those working with them. Many of those doctors sought professional help for their problems, but they misperceived their problems as something other than addiction—depression or mid-life crisis. The people they went to for help were no better at diagnosing the illness. Forty percent of the doctors surveyed were told by psychiatrists that they were not alcoholics—not addicted— even after the doctor-patients described their drinking and drug-use habits. Some of the psychiatrists even offered the addicted doctors other mood-altering drugs as substitutes.

There appear to be good reasons for that denial, at least on the surface, as well as good reasons that doctors helping doctors fail to diagnose PAD. As its victims, doctors fear that admitting to addiction would end their careers: Patients would flee, colleagues would shun them, hospital privileges would be cut off. On the other hand, doctors who are faced with attempting to diagnose a fellow doctor who has PAD may be unable to recognize it because it is not taught in medical school and because PAD often carries symptoms of other diseases that are taught in medical school. (This leads, for example, to the not-uncommon diagnosis of epilepsy for alcoholics who suffer from convulsions.) Moreover, doctors are taught that they are infallible. One doctor may be unconsciously disinclined to diagnose PAD in another doctor as long as it is still stigmatized as a disease of moral depravity.

Dr. Reed recalls how his large and lucrative family practice finally came to an end due to his failure to seek help. "In 1956 I went to Europe and contracted hepatitis," he told me. "When

I landed in New York, I was yellow. Being a doctor, of course, I knew that if you have hepatitis, you don't drink. But I drank anyway. That was the first real indication I had that something was definitely wrong with me. Naturally, I ignored the warning and went ahead with my life." All the addicted doctors I spoke to could recall a moment in their lives when they asked: If I'm so smart, why am I doing this? Through the miracle of denial, they simply pushed the question aside and went ahead. Dr. Reed went plunging ahead into his personal hell, which involved seventeen more years of drugs and drinking before he was finally burned out.

"In 1973 I knew there was something dreadfully wrong," Dr. Reed said. "I told my wife there was something wrong. I was depressed. I was sick." And so he did something that addicts have been doing for centuries, something that has been elevated to a thematic genre in literature: He took what's known as the "geographical cure," in which the afflicted person simply moves, hoping that everything will be different in the new location. Dr. Reed moved to South America and worked in a mission. And everything, indeed, was different. Well, almost everything. Like the dying hero of *Under the Volcano*, he lurched through his year in the wilderness, giving one pill to the patient and one to himself—one for you, one for me—until he was on the verge of death. He fed his addiction "mostly with drugs, but occasionally I'd get a fifth of Smirnoff's and really go at it."

Looking back now, he can see that he was in the final throes of an advanced and potentially lethal case of primary addictive disease. He was quite far gone and should have been in a hospital. When he returned after a year in South America, his partners had already eased him out. There was a new general surgeon in place at his prominent North Shore practice, and Dr. Reed's services were no longer required. He was free to destroy himself. Looking back, Dr. Reed expressed his amazement that no one told him, and no one offered help.

Today, Dr. Reed is grateful that he was not allowed to perform surgery any longer. "I didn't kill anybody," he said. "But I know somebody who had an extra operation he could have done without. . . ." And he trails off into a wistful introspection. In fact, his surgical privileges were suspended at the hospital and never regained. But by that time he had already decided that he no longer wanted to practice surgery. He wanted to work treating doctors with PAD.

The problem then and now has been getting doctors to admit that they have a problem and must seek treatment. As G. Douglas Talbott, M.D., a pioneer in the treatment of addicted doctors, put it, "Ignorance about alcoholism and drug addiction abounds even among health professionals."

❖   ❖   ❖

Dr. Herb Trace is not only a recovering drug addict himself, but his medical practice consists of treating drug addicts who are also doctors. I went to visit him at his spacious suburban home just outside Chicago one evening. He sat in a cushioned chair, the wall behind him decorated with an array of Indonesian and African masks, souvenirs of his travels around the world.

He looked distraught as he sighed and folded his hands across his stomach. He said, "Today was a hell of a day. People were going crazy left and right. We found one of our doctors dead tonight at Saint Francis Hospital." What did he die of? I asked. "Why, alcoholism, of course!" Dr. Trace said.

More is known about PAD today, from its gross symptoms to its neurochemistry, than ever before in the history of medicine. Doctors can trace physical addiction to a location in the hypothalmic instinctual center in the brain and even explain that it results from a chemical imbalance within the body's own pain-mediating system—"a biochemical defect in the hypothalamic instinctual control center in the endorphin and enkephalin systems," wrote Talbott. Yet few doctors (other than the fairly small number of specialists in addictionology who have recently arrived on the scene) are able to recognize primary addictive disease either in themselves or their colleagues. (One of the best-known psychiatrists in the country, Mark Gold, who heads the treatment center at Fair Oaks Hospital in Summit, New Jersey, told me that one of his closest friends was addicted to cocaine and Dr. Gold didn't detect it.) Addiction is a remarkable disease that tells the patient he has no disease. Then it gives him the tools with which to conceal the disease not only from himself but from others. At least for a time.

While there are no reliable data to hint at its prevalence among physicians, it is clear that doctors enjoy no special protection from PAD. Many addiction specialists such as Dr. Trace believe that professionals, including doctors and lawyers, are more susceptible than the general public. Researcher Le-Clair Bissell says, however, that doctors are not much different from others in their *susceptibility* to PAD; they are only different in that they have more ready access to (and therefore more frequently become addicted to) narcotics. Although the Doc Holiday image of the physician-tippler is one that has been readily assimilated into literature and movies, there is no evidence to show that doctors are any more naturally inclined to become addicted than anyone else is.

Whether or not doctors are more susceptible to PAD than the other professionals, they may risk more danger once addicted. PAD and suicide go hand in hand. "Overt suicide attempts before the first interview were reported by seventeen percent of the men and thirty percent of the women," Bissell writes of one of her surveys of addicted doctors. She describes one of her subjects "who was discovered dissecting out her femoral artery. . . ." (Physicians have better skills, tools, and methods for doing themselves in: One doctor told of putting exactly the lethal dose, according to body weight, of cyanide in his bottle of scotch, and then calmly sitting down to drink himself to death. Luckily, he was discovered before the end.) The overuse of various drugs, including alcohol, can promote profound depression as a side effect.

"Typical stories," Bissell wrote, "described long-delayed diagnosis and useless encounters with would-be helpers who lacked the training or expertise needed to recognize or manage the addictions. Repeatedly, we heard accounts of years of inept management before admission or referral was made to a specialized treatment facility and effective help was found."

Bissell goes on to add that only three of her one hundred respondents in a survey "had been taught about AA in medical school. . . . Most were unaware that AA's cofounder had been a physician."

Primary addictive disease has a psychosocial component as well as a biogenetic one. Most researchers today believe that the genetic disposition to PAD is not in itself sufficient to bring on the symptoms of compulsive drug or alcohol use. Social and psychological factors must be present to trigger the disease. For example, high rates of PAD correlate with "Relative affluence, exposure to the sophisticated environment of urban areas, distancing from the more abstinence-oriented fundamentalist religions, social settings in which drinking is accepted, very high (as well as very low) educational level . . ."

Today there are strong movements afoot in the medical community to address the dual problem of doctors who are ignorant of PAD and of doctors who have PAD (or have an addicted colleague) and are in turn ignorant of that crucial fact. Sometimes both problems are attacked simultaneously, as in the Georgia Disabled Doctors Program, upon which the Parkside Recovery Center at Lombard, Illinois, was modeled.

Talbott's program was the first of its kind, but nearly every state medical society now has, or is affiliated with, a program that can provide treatment for addicted doctors (who are described variously as impaired physicians, disabled doctors, and simply people with addictive disease). Curiously, although the decades of the seventies and eighties saw the elevation of PAD to the status of a full-fledged medical problem, the treatment is for the most part non-medical in nature. Not even the diagnosis follows traditional lines. "It is the only disease that cannot be diagnosed by smelling, hearing, seeing, or feeling," Talbott wrote. "Biopsy, blood test, radioactive flow studies, and

CAT scans are worthless as detectors of the cause or often even the presence of substance abuse."

The fact that doctors, just like the rest of the population, suffer from PAD has been known since at least 1869, when Sir James Paget reported on some of his medical students at Saint Bartholomew's Hospital and their "habits of intemperance or dissipation." But no medical treatment was ever found, and psychiatry has done no better in treating what its practitioners perceived as the root causes, the underlying psychopathology, of excessive drug and alcohol use. The label "primary addictive disease" is now used to emphasize that compulsive drug-taking is not a symptom of some other disorder; it is itself a primary disease. In other words, addicts don't drink or take drugs *for any reason.* The drug itself is the reason. And taking it is the major symptom of the disease.

Yet even today, many psychiatrists approach such patients with this strategy: Let's just see what underlying psychopathology is making you take all those pills (or drink all that booze or smoke all that weed or shoot all that morphine). Such wasted (if well-meaning) efforts have set up a situation that can make it even more difficult for addicted doctors and other professionals to get help.

Not until Alcoholics Anonymous was formed in 1935 did a workable treatment for PAD evolve, and that program remains today the only known method of maintaining addicts in a drug-free condition for long periods of time. All treatment programs, whether for doctors or for the general public, are aimed at one ultimate goal: getting the patient into Alcoholics Anonymous (or a related program) and keeping him involved with the program of recovery to avoid relapse. There is the subtle, underlying, undeniable fact that AA accomplished what the medical arts throughout history had failed to do and what psychiatry over the last 150 years had been trying and failing to do: stop the addict from taking drugs. Prior to AA addicts were locked up in mental wards, or else they simply died of their disease. An unintended side effect of AA's success was a turf battle. Was AA threatening to take over something that rightfully belonged to the world of medicine? Making this tension worse, AA achieves its results (i.e., mitigating a medical condition) without medical intervention.

Some people recoil at such an "unscientific" approach when they first hear how a medical problem is treated. As Dr. Talbott has said, "The substance abuser has a biogentic disease. He or she is not responsible for being an alcoholic but *is* responsible for recovery or for not ever using mood-altering drugs again. Taking drugs away from a drug addict or alcohol from an alcoholic is easy, but that does not prompt recovery. Recovery is the development of non-chemical coping skills so he or she can achieve sobriety. Sobriety is not just a state beyond abstinence from drugs but is freedom from the drugs with peace and serenity." Alcoholics Anonymous provides what its proponents refer to as a spiritual program that leads to serenity and teaches those coping skills. The medical community, especially psychiatry, has been slow to catch on: This works; it may be the best answer until something else comes along. But today attitudes are changing, and a new generation of doctors and psychiatrists is coming of age.

Dr. Daniel H. Angres is medical director of the Parkside Recovery Center at Lombard, Illinois, where some of the pioneering work in treating physicians is taking place. About forty percent of the patients are physicians. The rest are from other professions. Dr. Angres is young and dresses stylishly. His modern office looks out onto a small man-made pond that gives the suburban setting the feel of a country retreat. Dr. Angres is also a psychiatrist. Or perhaps we should designate him, along with Mark Gold and their whole generation, as *new psychiatrists.*

"Treatment is a preliminary process to facilitate entry into AA," Dr. Angres told me. "Some need it. Some don't," meaning that some doctors, if they get to AA in an early enough stage of the disease, can successfully begin recovery and never relapse (i.e., go back to drug use).

"I don't have a problem understanding a medical condition that requires non-medical treatment," he assured me. As well as recovering from PAD himself, Dr. Angres is also a heart patient with coronary artery disease. He thinks the comparison between the two diseases is a useful one. "In both cases we have real medical problems that may be treated in holistic, non-medical ways. For example, for heart disease, we may prescribe lifestyle changes, such as diet, exercise, reduction of stress—all non-medical methods of controlling a medical condition. The same is true of alcoholism and drug addiction. The spiritual approach is what works." He cited the necessity for patients to undergo a radical change of mind and heart, leading to self-examination, acceptance, and personal accountability, in order to achieve the serenity Dr. Talbott referred to.

According to Angres, an addict is a person who has learned that pain, discomfort, anxiety, conflict can be eliminated instantaneously by the simple act of taking a potion, powder, pill, elixir, injection. It is a tough act to follow. To do that without drugs requires a kind of spiritual enlightenment that in previous centuries only full-time mystics were able to get. Tibetan lamas sought nirvana. Monks brought enlightenment through prayer and meditation and conscious contact with God. And today people out in the Chicago suburbs, working together at centers such as Parkside, Evanston Hospital, Glenbrook Hospital, Lutheran General, Martha Washington, Skokie Valley, are all seeking that same state, which is the only mental and emotional condition in which they can live without their previous omnipotence—the ability to kill the pain of life instantly, on demand.

Some doctors, blessed with a logical, scientific turn of mind, think that this prescription sounds awfully fishy. "But it's no more peculiar than telling a patient to jog and eat broccoli," Dr. Angres says.

❖   ❖   ❖

In high school, Dr. Nick Walcoff wrapped his father's red and white Ford around a tree after a drinking spree with some of the older guys. His father, also a doctor, paid off the cops to smooth things over. During premed Walcoff struggled with hangovers. But he was young and resilient and made it through. In medical school it was not uncommon for him to lose part of an evening to a blackout, but he managed to get the work done.

I met Dr. Walcoff in his office in the North Shore hospital where he now runs a program treating people—many of them Chicago professionals—with PAD. This was a real doctor with real status in the community and a unit full of patients just outside the door behind which we were talking. As a consequence, I could hardly believe that the person he described to me was the same one now sitting before me. "It was at that time," he recalled of his premed years, "that I met the girl who was to become my wife. I remember once she was coming to town, and I stopped to have a few drinks with the guys on my way to pick her up. I ended up drinking so much that I passed out and never got to the train. Here was this beautiful, wonderful girl, and I was completely, helplessly in love with her. And yet it was more important for me to drink than to meet her at the train." Most such incidents are viewed at the time as youthful folly. Dr. Walcoff can now see it as a clear indication that something was dreadfully wrong.

Once he entered his residency, Dr. Walcoff recalled, drug companies sent samples, "and some of us would eat our mail and some of us would read it." Soon he was on a regular course of self-medication with amphetamines. "I believe now that in part I was suffering from self-esteem problems and depression, and by mixing alcohol and amphetamines I found I could get relief." Of course, the rebound effect from amphetamine is depression, which requires more amphetamine, which causes more depression . . .

The drugs and alcohol affected Dr. Walcoff's performance even before his residency was over. "Showing up late for surgery is not the way to get ahead," he said. In 1970, after four rocky years of surgical residency, he was drafted and went to Vietnam as a major. "When I realized I was going, I ran around all over town stockpiling amphetamines to see if I could get enough to last me my whole tour of duty there. I was clearly behaving in an addicted way then. Of course, it was impossible to get enough to last me. I ran out about halfway through." Another important signal that he ignored: He experienced withdrawal symptoms when the amphetamines ran out in Vietnam. "At that point I started smoking grass." All the while he kept on drinking.

With respect to his functioning in Vietnam, he said, "I was a good surgeon. There is no question that I was operating under the influence, but I don't think anyone got hurt. I do recall one night when I wasn't on call—I was free—and I was smoking a lot of grass. Then we had one of those mass casualty situations, and we were all called in. I operated all night long, and I really don't remember what I did." Doctors tell me that performing surgery in a blackout is a clear (and not uncommon) signal by which a physician can self-diagnose PAD.

Returning to the United States, Dr. Walcoff stopped taking drugs and alcohol and gave up surgery in favor of a psychiatric residency. "I felt terrific because I was making a major change in my life. But midway through this course my younger brother committed suicide, and there was clear indication that he was alcohol and drug addicted." Rather than swinging Dr. Walcoff away from further use of drugs, the tragedy had the opposite effect. "It gave me a reason to start using again." Such paradoxical twists of logic are the staple fare of people suffering from PAD. Soon he was back to the old pattern of use in dealing with stress, and it quickly began to effect his home life. By that time he was married and had children, though he had little time for them.

At the age of thirty-five he had a heart attack, followed by quadruple bypass surgery. "I was scared for a couple of years and tried to minimize my amphetamine use," he said. But one day a patient brought in a bottle of Ritalin and left it, and Dr. Walcoff tried one, once again "to cope with feelings of isolation and depression." This brain stimulant, normally prescribed for children with attention deficit disorder, was the key that fit

Dr. Walcoff's lock perfectly. "I rapidly went from using a normal amount, say twenty milligrams, to using incredibly high doses. I was up around two thousand milligrams a day." And this despite the fact that he was well aware that even a normal dose of Ritalin, a cousin of the amphetamines, could be deadly for a coronary heart disease patient. "This is where the insanity really comes in," he said, recalling a moment like Dr. Reed's continued drinking in spite of hepatitis. "I just kept on taking it.

"Like most doctors, I maximized my efforts to conceal my addiction and was pretty successful at it." He was filling prescriptions all over town, and sometimes a pharmacy would call and get one of his partners on the phone by chance. Once or twice his colleagues asked him, "Are you taking this stuff?"

"Once in a while," he would say. "Nothing I can't handle." And the incident would be forgotten.

"I never had trouble filling prescriptions," Dr. Walcoff told me. "Sometimes a pharmacist would even ask me if I wanted more. But ordering ten thousand amphetamines at a time was not consistent with my denial system," he added with a wan smile.

By 1980 he was not functioning. "I was triple-scheduling patients and forgetting. I had a beard, I had lost a lot of weight, and I looked haggard and very sick. I have photographs to substantiate that." Yet still no one said anything to him.

Dr. Walcoff's crash came in 1981 when he went off to Maui for vacation. He had decided to remain drug free, but he couldn't stick with the plan. "At the last minute I went into a panic and went around filling prescriptions for Ritalin all over town." In his haste, he went to the same drugstore twice in a period of three hours without realizing it. He was reported by the pharmacist. When he returned from Hawaii his lawyer said, "You are very sick. You ought to be in a hospital."

"It was the first time anyone had said that to me, and it wasn't a doctor; it was my lawyer," Dr. Walcoff said sadly. It was a common refrain I heard from doctors, and whenever they said that, they looked a little baffled: Why didn't someone tell me how sick I was? Addicts start out believing that they are sailing away in a luxury liner, but they are already in the lifeboat, drifting out to sea. When they finally fall overboard, they can't understand why no one even throws them a ring.

Dr. Walcoff, like Dr. Reed, went away for four months to a special treatment center for doctors, such as the one Dr. Angres runs in Parkside. Special treatment facilities for doctors with PAD, and even special AA groups whose members are all doctors, are becoming common today. It is in part in recognition of special needs and issues peculiar to addicted doctors. But it is also to put them at ease about seeking help and to make it easier for them to re-enter the normal world.

Just as there has been an anti-AA bias in the psychiatric and medical communities, so there is sometimes an anti-medical, anti-science tendency within AA. First, medicine and psychiatry failed where AA succeeded. Second, many people get to AA and successfully begin recovery only after spending many years and a lot of money on psychiatrists who have led them astray, misinformed them, and even made their addictions worse by giving them more drugs. And third, doctors by their own admission often become egocentric, setting up an easy target for a group of people attempting to practice humility, modesty, and patience. Naturally, those stereotypes on both sides are exaggerations, but problems nevertheless arise for doctors seeking help from AA. Some have had bad experiences in attempting to be open in talking about themselves at AA meetings.

Dr. Reed warns the doctor who has been newly inducted into AA that even in that brotherly love fellowship of sharing there are limits to what one can reveal and still remain in good odor. "I once went to a regular AA meeting—not a doctors' meeting—and I talked about an incident in surgery," Reed recalled, "and did I catch hell! There was some serious doctor bashing going on after that meeting, and I realized that all was not sweet understanding, not even in AA." People in AA may be seeking spiritual enlightenment, but they are still people.

Since then Dr. Reed has kept his more serious professional blunders to himself, sharing them only with one or two carefully selected confidants. This need for an understanding forum of one's peers is one of the reasons that AA groups for doctors have proliferated. But the idea is not a new one.

The first recovery group that was designed strictly for doctors began in 1949. Known as International Doctors in Alcoholics Anonymous (IDAA), it is still in existence today and meets once a year. Herb Trace says that for doctors recovering from PAD, "it's our spiritual bond." It has approximately twenty-five hundred members. At last year's IDAA dinner in Lexington, Kentucky, there were seven hundred doctors. (IDAA includes both M.D.s and Ph.D.s in the health care field.)

At the time of its inception in 1975, the Georgia Disabled Doctors Program, founded and run by Dr. Talbott, was established in part because "traditional one-month treatment programs are inadequate for disabled doctors." Doctors need special treatment for a variety of reasons, not the least of which is what Dr. Talbott calls "incredibly high denial." Dr. Angres lists his "four M.D.s" to explain why doctors need custom-tailored programs and don't necessarily get the best benefit from recovery programs aimed at the general public.

"M-Deity is the first," Angres says with a slight smile. "Doctors are trained to think they're God." Massive Denial, Militant Defensiveness, and More Drugs are the other three. "In addition, the physician is licensed for the care of others. His accountability is essential to his recovery if he is to continue to practice," meaning that there has to be some way to determine with a high degree of certainty that he is no longer taking drugs.

Because of the issue of accountability, doctors who treat doctors are careful to distinguish between treatment and self-help. Treatment is medical intervention—or at the very least, intervention by medically trained people. The object of treatment is to get the patient-doctor to the point that he can make use of AA, the self-help program for people suffering from PAD.

Treatment is something that can be documented and proven—to show the public and the authorities that the doctor is getting better. Self-help cannot be documented.

Most physicians agree that AA has no role in this process of accounting for a doctor's sobriety. The entire program of AA is based upon self-reliance and personal responsibility. No record of attendance is taken at meetings. No one is looking over the shoulders of the members. People can go to meetings and then go out and drink and then go to more meetings, without ever telling anyone. Some people do. And while that does not lead to very effective recovery, neither does it result in any sanctions. Nor does it guarantee that a doctor is staying sober.

Today most states have medical societies that will act as advocates for the doctor with PAD in his relationships with the state licensing body—especially when the physician has already gotten himself into trouble, perhaps by having his hospital privileges suspended. But those societies need verification that recovery is proceeding properly. There needs to be some hard evidence that a doctor is successfully following his program—that he is staying sober, getting better. That's where the special treatment programs come in.

"We take urine drops," Dr. Trace said of his Evanston program, "and we take attendance." All reliable treatment programs for doctors place emphasis on clean urine samples, taken at random, perhaps twice a month. Urinalysis is a method of detecting the residue of drugs that may have been taken.

The physician entering Dr. Angres's program in Lombard signs up for an initial stay, lasting from four weeks to four months, with a mandatory twenty months of what is called aftercare. This is different from the way non-physician addicts get help. Many go into AA on their own and chart their own course to sobriety. Others may go through a two- to four-week hospital stay, after which they are on their own, able to go to AA or avoid it as they please. Doctors in Angres's program don't just promise to be involved in the intensive, closely-monitored two-year sequence; they sign contracts.

During that time a number of goals are accomplished: detoxification and stabilization, if necessary; education about PAD; introduction to group therapy and AA groups, including a weekly peer group (other doctors) as well as a non-peer group. It is essential that the doctor with PAD get the benefit of AA groups composed of other doctors. The reason is obvious: To have a lay person telling a doctor about a medical condition would simply not carry the weight necessary to break through denial. But it is equally essential that the doctor with PAD meet with "ordinary people," so that he doesn't get the idea that his special position in society gives him special rights where this disease is concerned. Addicts come to think they're God, because they have a kind of omnipotence, the power to alter the world at the drop of a pill (drink, injection, etc.). Doctors think they're God because they have the power over life and death, the power to heal by laying on hands. Addicted doctors really have a problem with the question of who is God (or perhaps more relevant, who is *not* God).

Many doctors are worried before seeking treatment—worried that someone will find out, worried that they'll lose their practice, worried that patients will flee in fear if they learn that their physician is an addict, worried that they'll lose their license to practice or prescribe. "All those worries are true," says Dr. Angres, "if they don't get help." And if they do get help, all those worries disappear.

Doctors don't need to worry that someone will find out about their addiction. Anonymity is fanatically guarded in AA groups for doctors as well as in treatment programs. Most doctors, by the time they need treatment, are on the point of risking their privileges to practice anyway, though they might not realize it. With treatment, the doctor with PAD can have a long and fruitful continuation of his career—with the blessing of the state and the medical community.

It is rare for a doctor in AA to find that his practice goes badly, says Dr. Trace. In fact, many believe that Alcoholics Anonymous helped them professionally. "I believe we make better doctors. At least you know that we weren't out drinking last night."

❖   ❖   ❖

Two things are changing the way physicians look at PAD—and at each other. The Chicago-based American Society on Alcoholism and Other Drug Dependencies (AMSA-ODD) provides certification for doctors in treating PAD. At one time the medical arm of the National Council on Alcoholism, this organization conducts a day-long exam for doctors who wish to treat PAD. There are no residencies or fellowships yet, but AMSA-ODD is working toward fellowships and looks forward to a time when addictionology, as some call it, will be at least a recognized subspeciality. "It's difficult to change a medical school's curriculum," says Executive Director Emanuel Steindler. AMSA-ODD conducts its own review courses for doctors who wish to prepare for its exam or would like to learn more about recognizing and treating PAD. So far, AMSA-ODD, with three thousand members, has certified thirteen hundred physicians, with an additional six hundred expected to take the exam.

One of the aims at AMSA-ODD, equally important in their view as certifying those who wish to treat PAD specifically, is to educate other doctors so that they can recognize it in their patients. "It's so prevalent in the general population," says Steindler, "and it's so commonly misdiagnosed." PAD is routinely diagnosed as essential hypertension, epilepsy, depression, borderline personality disorder, adult onset diabetes, and a wide variety of other disorders—the symptoms of which disappear when the drug causing them is removed.

Steindler credits state medical societies with a big role in getting help for physicians. "Until the state medical societies made it all right for a physician to come forward, the doc had nowhere to turn," except perhaps to face the punitive measures of the licensing body. That situation served in many cases to

discourage doctors from seeking treatment in the past. Even today, with programs of advocacy and self-help in every state,
most doctor-therapists believe that physicians with PAD are
tough customers for treatment. Intervention still seems to be
the rule rather than the exception.

Here's how intervention works: One day a physician who
has been overusing drugs or alcohol will get a call. "We are
from the state medical society," the caller will say. "We need to
talk to you immediately about a very important personal matter of professional business. It is too personal to discuss on the
phone. We'll meet you at our office or your office or your home."

As soon as the meeting can be arranged, preferably that day,
"Impaired physicians are told the intervenors cannot hurt them
but can help them by protecting the professional status, the
hospital staff privileges, and integrity within the medical society and professional community," wrote G. Douglas Talbott,
who helped pioneer the use of this method to get physicians
into treatment. "Additionally, an advocacy position with the
licensing board and Drug Enforcement Agency is also provided.
On the other hand, the dangers of malpractice, investigation by
the DEA and the licensing board, as well as revelation of poor
medical practice within the local and national media are carefully explained to him or her. This is done by two intervenors
who are peers of the impaired physician." (Often one or both
of them is a recovering addict himself, since part of AA's program calls for its members to help others who are still suffering
from PAD.)

In one study done by Talbott, seventy percent of eight hundred doctors had come to treatment with real or threatened license problems. Only thirty percent had come prior to reaching that degree of impairment from drug use. "It requires a
crisis to get most physicians to treatment," Angres agreed.
"Absolutely," he added.

One thing everyone in the field of addictionology agreed on:
A lot more education is needed, not only because people are
suffering from PAD, but because the people treating those

people are also suffering from it. And no one seems able to tell, even when it comes up and slaps him in the face. Talbott wrote:

> Alcohol is the base of both iodine and mercurochrome as an antiseptic. As a sedative hypnotic, it is an excellent sleep inducer—in the garage, out on the lawn, on the beach—it will induce sleep almost any place. As a tranquilizer, alcohol works almost every time on everybody far better than does Librium or Valium. Suppose someone announced the discovery of a drug—C_2H_5OH, ethyl alcohol—that could serve as an anesthetic agent, antiseptic, sedative hypnotic, and tranquilizer. That would be the greatest drug ever discovered. However, under every scientific and pharmacological constraint existing today for the protection of society, alcohol most certainly would be a class 2 narcotic and would be available only with a Government Narcotic Registry Number. After all, C_2H_5OH minus water is equal to ether. The brain has no idea whether the body is in an operating room inhaling ether or in a bar having a six-pack of beer. The brain is getting the same ether message.

Yet we use so much of this drug that tax from the sale of alcohol provides the second largest source of revenue to the U.S. government.

❖   ❖   ❖

Dr. Trace hung up the phone after barking orders at an addicted doctor on the other end of the line who was resisting treatment. He sighed and smiled. "When we have our doctor's AA meeting, we joke about it. We call it the Meeting of the Gods. We secretly think we're better; that's why we need to meet with other doctors. But we're just as vulnerable. And we have to pay for our mistakes. We also have terrible guilt about it. 'How could we have gotten this disease—we of all people!'" He smiled knowingly.

He described his own "crash," as he called it, which brought him to treatment. "In 1974 I had a blackout and ran around the

house nude and scared my wife half to death. I was a burnout,"
he said.

Russ Reed sought help from Jim West, who is now head of
the Betty Ford center. West sent Dr. Reed away to a recovery
center for doctors in New Jersey, where he spent four months,
and Dr. Reed brought what he learned there back to Evanston
to begin his own practice. Most doctors in AA feel that they
were always looking for something. Being in AA, they say,
marks the end of that quest; they find what they were looking for. Enlightenment, serenity—whatever one chooses to call
it, the way of life promoted by their activities in Alcoholics
Anonymous reduces anxiety and helps them to function more
efficiently—not only because they're drug-free but because
they take things as they come, with equanimity. Because they
are no longer trying to change the world, the world is no longer
such a burden to them. That does not mean it's easy.

One of the biggest obstacles a doctor in AA faces is guilt, Dr.
Trace said. "The guilt was terrible. What right do I, a doctor,
have to get sick, especially a self-induced sickness? The first
thing that helped begin to alleviate that guilt was the fact that
there were other doctors there at the treatment center." Trace
and other doctors believe that is another important reason for
having special AA groups for doctors. "Subsequently I was introduced to the disease concept of addiction, which relieved
some of the guilt as well." "But," he admits, "it is an ongoing
process and one that takes a very long time." Regaining self-
esteem can take the rest of a doctor's lifetime. "I felt dirty for a
long time," he said.

Before getting to AA, Dr. Walcoff said, he felt hopeless. "I was
so ashamed, so guilty. I thought addicts and alcoholics were ter-
minally ill and didn't get well." And this was coming from
someone who was quite successful on the surface. His practice
never completely fell apart. His surgical privileges weren't suspended. "Almost everything I've done I've been successful at,
but I never believed it or saw it that way," he said. Now, being
in AA, he has become able for the first time in his life to appre-

ciate his own accomplishments and to see them for what they are. As a psychiatrist—or any sort of physician—that ability to have a realistic perspective helps his work tremendously.

Dr. Walcoff, like every other doctor I interviewed, believes that his AA experience has made him a better practitioner. When he was in the throes of PAD, he experienced "an almost paralytic lack of emotion, which in psychiatry is not very helpful to the doctor-patient relationship." The spiritual element of AA deepened his empathic response, took him out of himself, and allowed him to help others. Moreover, he is no longer depressed, and so he has no need to medicate himself for depression.

"I had a very profound experience the first time I went to an AA meeting," Dr. Walcoff recalled. He was in Georgia at Dr. Talbott's treatment center, where he learned the skills he brought to Chicago to begin his own treatment center. He was very sick at the time. He felt his life, his practice, were over. And then he entered his first AA meeting. "What it felt like was an enormous sense of relief. I had found a group of other doctors who had gotten there the same way I had. I was overjoyed. I was no longer alone, no longer isolated. But it was only much later that I recognized that as a spiritual experience."

Dr. Trace agrees that the AA experience teaches a way of life that helps him be a better doctor. "We become more compassionate," he said. "We are taught tolerance, taught how to be calm, how to accept."

Dr. Trace also believes that "going through the experience of drug addiction actually makes us better doctors. After an experience like this, you understand people better." It is like the classic hero cycle in literature. "Anyone in life who goes through a major catastrophe *and recovers from it* will come out with more compassion. We are good doctors. When we get abstinent, we are very good doctors. Our motto is: We clean up awful nice."

MARION PRISON

Next to killing someone or trying to escape, the most serious offenses that a prisoner in the U.S. Penitentiary at Marion, Illinois, can commit are drinking and being caught in possession of money.

There are many ways to make alcohol in USP-Marion, but the simplest is to take two small boxes of Kellogg's corn flakes and dump them into the toilet bowl in your cell. Let them fester for a week, and the result will get you drunk. Some inmates are more ambitious than that. From the prison log: "August 5, 1982: Approximately four gallons of brew found in cell of Ronnie Bruscino, 20168-148."

It is part of the magical transmutation of elements that occurs in the most maximum state of incarceration in America today. After an extended period of being locked up with nothing to do, cut off from the sight of other human beings, the sights and sounds of normal life, you begin to see the world transform itself. Nothing is as it seems. One thing changes into another. If you stare at a typewriter for long enough, with nothing else to occupy your mind, nothing else to stimulate your senses, the platen rods begin to look like shish kabob skewers. Then one day you find yourself with one of them in your hand, and it has been sharpened, and you've wrapped a sweatband around the blunt end for a better grip, and you are plunging the point into someone's chest. Jack Henry Abbott, convicted murderer and author of *In the Belly of the Beast*, wrote, "It is like cutting hot butter, no resistance at all."

The guards come and take you away. The administration orders the typewriters removed from the library, and you are locked in your cell. You are left with nothing but the steel bunk, the three walls, the air vent, the grille. But after you've stared at the air vent for months on end, it too begins to change. Instead of the metal frame and duct, you begin to see long, gleaming isosceles triangles. You get a four-inch bit of hacksaw blade that someone at Lewisburg Penitentiary swallowed before he was transferred here and expelled from his body upon arrival, a scrap of metal that has been passed from man to man, mouth to mouth, hand to hand, by the fleeting practiced prestidigitation of inmates making contact on the way to the shower or the visiting room. You spend weeks gently sawing at the edge of the air vent with this tiny bit of serrated metal; and each day you putty the cut you've made, using a mixture of Dial and Ivory soap, blended to match the flesh-colored paint that seems to obscure everything in this prison. And when you've finally sawed the shank of metal free from the edge of the vent, you spend another week (or two or three) on your hands and knees, feverishly rubbing it against the concrete floor whenever the guards aren't looking, until it becomes pointed like that isosceles triangle you dreamed. Then you work on it some more until it is sharp enough to shave with.

You ignite a book of matches and melt your toothbrush to make a handle for the pristine knife.

Then one day you find yourself plunging it into someone's chest. And the guards take the metal beds away and replace them with concrete slabs; and they throw you in the hole with nothing but a Bible and your underwear and a bedsheet. So you soak the Bible in the toilet until it is water-logged and weighs fifteen pounds, and you wrap it in your T-shirt; and when the guard comes to get you for your weekly shower, you hit him with it and fracture his skull. All these things have happened at USP-Marion.

Another entry in the prison's log:

April 2, 1980: While being processed for a U.S. District Court appearance, inmate Bryan, Joseph 15562-175 was found to be in possession of two (2) handcuff keys made from a "Doodle Art Pen." They were found hidden in the hollowed out bottom of his tennis shoe. The keys were made to fit the S & W handcuffs carried by the U.S. Marshall's Service. Bryan was in the Control Unit (H-Unit) at the time the incident occurred.

How does a Doodle Art Pen become a cuff key? These are the secrets of solitary confinement at Marion that no visitor can learn. A U.S. Circuit Court Judge wrote, "On at least one occasion a [Marion] prisoner had smuggled a homemade bomb into the courtroom via a 'keister cache' lodged in his rectum. When the bomb exploded, a correctional officer lost three fingers on his right hand."

As I walked the corridors of Marion one day, I stopped to greet a prisoner in his cell. "What's happening?" I asked.

"You want to know what's happening?" he asked in outrage. "Get in that cell next door for about ten years; you'll find out what's happening."

At Marion, reality is kaleidoscopic. As I learned, a visitor does not visit USP-Marion; he is led through a warp that winds its twisting way among three dimensions the way a cavern winds through the earth. One dimension is inhabited by the prisoners; one is inhabited by the guards; and the third is inhabited by the prison officials—the warden, associate wardens, and so on down the line. Whether Marion makes you crazy or your own craziness gets you sent to Marion, once you arrive, peculiar things begin to happen; and they happen fast and all the time.

The Administration

USP-Marion is the modern-day replacement for Alcatraz. It is supposed to be so secure that the Bureau of Prisons (which provides administration for all Federal prisons) invented a new level of classification for it: It's called Level Six, the only place of its kind. Marion is the end of the line. Since there is no Federal death penalty, incarceration in USP-Marion is considered the most severe punishment that our government can mete out.

Marion sits on acres of rolling manicured lawn. To reach it, I drove about fifteen miles east of Carbondale, Illinois, and then followed the access road toward a sky-blue water tower. The tinted glass and clean lines of the cast-concrete gun towers make them look more like airport control towers than battlements. The low, louvered buildings of Marion were surrounded by a dancing silver aura that confused my eye as I approached. It was like the first brilliant reflected sunlight I've glimpsed driving toward the ocean. Then I rounded a curve, and the scene snapped into focus: thousands of yards of razor wire, each individual razor blade picking up the sunlight and reflecting it back the way rippling water does.

The light was like a glittering energy barrier around the sand-colored concrete buildings.

I couldn't tell from the road that the modern prison factories were abandoned, the new cafeteria idle, the gymnasium as silent and empty as the chapel.

In the bright, air-conditioned anteroom beside the entrance to the warden's office, a secretary sat before a large plate-glass window. Behind her was a big poster with the inscription CAUTION: HUMAN BEING—HANDLE WITH CARE. Her window overlooked the freshly mowed expanse of lawn where a helicopter had landed May 24, 1978, during an escape attempt. Barbara Oswald, a friend of one of the inmates, had hired a helicopter and then pulled a pistol and ordered the pilot to land inside USP-Marion. The pilot wrestled the gun from Oswald and shot her six times, killing her. He landed the helicopter on the grass; and when he opened the door, her body tumbled out onto the green lawn right in front of this window.

"This is the prettiest spot to be in the fall and spring," the secretary told me. "There's a lot of dogwood and redbud that come out," she said, pointing at the treeline in the distance. Between us and the treeline, a hundred yards of silver razor wire curled up and over the fence like an ocean breaker.

On February 14, 1979, two inmates actually climbed over that barrier after wrapping their arms in newspaper, which would seem to confirm what the administration says: that the typical Marion prisoner is a desperate and violent man, always on the verge of escape. To support that point of view, officials display homemade weapons—pen bombs and hacksaw blades and handcuff keys—evidence that those who are put in USP-Marion are a special breed.

John Clark, executive assistant to the warden, summed up administration policy this way: "It's a matter of who's going to run the prison, us or them."

"All of 'em are total sociopaths," said acting warden D. B. Bailes.

Marion officials stop just short of saying that there is such a thing as a born criminal, the notorious criminal type that went out of vogue among penologists and criminologists a hundred years ago.

❖   ❖   ❖

Not many people are sent to Marion directly from court after being convicted. Most are sent there for "failure to adjust" to institutional life, which means that the prisoner has done something at Leavenworth or Lewisburg or Lompoc or some other Federal prison that made those officials feel that the prisoner needed the more secure and repressive atmosphere of Marion to make him adjust. In addition, state prisoners who fail to adjust to state institutions may be sent to Marion. Precisely what it takes to get into Marion is the subject of controversy. A U.S. magistrate in the Southern District of Illinois, in a recent decision involving transfers to Marion, cited a case called *Meachum v. Fano*, saying, "Therein, the Court held that prisoners may be transferred between or among institutions arbitrarily—for no reason at all."

It is equally difficult to say how a prisoner gets out of Marion.

When I saw it, the airy prisoner mess hall was equipped with a contemporary salad bar, red tile floors, and stainless-steel cafeteria equipment that gleamed in the noonday sun pouring through the glass-brick skylight thirty feet above. Light-orange and yellow decor made it look as if it might have been a modern hospital or university cafeteria. Some of the tables set up in a small area of the dining hall had blue-and-white checked tablecloths on them. The room was frankly inviting, and the food was more palatable than what I was served in my college dorm.

Only no one ate there. No one except a handful of men who had recently been singled out to leave Marion, having gone through a mysterious process that no one could explain—not prisoners or officials or guards—by which, the warden insisted, one can work his way out to the regular prison system.

I watched half a dozen prisoners line up for chow one day, dwarfed in that enormous echoing cafeteria. One of them, a highly educated man considered to be an escape artist, tried to explain how he achieved his status in this elite group eating lunch in the mess hall. With a wry smile, he said, *"Abreit Macht Frei."*

What he was saying was that Marion is the hole; people disappear into it.

There are many differences between a normal maximum-security prison (where you might be sent for murder or bank robbery) and Marion. One is cell time. A normal maximum-security prison operates this way: At 6:00 A.M. your cell door opens and you run down to the mess hall for breakfast. You then go to work in a prison factory or on an outdoor work gang. All this time you are moving around freely, within the confines of the outer wall of the prison. You go to lunch in the mess hall. You have recreation in the yard or go to the gym to punch the heavy bag or lift weights. There's a four o'clock cell count, during which time you must be in your cell. You hit the chow line again in the evening. And at some point you are locked into your cell for the night.

At Marion prisoners are locked in their cells twenty-three

hours a day. One hour a day, one man at a time is removed for recreation. (The exception is the elite group mentioned above.) There is disagreement about precisely how and why this condition, known as lockdown, was put into effect at Marion; but it was, on October 28, 1983, in an atmosphere of general disruption that had been building since the summer and culminated in the killing of two guards and one prisoner. The Marion lockdown is now the longest in two centuries of U.S. prison history.

Asked who has been incarcerated at Marion to justify these conditions, the administration will list such criminal luminaries as Joe Stasi, the French Connection; Terrance Alden, the Bionic Bank Robber (so called because he could stand flatfooted and jump right into a teller's cage); and Alton Coleman, a kidnaper who went on a six-state murder spree in 1984 and was eventually caught in Evanston, Illinois. Numerous others had cop-killing, rape, murder, armed robbery, bank robbery, and multiple escapes on their records before they got to Marion. One quarter of the men at Marion have committed murder while in prison. The average sentence is forty-one years, while some are serving multiple life sentences. Marion houses numerous members of the white supremist gang known as the Aryan Brotherhood, including the infamous Joseph Paul Franklin, who bombed a synagogue in Chattanooga, Tennessee.

One Marion inmate was serving a Federal life sentence, to be followed by a state death penalty after his release.

The administration of Marion, as well as the Bureau of Prisons, maintains that the population of USP-Marion, being radically different from all other prison populations, merits such radical conditions as total lockdown and justifies the forty thousand dollars per year per man that it costs to maintain those conditions.

Executive assistant John Clark and acting warden D. B. Bailes explained the official point of view to me as we sat on green leather couches in the gold-carpeted warden's office one sunny summer day. (Warden Jerry Williford was on leave.) Bailes was a tall, fit-looking man in a conservative gray suit, with a bald head, a big smile, and an easy manner. Clark, a former Catholic priest, was a large, bespectacled man, partly bald, with curly brown hair. He wore shirt sleeves and a tie open at the neck. He had an unflinching stare and did not laugh easily. Both prison officials had the look of hard-working, unpretentious businessmen. An architect's model of the prison was on a coffee table in the middle of the room. It had two main concourses—called East Corridor and North Corridor—from which the louvered concrete cell blocks extended like fingers.

"We don't know what causes crime," Bailes said. "We don't make any pretense at rehabilitation."

Clark said, "One of my theories about prisons is they're drama schools where people learn to act rehabilitated. They tried here for several years to operate more or less as a normal penitentiary when they didn't have a normal penitentiary population. They finally decided that just wasn't realistic."

I asked how long-term isolation affects prisoners.

"After so many years, they begin to break down," Bailes admitted. "But," he added, "the prisoners let you know when one of 'em is getting flaky," so that the affected inmate can be taken out for psychiatric treatment.

The primary emphasis was that these were desperate, dangerous men who would do anything to escape and who had no regard for human life, not even their own. Many prisoners have contraband already in their intestinal tracts when they arrive at Marion, having inserted it or swallowed it before leaving a less secure prison. Drugs, syringes, handcuff keys, and even hacksaws and carborundum rods are routinely found, Bailes said. Most prisoners are now X-rayed before being allowed into Marion. Some are dry-celled: put into a cell with no running water, so that their feces may be inspected.

"But that's not foolproof," Bailes told me. "They'll reswallow it." To detect contraband, Bailes prefers a method he calls the "finger wave." Physicians call it a digital rectal examination. "We don't have an alternative," Bailes said.

Richard Urbanik, one of Marion's two resident psychologists, introduced himself by saying, "I'm considered the most liberal person here." He confirmed Bailes's assessment of the

Marion population while admitting, "This would be a very harsh way to treat the normal prisoner." Urbanik called his 335 patients "the most vicious group of people in the United States," but disagreed with acting warden Bailes's opinion of their psychological problems. He claimed that the odds are "relatively low" that this type of inmate would suffer from a two-year lockdown. "The Marion prisoner is antisocial severe," Urbanik said. "The Marion prisoner is different. Different behaviorally. They don't feel anxiety. They don't have the capacity. That's been shown in many research studies. Psychopaths don't learn under punishment. I'm a psychologist. We look at behavior. We're not really worried about whether there's a mind."

Urbanik characterized the situation at Marion as "basically like your four-year-old being put on his bed for misbehaving." He said that immobilizing a prisoner in a six-by-nine-foot cell twenty-three hours a day does not affect him. The fact that the bureau sent him to Marion means that he is severely antisocial, and "his being antisocial buffers him against the normal effects, although," he added, "there hasn't been a lot of research into the effects of long-term incarceration."

Precisely what a Marion prisoner is and what he is not, precisely how much he can tolerate before the punishment serves to make him more violent instead of less so, are the subjects of heated debate and of at least one lawsuit that was recently settled in favor of the bureau. The official position of the Bureau of Prisons is this:

> It is the mission of the Unites States Penitentiary, Marion, Illinois, to provide for the safety of inmates, staff and the public through appropriately designed correctional programs and procedures for those inmates identified as the most difficult to manage. . . . Marion's success in controlling these dangerous and disruptive offenders at one location allows other facilities to continue to function as open, working institutions. . . .

In the recently-settled lawsuit (*Bruscino et al. v. Carlson, et al.*), a U.S. magistrate called the methods at Marion "prudent," while characterizing complaints by prisoners about conditions there as "vicious and unjustified attacks."

The Staff

The prison log indicated that doors were frequently found mysteriously unlocked. Everywhere I went inside Marion I saw locks being changed. It's not like changing a dead bolt; Folger Adams locks have to be burned out with a cutting torch and new ones welded back into place. The halls of Marion smell like hot flux.

The heavy Folger Adams keys come with a silver cover that snaps into place when the key is not in use, because for some of the inmates, just one glance is enough: They can memorize the steps and then cut a copy out of anything—plastic, metal, wood, glass.

In the guard office at the end of each cell block is a board with little cards on it. Each card has a prisoner's cell number and a note that might say, "Killed Staff" or "Caution!" or "Bad Fight" or some other warning. One had a skull drawn on it.

The guards go around tapping the bars with rubber mallets once a week to check for any odd sounds and look for metal filings. Someone is always cutting his way out.

Nail clippers and Bic razors are kept on little numbered hooks in a locked case at the end of the range.

There is a wire litter for carrying wounded.

The attitude of the guards toward the prisoners is implicit in the language they use. Beating a prisoner is called "counseling." The inmates don't eat; they feed. When the stress of continuous solitary confinement becomes too much for an inmate and he does something rash—anything from refusing to go back into his cell after a shower to hitting a guard with his shackled hands—they say he "went off." As an unexploded bomb will finally go off if you agitate it enough.

The guards understand the stress. They suffer from it, too. It is possible to get the idea that the guards (who prefer to be called correction officers, in keeping with bureau policy) are hired by the pound and are nothing but big, ignorant bullies; but that, like most stereotypes, is not the entire picture.

Not only do the guards understand the nature of stress— theirs and that of the prisoners—but they also have a deep and subtle understanding of their relationship with the inmates. Most of them expressed undisguised loathing for them.

One guard, who had been at Marion for fifteen years, said, "The only thing wrong with this system is that we don't have the death penalty." He was a controlled and good-humored man most of the time, but when he spoke of inmates, his whole body tensed. He trembled as he told me, "I hate inmates." One of his best friends was a guard named Merle Eugene Clutts. He was murdered by inmate Thomas Silverstein.

It wasn't always that way at Marion, said J. B. Killman, a guard who had been at Marion for seventeen years. "You never completely relax around inmates. But it used to be inmates would speak to you. We were on a first-name basis with them." He recalled a time when the staff and inmates lived in a kind of uneasy detente. "They had things to do then. There was leather craft. They'd have movies on Friday nights with hot buttered popcorn. Basketball. Outside entertainment would come in. Sixty people worked in the kitchen and dining room. It was a nice institution back then. It started to change in the late seventies when a different type inmate began to come here."

What Killman noticed was one of the periodic shifts in penological practice that has been taking place since the 1600s. Prisons go back and forth between rehabilitation and repression. In the 1930s, Alcatraz was the repressive model of a prison. It caused a scandal (as such prisons eventually do), and during the 1960s the United States tried rehabilitation. Since that never works, the pendulum swings back. Marion is the new repressive model. When it causes enough of a scandal, another rehabilitation model will replace it.

❖   ❖   ❖

The guards know that the administration holds the view that everything that happens to a prisoner is his own fault. But they also know that they can control inmate behavior to an extent. Probably without being aware of it, they are masters of practical behavior-modification techniques. A guard can make an inmate go off or he can help to defuse him before he goes off. A guard can overlook a rule infraction. (You can be thrown in the hole, for example, for having an extra pair of socks.) Or he can overlook the fact that your toilet doesn't work; he can make you live in your own waste. Of all the powers that anyone has in the world over us, no one has the broad discretionary powers of a prison guard. The guards know their own power, and like all people everywhere, some abuse it, some respect it.

They carry black Lifetime riot bludgeons, three-foot-long weighted hardwood bats with a round steel ball protruding from either end. The metal ball is there so that the bludgeon won't break ribs. The steel ball separates the ribs, tearing the intercostal muscles, and then pops out. While the pain from it can be intense for weeks and months afterward, the bludgeon tends not to leave obvious marks. But if a guard really wants to hurt an inmate, he doesn't need to touch him. Under the right circumstances, he can take his life simply by letting one inmate out while another is handcuffed and helpless.

And yet the guards and prisoners are often nothing more than reflected images of one another. Often they come from the same backgrounds, and the factor deciding who becomes a prisoner and who becomes a guard is often blind luck. One former Marion guard, speaking of his job at another prison, told me of a case in which one of the inmates turned out to be a boy he'd grown up with in a small town in southern Illinois. He caught the inmate with drugs and had to report him. "He was my best friend as we were growing up," the guard said. "We just took different roads in life. Because my friend was busted by me, he was beaten, raped, and turned into a punk for the rest of the inmates. I was told by my captain that I was a rotten son of a bitch for setting up a friend like that."

One of Marion's two prison chaplains, Gavin O'Conner, said, "Most prisons operate on the good will of the inmates."

Executive assistant Clark agreed. "At any time the inmates could take over because they've got you outnumbered."

Any guard who has been in a prison takeover or riot knows that. Several of the guards I talked to had been surrounded by prisoners at Marion, and they described it in the same terms I had heard used in descriptions of men surrounded by the enemy in war. In a typical prison situation (the way Marion was before the lockdown), the guards—one or two or three at a time—wade in among the unrestrained prisoners—dozens, sometimes hundreds—and simply hope that nothing happens. They avert fear by blocking it from their minds. Once the idea of fear enters, however, they are marked men.

One such marked man was David W. Hale, who had been a prison guard since he was eighteen years old. At the age of twenty-eight he left Marion. The administration, which was forced to ask Hale to resign when Hale admitted beating prisoners, says he was an officer with many problems. The stress got to him, they say. He began abusing his powers, mistreating prisoners, and refusing orders from his superiors. The U.S. magistrate in the *Bruscino* case (which involved a long list of complaints by prisoners about conditions and practices at Marion) said, "The Court has serious reservations regarding the entirety of the testimony of former correctional officer David Hale."

Others, including former guards who knew Hale, claim that the administration was angry with him for what they called "spreading rumors to frighten other officers." Inmates, Hale claimed, were telling him that they were going to kill guards and take over the prison. Hale was on the yard one day before the lockdown, when he was surrounded by inmates. He called 222, the emergency number—"dialed deuces," as the guards say—but no one came. A guard of twenty years experience stood and watched. It was at the discretion of the inmates that Hale lived to tell about it.

Hale and others have claimed that the Bureau of Prisons was intentionally trying to provoke an incident at Marion, which would provide an excuse for a protracted lockdown. That would, say the guards, serve the dual purpose of getting the administration a bigger budget and realizing the ultimate repressive model of a prison: total control.

When I met Hale, he was living on unemployment compensation with his wife and children in a frame house beside a pond, an hour's drive from Marion. Young and boyish, he seemed deeply disillusioned with what he had fully expected to be his career for life. "When I started working there," he said, "it was like any other penitentiary. The inmates were all out; they were working in the factories. Sure, there'd be stabbings, fights, and stuff, but that was to be expected. The staff was never involved. It was between inmates. And then [former] Warden [Harold] Miller started taking more and more stuff away from inmates. Like you're going to work longer hours, we're going to cut your pay; you're gonna have less time on outside recreation. And he just kept taking and kept taking until finally the inmates went on strike."

Hale said that the atmopshere at Marion in 1979 and 1980 was one of increasing terror and intense frustration for the guards; there were almost daily assaults on the staff, but the staff could not fight back. The administration did nothing to try to stop the disruptions and would not allow staff retaliation, even though, according to Hale, inmates were often shackled to their bunks or beaten for minor rule infractions.

Hale finally decided to take matters into his own hands. He felt that if the staff didn't respond to inmate aggression, the prison would go out of control and there would be widespread killings of guards. Hale was going to beat an inmate who had assaulted a guard to demonstrate that these attacks would no longer be tolerated. The lieutenant stopped him, and Hale requested to be taken out of the cell block at that point. The significance of his action was not lost on Hale's fellow officers: It was tantamount to desertion in the face of the enemy. It was career suicide.

Hale said, "I was so mad I was crying, because I knew what was going to happen and nobody was going to listen to me. I said, 'Why don't you tell these officers that these inmates are going to take this place over and they're going to kill every fucking one of us? And you people don't care. We're like a bunch of meat on a hook you're dangling in front of them to see what they're going to do.'"

Roger Ditterline became a guard at Marion in 1980 after six years as a state trooper. He is now retired with total disability. He was one of three officers stabbed when Robert Hoffman was killed by inmate Clayton Fountain. He said, "There weren't any controls. When you have this many murderers, rapists, people doing hard time, antisocial characters, you try to keep a lid on them fairly tight, but it didn't seem to be that way." At that time the guards did not even have riot batons. "We were moving these guys all the time up there with their handcuffs locked in front of them. Now, that goes against everything I was ever taught in law enforcement."

One day before the lockdown, when prisoners were allowed to walk freely to the mess hall for meals, Ditterline found himself surrounded by seventy or eighty inmates when he and another officer were sent in to get a bowl of beans a prisoner had taken from the cafeteria to his cell in defiance of the rules. The prisoners could have killed the two guards, but they did not. Some say it is this very balance of terror and respect between guard and prisoner that makes a normal prison system work. The guards cannot brutalize prisoners too much, because they know that one day they may face being surrounded by those same prisoners and be judged on the spot. When that even strain between guard and prisoner goes out of balance, the system breaks down; and riots or takeovers result. Ditterline, Hale, and other Marion guards believe that the administration and the Bureau of Prisons may have intentionally allowed Marion to go out of balance.

Ditterline said, "It seemed like the administration was trying to get something to happen, and we couldn't figure out why."

Ditterline and Hale said that under Warden Miller, rule changes seemed capricious and designed to frustrate prisoner and guard alike. One day the guards would be ordered to remove all sugar packets from the cells. The next day it would be salt. One day razors were issued; the next day they were prohibited. "It was crazy," Ditterline said.

During the winter months, when the wind blew through the louvered windows along the ranges, the administration would allow inmates to hang blankets on their cell bars to stop the wind. The inmates would get used to that for three or four weeks, and then a memo would come from the warden's office: Immediately confiscate all blankets hanging up.

Although the guards may have seen a conspiracy, it could just as easily have been the typical workings of a bureaucracy.

Jim Hale is another former Marion guard (no relation to David Hale). The day after the killing of officers Clutts and Hoffman at Marion, he claims that he began carrying a knife for his own protection because he felt the administration was not sufficiently concerned about staff safety. He was forced to resign when a fellow officer reported him. It is illegal for a guard to carry any weapons other than those issued by the prison, such as the riot batons (or guns in the gun towers).

When I visited Jim Hale, he was living in a motel room on the outskirts of Marion, Illinois, in a room not much larger than a prison cell. The shades were pulled tight against the white hot light reflecting off the highway outside, and the room was dense and dark with his belongings. The air was still and thick. Clothes, combat boots, dishes, and magazines were everywhere. He had an unusually large number of knives. There was a Bowie knife on top of the television and a machete propped up by the door. A Gerber boot knife was on the night-stand. The closet shelves were stacked high with junk food, and Hale and I sat on the bed while we talked. He was a large, soft man in his twenties and was wearing an undershirt. His pale arms were tattooed.

"The administration was just waiting and hoping for somebody to get killed so they could lock it down," he said.

"Why?" I asked.

"I don't know," Jim Hale said. "I can't really say much about that. Harold Miller has a reputation throughout the Bureau; you hear people talk about him: When they want a place locked down, they send Harold Miller there. And it gets locked down. When he left Marion [shortly after the lockdown began], he went to Lewisburg. Within two weeks after he got to Lewisburg, they locked the place down because they had a work strike."

Referring to the day when two guards were killed at Marion, Hale said, "The associate warden, a guy named Ken Stewart, told the crew that was working H-Unit [the hole] that night to go ahead and run it like it was normal routine. Take these guys to Rec; put them in the showers. Now that doesn't make a lick of sense. They should have locked that unit down—it doesn't have to be the whole joint, just that unit [i.e., cell block]. Lock that unit down and shake it down. It wasn't locked down; it wasn't shook down. OK, Tommy Silverstein killed a guard that morning. That made him a big shot, the way the cons think. Well, here's Clay Fountain sitting upstairs [in the same cell block]. And he's a rabid little bastard if there ever was one. There's no way in hell he's going to let Tommy Silverstein have all the glory for killing a guard. If he got the chance that night, he was going to have to have some of that glory. Well, he got his chance. Bob Hoffman was killed because of it."

Later I asked John Clark why Fountain had to kill a guard. He said, "To keep the body count up, I guess."

"Then why weren't normal practices followed?" I asked. "Why weren't the cells searched after the first murder of the day?"

"That's the first time I've ever heard that even mentioned," Clark said.

Jerry Powless was the officer escorting Fountain when Fountain stuck his hands into another inmate's cell. Fountain spun around with one cuff off and a knife in his hand. Before he could get to Hoffman, however, he had to face Powless and Ditterline. He plunged the knife into Powless's chest and Ditterline stepped between Powless and Fountain.

When Ditterline told me about this, his voice dropped almost to a whisper and tears came to his eyes. "I remember blocking a couple of the blows, but he nailed me a couple of times and I fell backward. I was kicking at him, trying to keep him at bay as best I could." Fountain rushed past Ditterline and Powless to attack Hoffman, fatally stabbing him.

"And you know who the first person through that front grille was?" Ditterline asked. "Hoffman's boy. His son. He saw his father die."

Hoffman's son was also a guard and the first person to respond when David Hale dialed deuces. When Clay Fountain saw him come in to help his father, he hollered out, "Come on! I've never gotten a father-son combination before." And then Fountain did a little victory dance down the range, laughing, amid cheers from the other inmates.

The Inmates

When a person has passed through five grilles, he can say he's been in Marion, and he can look back out to the front door and see what effect all that steel has on sunlight. The world he knew—the bright, new, air-conditioned front vestibule, which with its magnetometer and guard looks like an airport terminal—is dimmed and shattered into an alien logarithmic crosshatching on the mirror-polished floor. But even there he is still not really in Marion. He is protected from it by his mind, which keeps alive the images of what he just left outside.

On the other hand, if he were to stay in Marion for a very long time and had to move past those grilles, it would be very difficult to remember what was out there, the white parking lot glittering with red and blue and tan automobiles—models he has never seen, which will come into and go out of style before he is released—and beyond that, the Crab Orchard National Wildlife Refuge with more than forty thousand acres of forest and lake, deer and opossum, fox and quail.

When a prisoner goes off at Marion, he is taken from the east corridor "normal" population to the north corridor "special housing"; he passes those grilles on his way into solitary confinement. You have to wonder if the designers planned it this way, but a man going to the hole can actually see outside, almost into the parking lot.

I saw a young black man being dragged there, shackled hand and foot. He was moved along by three guards. One held the handcuff chain behind his back to jerk him flat on his face at a moment's notice, while two others held their clubs at the ready to strike him down if he made a move. As the prisoner passed the divided shafts of sunlight on the gleaming yellow linoleum, he strained to look out beyond the grilles. After long enough inside Marion, the inmates simply call everything out there "the street."

"Being in the hole twenty-three hours a day for two and three years is a son of a bitch," said Garrett Trapnell, who is serving life for hijacking. "Some men are over in H-Unit today, and the only way they're ever going to see a skirt or ride in a car or eat at McDonald's is by killing somebody. So in our society, here, there's no punishment for murder. For murder you get rewarded. I've seen guys talking: 'I wanna see a girl, man! I wanna smell the world, I wanna see the grass; I wanna ride in a car. How am I gonna do that? I'm gonna kill this motherfucker.' An automatic trip—it's court time."

Dr. Frank J. Rundle, a psychiatrist who visited Marion, described "security conditions of a degree I have seen nowhere in ten years of visiting prisons around the United States." He added, "If more humane conditions are not soon restored there will be a catastrophe."

Joseph G. Cannon, a professor in the administration of justice at the University of Missouri in St. Louis, wrote, "I have worked in and around prisons and jails for the greater part of my life (now in my sixtieth year) and I have never seen procedures so extreme and so seemingly designed to degrade and aggravate the prisoners. . . . If the present procedures at this prison are permitted to continue, violence will be the consequence."

Craig Haney, a social psychologist specializing in prisons, said, "Unless the draconian and Orwellian conditions that now prevail [at Marion] are significantly abated, I believe that major outbreaks of violence will result."

What they mean is that one prisoner who escapes could pull a lever and let out eighteen prisoners on a range. Those eighteen could overwhelm the three to five guards at the end of the range and then let out an additional fifty or so prisoners. Those fifty could overwhelm guards on another cell block, and so on, until the entire prison was in the hands of the inmates. What they are saying is that even the tightest security must slip up once in a while, and then, if you haven't already developed the good will of the prisoners, you'll have a prison takeover on your hands. Marion could be the next Santa Fe. At that prison, inmates murdered thirty-three guards in a thirty-six-hour siege in 1980. Some guards were tortured with electric drills before being killed.

❖   ❖   ❖

I walked along the ranges, passing cell after cell. Hot moist waves of air moved through the flesh-colored bars like vapor sweat. There was the faint scent of burning paint and the resin binder of a grinding wheel. A lock was being changed somewhere on the corridor. The smoke drifted to us and mixed with the sublimated sweat that poured off guards and prisoners and rolled down the hall like a fog.

In some of the cells inmates had been allowed to fashion ducts out of laundry-bag plastic to direct air from the vent toward the bunk; these looked like giant condoms protruding from the walls. Each six-by-nine-foot cell had a vent and a bunk, a combination sink and toilet, and a cardboard locker about three feet wide and eighteen inches deep. The cells face out onto the range and a concrete wall with louvered windows. If the louvers are opened (at the guards' discretion), the prisoners can see across to the next louvered concrete cell block. The prisoners cannot see one another; they carry on conversations by shouting up and down the ranges.

Sometimes the inmates would not even look up to see who was there as I passed. At other times they would loom up out of the darkness, tattooed and apparitional and white, like rare fish surfacing from the ocean depths. A skull and death's head mask came up out of one cell, and I read beneath the blue hallucinations the words WEISS MACHT, German for "white power."

Then I saw that it was tattooed on a man's stomach, and I shifted my eyes to see his face. He might have been in his middle thirties. His head was nearly shaven; his well-developed upper body was covered with tattoos. He had so many tattoos it appeared that his clear, pale skin was turning blue from within— the last stages of some disfiguring disease. He looked up from a copy of Edward Abbey's novel *The Monkey Wrench Gang* and stared out at me. Swastikas had been hammered into his skin here and there, single-needle work; skulls and images of the Grim Reaper squirmed on rippling white flesh. There was a deep mass of scar tissue on his left arm near the elbow, and I asked him what had caused it. He said he'd removed a tattoo. I asked why.

"I thought it might cause me some trouble in here," he said.

"What did it say?"

"Oh, nothing. Just some initials."

"What initials?" I asked.

"A. B.," he said.

I walked away. I didn't get it until I had seen two or three men adorned as he was. Then it hit me: Aryan Brotherhood.

Some inmates came right up to the bars talking, as if I had been there all along. They did not touch the bars. They behaved, in fact, as if the bars were not there, passing papers through the bars, shaking hands with a casual, graceful ease that could have come only with long practice. An eight-and-a-half-by-eleven-inch sheet of paper was deftly folded with the fingers of one hand, then passed through the bars and unfolded again as if by magic.

Henry B. Johnson, a mild-mannered, clean-shaven black man wearing black horn-rimmed glasses and a forest green knit ski cap, came up out of the darkness of his cell, chattering softly in a long enunciated drawl, and didn't stop talking until I walked away. ". . . Leavenworth, Atlanta, Terry Haute, Lewisburg, El Reno, I done twenty years flat. They say I robbed a Safeway, a stickup, armed robbery, right? I originally started my time in the state of Virginia, then transferred to Federal system. I came here, moved to El Reno, El Reno to Leavenworth, Leavenworth to Atlanta, Atlanta back up here, to Terry Haute, back to Atlanta, Atlanta to Lewisburg, Lewisburg back here, Otisville to Lewisburg, and back. Now, the flux of the situation that I like to bring to hand is this here: The reason that the prisoners are locked down in this facility has nothing to do with the prisoners per se. It's the economics of the thing, the politics. You know anything about politics? Here's what I'm saying: What took place in the Control Unit—which is the last stop in this particular facility, right?—has no bearing on the population in this particular facility, right? It was an isolated incident. Now it's my understanding that the alleged officers that they claimed was murdered in the Control Unit should have been dealt with at that end. Since then, the past twenty-one months, we've been locked in our cells twenty-three hours a day, right? And a long period of incarceration without proper medical diet breeds psychosis. You know what psychosis is? It makes one become predatory, compulsive—his behavior is other than normal. So what I'm saying is if they plan to relieviate the situation, try to get things back into control, they should open the facility up. In my particular case, right now, I'm seven years overdue for being released. I come in when I was eighteen. I'm thirty-nine now."

Paper is the currency of prison; it was paper that got them into this fix; and paper, they hope, will get them out. An administration memo can grant a privilege or take it away. Almost all the prisoners I spoke to showed me something on paper—a writ, a lawsuit, a plea, a letter, a shot (citation for rule infraction), even a poem.

Clark sneered at the legal actions brought by prisoners. "It's part of the way they structure their time," he said. It is also their only hope.

On the other hand, the librarian told me of those inmates who simply request one legal volume after another—"sequence readers," he called them—one a day, until they've run through every volume on the shelves. He has to answer every request, or they'll file a suit saying they're denied legal counsel. As a result, with an inmate population of only 335, he processed ten thousand requests for books in 1984.

A lawsuit is no trivial matter. I visited one room in the prison stacked hip high with some forty thousand pages of documents involved in *Bruscino*. The case contended that the harsh conditions of USP-Marion violate a wide range of constitutional rights. The room was dark, abandoned looking, with a paper wasp pelting its body in vain against the bright metal mesh of a single window up near the ceiling. The long tables where researchers had sat, the high yellow ceilings, the dust, all contributed to the impression that this was what remained of a vanished civilization. "The only option they have at this time to change their self-imposed plight," said the magistrate in that case, "is to manipulate the judicial system for their benefit. This Court will not be a party to such manipulation." And, he added, "Conditions at USP-Marion, singularly or totally, are constitutional."

❖   ❖   ❖

As I walked the ranges, I saw one man sitting on the toilet, staring out. We might have been shadows on a scrim. The only privacy in prison is the privacy you create by refusing to see.

Another inmate sat bolt upright on the edge of his bunk with his face just inches from the television set, staring with rapt attention at the close-up face of a soap opera heroine. Channel ten is a closed circuit on which the prison broadcasts religious services and, now and then, the Jane Fonda workout tape first thing in the morning. It was once a favorite, but after two years of solitary confinement, the inmates have become inured even to that. Prison authorities decide who can have a television set or a radio—or any possession, for that matter. A list of approved articles is distributed. Anything not specifically approved is forbidden. In the hole, there is nothing.

A big, white, freckled kid with red hair cut marine style squinted, pacing angrily in his cell. He looked as if he were about to hit someone, only no one was in there but him. When I approached, he spun on me accusingly, his fists balled. "There's no sense in me talkin' to you," he said. He had an eye tattooed in the center of his hairless chest. He was almost shouting. "I've been here for five years!"

Another man rushed the bars, saying, "Yeah, don't believe anything they tell you. They're just covering their own asses. I was roughed up in Lewisburg and protested. I fought back. I was charged with assault and sent here." Behind him on his shelf was a copy of *Art through the Ages*. Some prisoners are allowed to have books sent to them from outside. "Now what sound man is going to attack ten officers?" he asked.

Michael Price had WEISS BRUDER tattooed across his stomach and a little swastika needled into the tender flesh just outside his right eye. Elsewhere on his body: a skull, a Grim Reaper, and the word DAGO. I thought it remarkable that a white racist would use ink to make his skin darker.

Glen West said he'd committed robberies, escaped from prison, and taken policemen hostage since his career of crime began. "I'm not saying I don't belong in here," he told me as I passed his cell. "I don't care where they put me. But isn't it funny that the Bureau of Prisons hires nothing but perfect people? None of them make mistakes." He couldn't read when he was first put in prison. He taught himself during the rehabilitation fad.

He handed me some papers. They magically folded on his side of the bars, passed through, and unfolded again in the air before me. It was a trick as neat and unconscious as a cowboy rolling a cigarette with one hand. I read the BP-DIR-9 form, "Request for Administrative Remedy," which has two parts, one labeled Part A—INMATE REQUEST—and the larger labeled Part B—RESPONSE. In the top portion West had written:

> I have been told by both the Warden and now the counselor that even though we have a cabinet in our cell which can be used as a table to eat our meals on they won't allow us to. We are being told to either eat out of our laps or off the floor. This simply because they think the cell looks neater if the cabinet is where we can't use it. We can't eat out of our lap like a sea otter because often the trays have food or water all over the bottom of them. Besides to say eat out of your lap because we like the way the cabinet looks over there is ridiculous. Why not just give us a bowl and we can eat off the floor like a dog.

The warden wrote back, "This is in response to your request for administrative remedy receipted 5/31/85, in which you request to be allowed to use your storage locker to eat off of. Lockers presently issued to inmates are designed for storage of personal property, also a shelf for televisions. Shelves are presently being considered for placement in each cell which will serve the purpose for eating, writing, etc. Accordingly, your request is denied."

It's the sort of treatment that is so difficult to define, so gentle is the method, like the Chinese water torture, or the death of ten thousand cuts. Each cut is so clean that you never feel a thing. Psychiatrists fear it will drive men to violence, make men go off, and one day make Marion as famous for carnage as Santa Fe.

I watched an inmate go off one day at Marion. (The administration calls it "acting out.") He was a black man in his mid-thirties. He'd been let out of his cell for his sixty minutes of indoor recreation, and he was walking up and down the range in his bare feet, cackling and howling, refusing to be locked up again. He didn't realize he was more locked up than most of us will ever know. Freedom to him was an hour out on the range: A yellow-painted steel screen at the far end covered a ventilation shaft; a sliding grille of prison bars blocked his way out past me and the guards. Still he wouldn't go back into his cell—I guess freedom is a relative thing—and no one was about to go in there and talk to him until the riot squad came. So he was allowed to hoot and carry on until he wore himself out. Then the SORT team came and did a forced cell move on him: held him down and carried him away. SORT stands for Strategic Operations Response Team. Inmates call it the Goon Squad. When the SORT team comes to get you, all your possessions are removed and taken to the second floor of the hospital, where they're stored in an abandoned ward.

After the guards were killed, inmates say, there were widespread recriminatory beatings of the prisoners by the guards. Mike Sizemore, a young white man, was one of the alleged victims. He told me his version of the events: "Shortly after the lockdown they moved us early one morning. I was dressed in shorts, T-shirt, and shower shoes, nothing else. And this was the middle of November and all the windows were wide open and they were writing up shots left and right." A prisoner is never given explanations, such as why he's being moved, or to where, or why he's being made to stand nearly naked in a November breeze. "I asked if they could close the windows," Sizemore said, "and the guy jabbed me through the bars with his stick and told me to shut up."

The next day the SORT team came for him.

While they were moving him, someone "hit me in the back of the neck and knocked me to the floor. And then it started. It was a long way to the hole. They beat me up all the way, throwing me into the walls. They still didn't handcuff me, but I saw no point in fighting back. I'm not a man who will let a man smack me in the face and not do anything. But they were all dressed out [in riot gear], and I couldn't have hurt them if I tried." When they got him to H-Unit, the hole, the guards punched him around some more, Sizemore said, and asked why Clutts and Hoffman had been murdered. Later a physician's assistant happened to be passing his cell and Sizemore asked to see a doctor. He was told he could not see one.

The U.S. Court ruled in the *Bruscino* case that such charges by prisoners were untrue and without foundation in fact.

❖   ❖   ❖

By a mysterious paradox of the rule system, if you go off frequently enough, unless you kill or maim someone, the guards finally back off and leave you alone. Describing "the process of dissolution" that takes place after long incarceration, Jack Henry Abbott in his book *In the Belly of the Beast* wrote, "The pigs can sense it and they pass the word. They place you on the *pay-him-no-mind* list. You are allowed to roam the prison and do and say *anything* you care to and the guards overlook it; ignore you as if you were not even there. Only if you commit an act of violence do they pounce and drag you to the hole."

Danny Atteberry, known as Schemo to his friends, is a white inmate with long black hair hanging down past his shoulders. He paced his cell, bobbing and smiling and laughing. He had set his steel bunk on end in an attempt to make the most of the fifty-four square feet of floor space. Atteberry had hung his clothes on the steel bedframe and rolled up the mattress in a corner. Like so many inmates I saw, Atteberry was doing his paperwork when I walked up to his cell—preparing or reading or researching various legal documents. Tom Krajenta, unit manager and immediate superior of all the guards on the unit, stood behind me, facing Atteberry, as we talked. I asked Atteberry why his cell was arranged the way it was.

"I'm living in the bathroom, in the shitter," he said. He

laughed: A-hilk! "I mean this is where I've got to live. There ain't nothing I can do, I'm in here twenty-three hours a day. And so I'm gonna live however I want. Now, they're putting guys in the hole if they don't set their bed up here, if they don't put their TV back." A-hilk! A-hilk!

"So how come you're not in the hole?" I asked.

"I generally stay in the hole. I've gotten like twenty shots in the last eighteen months for calling them turds and shit-eaters and maggots and for putting up a sign on my locker that says FUCK AUTHORITY. They take me away from my constitutional rights and put me in the hole."

"So how come you're not in the hole right now with your bunk up on end like that?" I asked.

Atteberry got a wild grin on his face and edged closer to the bars. "Because they're treating me real nice. They don't want to put me in the hole for some reason. I don't know." A-hilk! A-hilk!

I turned to Krajenta and asked why Atteberry wasn't in the hole.

"In this unit the regulation as far as the actual furnishing— we just don't enforce it. The other unit manager or I have the discretion to say if you don't have your bed down you're going to go to the hole, but I haven't done that in this unit because I don't have any problems in this unit."

"I'm the only one that fucks up," Atteberry added. A-hilk!

"How do you feel about being called a turd by Atteberry?" I asked Krajenta.

"I just totally disregard anything that comes out of his mouth."

I asked Atteberry what he'd done to get into prison in the first place.

"I was a youngster. I've been here seventeen years. I went down when I was twenty-two on a robbery charge. After that I escaped and caught a robbery and assault on a police on escape. And then after that I took hostages and stabbed nurses in a prison takeover in 1974 in Walla Walla, Washington."

I asked him how long he might be in prison, and he said he didn't know.

I went down into I-Unit, a cell block containing seventy-two strip cells, what used to be called Oriental cells at Alcatraz, with nothing in them but a toilet and a bunk. B-Range of I-Unit contains the boxcar cells, which have closed fronts to cut off sound and ventilation. There are the bars, as on a regular cell, and then a few feet in front of that—just far enough so that the prisoner can't reach—is a second set of bars covered with plexiglass. A door can be closed so that the inmate's screams are muffled, so that air flow is cut off, so that he can't throw food or feces out of his cell. As I walked down the range, I could hear the last man in the last cell hollering, "Hey! Lemme speak to you for a moment! Hey, newspaper boy! Open the door! Open the door!"

"The door's open," I told him.

"Oh," he said, as if he'd just noticed.

I went through the door and stood in the small space between the two sets of bars.

"My name is Abdul Salam, a.k.a. Clark." A piece of paper materialized on my side of the bars. It said he was once Jesse James Clark but had become Muhammad Mustafa Abdulla. He was an enormous black man, perhaps 230 pounds; but very little of it was fat. In the middle of his stomach he had an enormous scar blooming like a pale flower from the dark flesh of his navel. Smaller scars adorned his arms and upper body. "Now, tell all the women that they gonna send me to Springfield," he said.

"Can we take your picture?" I asked Abdulla.

He hollered up at the ceiling, "Hey Price-Bey! Hey Price-Bey!"

A voice drifted down from D-Range above us: "I heard dat."

"You gonna let 'em take a picture of you, man?"

"Yeah, I am!"

"OK," he said. Abdulla's cell was littered with clothes and bits of torn-up paper. The walls and ceiling had been smeared with something dark. He showed us his prayer rug and Koran. He insisted on putting on his shirt and shoes before having his photograph taken, saying he was a religious man; and he held his worn, green-bound Koran and posed deliberately for each shot. One of his sneakers was laced halfway up and untied. The other was completely unlaced. As he moved his enormous bulk in that cramped and littered space, he lurched and staggered; though he never quite hit the walls or the bars. Even for Abdulla the bars seemed not to be there.

"Hey, Clark," Abdulla said to the warden's assistant. "I know ya'll sending me to Springfield for a medical, for a mental, and you know I don't have no mental problems. You ought to send me back to D.C."

"I'm not sending you anywhere," Clark said.

Abdulla suggested this caption for his picture: "I want you to put in there that I am trying to get back to D.C. and that any Muslim that desire to contact me that it's cool and I'm tryin' to do right but Marion is holding me here as a contract prisoner and don't want to turn me loose."

"Tell me about your stomach scar," I said.

"Naaah!" Abdulla said modestly. "I don't want to talk about that. You know, because that involved me getting shot and then I shot somebody else, that's all. But lemme tell you: They keep my door closed twenty-four hours a day. I been on lockup in this place right here for three months."

He kept on talking as the associate warden and I walked back up the range. Jesse James Clark was taken away the following week to the hospital facility at Springfield, Missouri, for a psychiatric examination.

While I-Unit is known as the most disruptive and rowdy in the prison, D-Unit, which the guards call Dog-Unit, is just the opposite. No radios or televisions are allowed on I-Unit. They are allowed on D-Unit, yet it's surprising how quiet D-Unit is. I never heard music as loud as you might hear it on any bus or subway. There was an almost monastic feel to D-Unit.

There were only forty-five men on Dog-Unit, although it can

hold seventy-two. One of them was Frank Lewis, a soft-spoken thirty-year-old black man, who looked weary and contrite. He had robbed a bank with someone in New York in 1977, and when I asked him to tell me about it, he said, "I'm not proud of it." He smiled slightly when I asked him to tell me if there was anything good about being in Marion. "It makes you think much more. Think about your life and how things are fucked up—how you fucked up. And you start saying, 'Wait a minute, I've got to do something about this.' Most of the guys here are in the hole. I've been around. I've been to plenty of institutions, and this one here is tight. It's very tight." He said he didn't mind Dog-Unit because it was quieter. "There's a great deal of maturity over here; guys can somewhat deal with it."

I asked Lewis to compare Marion with Leavenworth, which is where he was serving his sentence before being transferred to Marion.

"Ah, no comparison. At Leavenworth there's much more freedom. You can move around. There's a lot of programs, and you can pretty well occupy yourself. Here there's nothing, so if you can't read, you can't write, and you have no discipline, you're in trouble. It's dangerous in the sense that a lot of guys don't have any money, been down awhile, they've lost contact with their girlfriends; and a guy reaches a level of frustration. So it does present a large amount of danger. In fact that's why I'm over here, because the guys can handle it." Dog-Unit is designated for those the administration identifies as gang leaders.

I asked him if there was any violence when he robbed the bank.

"Well, a gun was used and the threat was there."

"How long did you get?" I asked.

"I got twenty-five years," he said, "because it was the second time."

"So what got you to Marion?" I asked.

"I got in a fight with some officers," he said. "Or a struggling match anyway. But it doesn't take anything major to come here."

It just takes something major to get out.

I visited John Greschner in the hole, which has many names: H-Unit (we were on A-Range), the Control Unit, disciplinary segregation, solitary, strip cell, Oriental cell. Whatever you call it, Greschner put it this way: "There's nothing in there but me." Even when an H-Unit inmate is let out of his cell for his hour of recreation, he is only put in a larger cell.

Greschner stood in the exercise cage as I spoke to him, an elongated steel-mesh box along the range of eighteen cells. In the box was an exercise bike, a chinning bar, and nothing else. If he requested a jump rope, I was told, the guards would give him one. Then again, maybe they wouldn't. Prison authorities gave me their point of view on a few of Greschner's activities since he was sent to Marion in 1976:

> November 18, 1979: At approximately 3:30 P.M. on "A" range of "H" Unit Greschner, John 2550-135 attacked and stabbed Logan, John Henry 87870-132 with a sharpened weapon fashioned from a round metal rod. Logan received approximately twelve wounds to the chest and upper part of the body. The wounds required that Logan be transported to Marion Hospital for treatment.
>
> April 28, 1980: Inmates John Greschner, Reg. No. 02550-135, and Clayton Fountain, Reg. No. 89129-132, escaped from their cells in the Control Unit by way of the air vent system in the rear of their cells. Using the air vent system, they gained access to the pipespace in the Control Unit and attempted to escape from that area. Squads of officers had to go into the pipespace using riot batons, plastic shields and tear gas guns to force the inmates to leave the pipespace.

When I saw Greschner, he was very pale and sweating from exercise. He had black hair and a goatee. His shirt was off, and he was holding it around the back of his neck to absorb the sweat. He pointed across the range at his cell. "I'm down here for insolence and use of morphine or heroin."

"How do you get morphine in here?" I asked.

"Well, that's what I was trying to explain to them, how do I get morphine in here? You know, they've got it locked down. I don't have any contact with anybody in the streets, I don't have any visits, I don't have anything." Balancing on the balls of his feet, he smiled and shrugged as we struggled to see each other through the steel mesh. Like the bars, it seemed designed to frustrate human contact. The bars and screens seemed always to be just at eye level and spaced so that you could never quite see anyone with both eyes at once. Like everything else at Marion, the effect was disorienting.

"But this is no good here," Greschner said. "They lay people on these shelves for years and years. As a matter of fact, they've got a new shrink here. He's been placed in this unit since the killing of the guards and the allegations by the prisoners that people deteriorate down here—long term isolation, sensory deprivation. There is no TV, no radio, and if they consider you're disruptive, even if you're in the cell and you can't get out of the cell, they will run in and jump you with a Goon Squad [SORT team] and beat that ass and tie you to a bunk. So they brought a shrink in here and the first time I seen him I asked him, 'You know there's a lot of things been happening here and you've been getting a lot of testimony [in *Bruscino*] by psychiatrists that these units are harmful. They aren't doing any good. Also, a personal friend of mine named Silverstein, who ya'll got for killin' one of these guards, was down here for years on end, and they knew that was going to happen with that guard because he told them it was going to happen with that guard if they didn't get that guard off his back. And I was there when he told the unit manager that after months and months and months and months of the harassment from that guard, Clutts, finally he says, 'I can't take it any more. If you don't get this guy off my fuckin' back, I'm gonna have to do it.' He told J. T. Holland that. That was the Control Unit manager. They never did it. I went to Leavenworth. Six months later I hear they got Silverstein for killing Clutts."

As Greschner talked, he became more animated, pointing his finger at the flesh-colored steel mesh that separated us. "Now, I have no problems with a guard doing his job. That's what he's here for, to make sure we ain't sawing windows out and all that. But when you start poking at a motherfucker and start fucking with a motherfucker all the time, you know, putting shit in his food, fucking with his rack, harassing him, shaking his shit down—you go in and you find pictures of your old lady, or your mom, with boot prints on 'em. Then you go to his superior and say, 'Hey, look, check this out, look what he's doing in there,' and they don't do nothing; finally, it reaches the point where you're either going to take it or you're going to do something.

"Now, I'm trying to explain this to this shrink. I told him, 'Yeah, I did almost nine years in solitary confinement, I went down to Leavenworth, yeah, I'm annoyed and fucked up, man, and . . . I'm doin' OK . . . but I'm fucked up and having a hard time navigating, man. I been away from people so long, you walk up and I don't know you, I'm kind of annoyed with you. . . .' You know what I'm saying?"

"Yeah," I said.

"And consequently, I'm down here for four months, and I get in a little old beef with this dude, man; I get in a killing. Now I'm back here. They gimme a double life sentence. And I'm saying, 'What do you think of that? What do you think of the detrimental effects of a unit like this?' And he says, 'You know what, Greschner? You just gimme good reason to keep you locked up in here forever.'"

❖   ❖   ❖

Being in the hospital was like being on the bottom of a swimming pool, an indistinct green coolness after the oven of the cellblocks. The physician's assistant in charge of rectal searches carried a radio and a set of keys like a guard. He said, "I have yet to see a beating here."

The dentist, a civilian drawing lieutenant-colonel's pay, said, "I've got the needle, the ultimate persuader." And he laughed.

I took the armored elevator to the second floor, a ward that used to house inmates but is now deserted except for one guard and one prisoner behind a steel door for his own protection while he's testifying. Federal witness protection. He squinted out through a slit at us. A walking dead man.

At the end of the corridor were two large hospital wards now piled high with upturned hospital beds, discarded IV stands, old duffel bags, and the belongings of prisoners who were being kept in strip cells.

I asked the fat, boyish guard, "What do you two talk about up here?"

"I avoid talking to most of these convicts," he said.

"Don't you talk to him at all?"

"When I have to."

"Why?"

"You start off talking about apples and pretty soon you're talking about oranges. The next thing you know you're talking about tangerines," he said. He turned the key and sent me on my way in the steel elevator.

I went out of the hospital and down the corridor and back out through the magnetometer and into the world. The parking lot, the cars, seemed dazzling and fantastic after days inside USP-Marion. As I stood on the brink of the Crab Orchard Wildlife Refuge, I thought how cruel it seemed to deprive someone of all this. Then I remembered one prisoner I'd asked what he thought his punishment should have been for all he'd done.

"What do you think they ought to do to you?"

"By the code that I live, I would have done something. I expected it. I'm not in here unjustly. I stabbed the officer and that's what I'm in here for. Wasn't nothing unjust about that. It was just something that happened at the time. I couldn't get around it. I have my own code of ethics I live by on the streets. I don't live by society's laws, so when society catches up with me, I got to be punished. I accept that. It ain't no big deal. I accept what's coming to me according to the society."

"Would you try to escape?"

He looked up suddenly and angrily, as if to see whether or not my question was serious. "Would I try to escape? Of course."

MAN IN CAPTIVITY

I

There exists at this moment among us an orga-
nized society of criminals. . . . They form a
small nation within the greater. Almost all
these men met or meet again in prison. We
must now disperse the members of this society.

—ALEXIS DE TOCQUEVILLE, 1831

The third floor of Division two at the Cook County Jail is
called Gladiator School. There are no cells, no bars, no air conditioning. Each dorm is a big hot cavernous room rimmed with
tile like yellowed teeth, linoleum floors, and fifty steel bunks
spaced so that when I sit on the edge of one, my knees touch
another man's knees. It smells of bleach and sweat. One wall
is dominated by louvered windows facing the yard through a
heavy steel screen and layers of dirt—an alien, dying light
makes it look as if we've landed on the surface of Mercury.

The guards are the drill instructors of Gladiator School. "If
you don't know how to fight when you come here, you'll know
how when you leave," an inmate told me.

The sergeant, a small, muscular man in his fifties, said, "I'll
put some blood on your ass if you act up, and if you give me any
shit, I'll beat your ass and send you to Cermak Hospital. I got
control here."

These are not well-seasoned prison inmates; they are kids

fresh off the street, pre-trial detainees (a fair number will not be convicted), yet already they seem embued with ideals, values, and codes that set them permanently against society; they seem utterly prepared for (and energetically enthusiastic about) the life of the outcast that most of them are well on their way to leading. The warden tells me that one-third of them will be dead before they reach thirty.

Some of the black men lather like horses, white froth building in the fur under their arms as they swagger about, fulminating with wrath, scowling at the room as if waiting for a challenge. At the front of the room by the gurgling blue light of the television screen, a few white boys hang here and there on the edges of steel tables where others play cards. They eye the room cautiously—they're a minority here. At a distance the whites look as big and wholesome as surfers, but up close, I can see: One big kid with curly blond hair has a deep incision from his hairline to his chin. He was handsome, but the street surgery bisected his nose, and the pieces have grown together slightly misaligned, Picasso style.

Some people—perhaps a majority—believe that Gladiator School—what one penal historian likened to the poetry of Dante made manifest—might frighten a few of the boys into giving up a life of crime, that once they are back out on the street, they will remember how bad jail was and not want to go back; but the facts prove otherwise. By the time those kids get to Gladiator School, they are already lifers. The threat of prison does not deflect them from their path; the memory of jail will not deter them.

Near the back of the room several young men were doing bicep curls using a large plastic bucket filled to overflowing with water. They had rigged a strip of bed sheet to make a handle and wrapped a towel around the bed sheet to keep it from cutting into their fingers. Most of them wore tattoos representing their gangs. Some of the work was so new that it was still scabbed over and peeling—ordinarily a sign of a jailhouse turnout, a new gang member recruited in jail.

There are occasionally those few who somehow wind up in

jail and are so badly frightened that it changes their behavior; they are the exception, but they do exist. Equally rare are the staff members who are sensitive to the problems. A staff member told me, "Sometimes people who find themselves in jail for the first time go into shock or depression or panic. They can't eat, they can't sleep. They don't shower. You see them pacing. We try to help them adjust to the new environment." Captivity is an experience of mythic proportions; it sometimes produces a transformation. (At one time, in the early 1800s, spiritual conversion was the whole point of prison.)

But in modern American prisons, conversion to normal social values is an exceptional (and unintentional) side effect of the system. Although conversion is possible, even in so-called hardened criminals, no method ever tried has been successful at systematically and predictably engendering such conversions, on demand as it were. In 1808 J. B. Treilhard described one method that was used off and on until the present day:

> . . . compelled to work, convicts may come in the end to like it; when they have reaped the reward, they will acquire the habit, the taste, the need for occupation; let them give each other the example of a laborious life; it will soon become a pure life; soon they will begin to know regret for the past, the first harbinger of a love of duty.

Road work, chain gangs, prison factories—nothing seemed to work with any certainty. Conversion seemed to come from within, spontaneously, as an inspiration.

Today our prisons are not set up for work. (Indeed, most prisons are set up to prevent useful labor, though many institutions make a show of the token convicts "allowed" to work in a small shop, while the majority sit idle.) As anyone experienced in religious or political work can attest, precipitating a conversion is a dicey affair: It can go for or against one's intended purpose. An inmate who is mentally or socially or emotionally marginal, who is barely clinging to the common values of society, has a chance of being converted into a vicious and dangerous criminal in Gladiator School.

I talked with many boys from the ghetto who came from homes with no parents, who had spent their lives threatened by violence in school and on the streets, who were constantly pursued by marauding gangs. Some were beaten, sexually abused. One lost his girlfriend to a gang shooting. Another lost his baby sister. Many took drugs from a very early age. In short, they fell into that marginal category.

In jail for the first time, such a boy might have one of two reactions: He might be elated that he has finally risen to adult status, signaled in his social matrix by "doing time," or he may be in such a panic that (since the guards won't protect him) he'll seek protection in the company of the gang members who rule his streets and all of our penal institutions. (Roughly eighty percent of prison population today is made up of gang members.)

Whatever his reaction, he will be pushed toward a return to prison, not toward the development of values that could help him move from the ghetto into ordinary society. In the first case, enduring the torments of prison is a ritual game of manhood, like the Spartan enduring the bite of the fox. Those warriors are a long way from being motivated to become "normal." In the second case, a boy finds it difficult to get out of the gang once he's out of jail (he's tattooed, marked for life). Having sworn allegiance, he is unable to duck the gang back on the street: Noncooperation in gang activities is seen as "disrespect," which carries severe penalties, sometimes even death. He is swept into gang activities, which are almost always illegal and highly public. The inevitable result is getting caught, returning to jail. Most of the "kids" in Gladiator School have records going back to the age of puberty. They were lifers by the age of twenty-one.

❖   ❖   ❖

A Mexican from the Insane Unknowns, part of the loose confederation of gangs known as The People, showed me his new tattoo. It had been done with a safety pin by another inmate, who liked to be called Lepke in honor of the founder of Murder, Inc., in New York. Lepke had a crude blue teardrop tattooed at the outside corner of his left eye. The I/U/K on the Mexican's left breast was chiseled out in clean German gothic lettering, but the blunt point had done so much tissue damage that the letters stood erect like the ritual scars of a Zulu warrior.

I find it helpful to view Gladiator School (and prisons in general) as a culture apart—as the name suggests, a camp where warriors are trained—with its own set of rules and traditions, where what we call civilized norms are suspended (or unheard of). That allows me to observe it for a moment without judging it. It is difficult to be a middle-class property owner, hard worker, regular citizen, and not feel hatred and fear toward these warriors. By emphasizing the relatively few crimes committed across class boundaries, law enforcement officials and the press make it seem that this lower class is waging war on the middle class—stealing, raping, even murdering. That is untrue. Most murders, for example, are committed by a person known to or related to the victim. Most theft occurs within or along class geographical boundaries. Svend Ranulf's book *Moral Indignation and Middle-Class Psychology* described how ordinary hard-working people come to hate the lower classes. It has little to do with crime committed by one class on the other, he says. We want to see them punished because we are working hard and they are not. Their slack-limbed, disorderly lassitude; the way they sprawl on the streets, taking up public space; the fact that they shoot off their guns on New Year's Eve frightens us and makes us crave some power that will force them to conform.

So police are hired to send them to jail. Prisoners, then, can be likened to the warriors of those tribes, those "small nations" suggested by de Tocqueville.

In fact, the roaming bands that formed the original underclass, which gave rise to penal codes and jails in the first place, were the very tribal people who were displaced, torn free from the land, first by the breakdown of feudalism and later by an organized agricultural business and the industrialization of Europe. The growth of civilization as we know it brought with it an idle class. Likewise, in the development of American society, similar new tribes of people have formed—dislocated, nomadic bands over which our cultural norms have no sway. Their world, their beliefs, their values, are as different from ours as those of the Plains Indians were from the European settlers. The parallels are intriguing. They speak with their hands, in sign language, and the signs sometimes cause bloody tribal wars. El Rukns, Vice Lords, Latin Kings, Insane Unknowns—even their names are like the names of tribes, and they refer to themselves as The People, which is what the Arapaho and many other nations called themselves. Their enemies are The Folks.

Prison is an attempt to fix them in space, these odd tribes. Since they don't speak our language, don't recognize our laws, are not afraid of our punishments—in fact, it is a sign of honor among them to be able to withstand our most exquisite tortures (the teardrop tattoo signifies one who has done time in our prisons)—since they are immune to those influences, prison cannot function according to the official mythology: as a sanction against lawlessness. But it does seem to function as an effective mechanism by which a part of the population is held in check. It also satisfies the middle-class desire to have the lower classes punished. Those in Gladiator School are destined to be, for the rest of their lives, either in prison or in the ghetto, which is the social correlative of prison.

Intended or not, that is the effect: Prisons take the chaotic element in society and reflect it back into the ghetto, where its destructive, disordering force is dissipated into the lower class population, which is thereby held in its place. This creates a barrier through which people cannot rise to disrupt the smooth working of the economic engine—that is, the middle class.

This is not to say that the middle class is at fault, that the people in prison are innocent of crimes, that we should be "soft on crime," or even that we should feel guilty that the prisoner class happens to be in prison some of the time. This is simply to describe what prison is—a mechanism.

To be sure, there are real criminals who commit real crimes, and there is a real need to do something to protect ourselves from them—at least to stop them from further crime. But the main methods of law enforcement are not directed at that sort of crime. The peace-keeping style of law enforcement is directed at the lower classes, who commit petty crimes in public places (e.g., drinking on the street) where they can easily be observed by the beat cop, the narco cop, the vice cop. The riddle of what is to be done with serious criminals, who do their work in secret and are generally not caught, is not being answered, because most law enforcement efforts are directed elsewhere. Prison is a relatively new idea of what to do, and not a very good one. Rousseaud de la Combe wrote in 1741:

> There were formerly penalties that are no longer practised in France, such as writing a condemned man's penalty on his face or forehead and perpetual imprisonment, just as one no longer condemns a criminal to be exposed to wild beasts or sent down the mines.

Because of the way crime is reported by the press, it is difficult to make the crucial distinction between the people whose very existence is defined by a perpetual state of inconsequential illegality, the poor, who can never adhere so completely to the letter of the law and are therefore always vulnerable to arrest and punishment, and the real criminal, who intentionally and purposely breaks laws for personal gain, vengeance, or wrathful evil-heartedness. Both types of people exist, but not in the proportions that the middle classes have been led to believe.

The middle class is as much a victim of this system as the lower class is (perhaps more cruelly misinformed, since the lower class tends to know it's getting screwed, while the middle class has delusions of being in charge). The middle classes did not invent and do not run the penal system. Yet it is not a conspiracy, either—or if it is, it is a very democratic one.

One thing we know for certain: Prisons in America are not there to punish lawbreakers. "A penal system must be conceived as a mechanism intended to administer illegalities differentially, not to eliminate them all," wrote Michael Foucault. He recognized the existence—even the essential nature—of "popular illegality." In other words, people are always committing petty crimes. The question is not so much which laws to enforce, but which group of people to round up and punish—and more important, with what goal in mind?

Segregation and criminalization as tools of enforcing class boundaries have been around for centuries and are well documented by social scientists in modern times. Joseph Gusfield described how laws governing drugs and alcohol are used to immobilize lower classes. John Irwin wrote about the "selective use of arrest" in the same way. Our modern urban arrangement is typified in each city by a ghetto for the poor, a jail with a large circulating population, and, at a more distant location, a prison. A certain portion of the ghetto population circulates through jail, prison, the streets, and back to jail, thereby creating a climate of disorder and danger in all three locations and immobilizing the population. A continuous supply of "new blood" is always available from the ever-growing pool of ghetto youth. They are thrown into various Gladiator Schools, where they are quickly made ready to perpetuate the cycle. Paul Rock described this system as "a limited restoration of neo-feudal styles of control."

The majority of inmates know this, if only subconsciously. They regard prison's corrective effectiveness with ridicule and hold the entire legal system in contempt. Likewise, police, guards, and deputies (like the middle classes from which they come) accept the evident function of penal institutions to provide a force to counter the rising tide of the lower classes. Only at the highest administrative levels is there any attempt to deny the system of class control and pretend that prison is a force effectively balanced against crime, a righteous exercise of the legal power to punish. A prison bureaucrat looked me straight in the eye and said, "I see no problem," and "We don't have complaints like that here," while in the file cabinet behind him were more than a thousand lawsuits filed by prisoners against the state. ("Oh, that's just how prisoners like to structure their time," he said, disdainfully.) Even among administrators, there were those who agreed that the prisons have no corrective function anymore; they were merely there to hold the people sent to them. But culture abhors a vacuum. Thrown in with others, we all learn something. The curriculum in Gladiator School is simple: Be bad or be dead.

❖   ❖   ❖

The Insane Unknown Mexican with the Zulu scars took my pen and wrote his marks in my notebook, a five-pointed star, "Insane Unknowns," and an upside down R attached to the letter K. I asked him what that last figure meant, and he said, "Royal Killer. I'm a Royal Killer. I kill the Simon City Royals." Killing is part of the culture taught in Gladiator School. It may seem alien to me, but my notebook and pen seemed just as mysterious to them. Life without killing is unthinkable: I asked one boy, an eighteen-year-old Mexican with curly hair and a nice smile, how he'd gotten there, and he launched into a long story about how his wife had just had a baby, and he'd only shot this guy in self defense. "I was walking down the street with my baby in one arm and this guy comes at me with a great big knife. So I shot him." I asked where he'd gotten the gun. "From my belt," he said with an odd look—like where else would you get a gun on short notice? I asked what he was doing walking down the street with a baby in his arms and a gun in his belt, and he said, as if I were really stupid, "You *gotta* carry a gun."

I met a Royal in maximum security. He'd been down three times for armed robbery and burglary, and he was going down again. He was a large man with a great reddish-brown beard and handlebar moustache combed stylishly out—he really looked like the Old West (or should I say the Crusades? Or the Peloponnesian War?). It is interesting to see how far from even the most rudimentary understanding of our social norms the people in the nomadic warrior class are. His name was Anthony Diamond, and he showed me his own hand-written summation, in which he intended to plead "the adrenaline factor" as a mitigating circumstance in his case, evidently unaware that that would make him an object of ridicule in a courtroom.

Diamond could not conceive how his mere appearance would work to ensure that he never got out of prison (or if he did, that he would be back again soon). He had smooth pink skin. He wore a white T-shirt and had tattoos from his neck to his waist. Blue chains ran around his biceps. There were jail scenes on his shoulders and stomach and arms. Diamond's entire back was covered with exquisitely wrought ladies and dragons and other tattoos. (They had been done with a good prison rig made from the motor taken out of a small tape recorder. A piece of guitar string was used for a needle, and whatever was handy was used for ink: Cigarette ash could be made into a crude ink; plastic spoons from the mess hall could be burned, the ash mixed with toothpaste and water. Inmates were sometimes able to get real ink from the officers.)

One of the biggest differences I noticed between the older warriors like Diamond and the young braves in Gladiator School was the attitude. The young ones were eager to prove how bad they were. They were champing at the bit, ready to get their battle scars and tattoos. The sanctions were actually incentives; they saw "going down" as a way to gain status. Back on the streets the tattoos marked them as men of consequence to their peers, just as they marked them for the police as members of the prison class. But captivity gets old fast. The old warriors had been in the system a long time, and they were tired of it; they always told me they were innocent.

So here is the question that plagues us: Can they ever understand our laws? Once a complete set of cultural rules and symbols has been marked upon a person's soul, is it possible to erase it and replace it with another entirely different set? Is it possible to alter that built-in governor that controls behavior?

From the late eighteenth century onward, in America there were two models of prisons, Auburnian and Philadelphian, and as different as they were, they both had as their aim this very trick of transformation: somehow to remake the prisoner and return him to a good and useful and contented place in society. Auburn followed monastic codes, forming a highly regulated society in miniature, which would prepare the inmate for the other society outside. As in the Society of Jesus, which the Auburnians sought to imitate, everything was regulated. The inmates rose, bathed, dressed, ate, worked, prayed, studied, and retired together in strict order and in silence. It was through this practice of discipline that the prisoner was to learn how to become a human being again. (The Jesuits also provided the model for military discipline leading to warfare.)

In the Philadelphia prison, "the walls are the punishment of the crime; the cell confronts the convict with himself; he is forced to listen to his conscience," wrote Abel Blouet in 1843. While Auburn sought to condition the prisoner to social disciplines, Philadelphia sought to trigger a fundamental metamorphosis within the soul and mind of the inmate by enforced solitude and isolation. Although the Philadelphia prisoner worked in the company of other inmates, the work was less important, took up less time, and was considered a luxury that could be withdrawn at any time. The method was, in effect, solitary confinement. Even so, the practice was based on a theory of rehabilitation, not punishment. "Walls are terrible, but man is good," wrote Blouet.

Or is he? Neither system worked.

❖   ❖   ❖

Gang members are notorious for unspeakably vicious crimes. One White Power Organization member, who was half Chippewa, half white, told me of his friend who went into an old man's house to rob him and inadvertently smothered him while trying to keep him quiet by sitting on a pillow he'd placed over the man's head. "He didn't have no remorse, though," he told me. "When he realized that the guy was dead, he just sat there on the bed with him and drank a beer. He set the can on the old man's back."

Tribal colors and symbols are deadly serious. When The People saw the signs of The Folks in my notebook, they nearly went off. One of them demanded that I rip the page from my notebook so that he could desecrate it. He wanted to urinate on the paper. On the street those same warriors might have shot me for it, as they have shot others for wearing the wrong color of shirt (a rival's colors, or their own colors worn in the wrong way) or for wearing a hat cocked to the wrong side, or as they shot up a car full of high school girls in Chicago last March for flashing the wrong hand signal in greeting, shot them to pieces, point blank, with shotguns.

Cases of mistaken identity are often ghastly. They may beat to death an innocent bystander for crossing his arms the wrong way ("crossing up" is a signal of gang affiliation—People cross right over left, Folks left over right). And they may raid a funeral home and drag the body of a rival gang member into the street to shoot it full of bullet holes in a ritualistic display of vengeance. It is no wonder that penal administrators begin to believe that walls are good; man is bad.

❖   ❖   ❖

They call it getting recreated. Out on the yard about 150 men are lounging around in twos and threes or walking giant ovals around the basketball courts, their heads propped together in private conversation. A few men shoot baskets. It is a mixed group, ranging from startling drag queens (in for soliciting and drug possession) to the impish, diminuitive boy with the misshapen face, who killed his mother, father, sister, brother, and the baby and burned the house down.

The rec yard is bordered by a junkyard, a surreal no-man's land, giant rusting sculptures of tortured metal and twisted wire. A blue-shirted officer with a pump shotgun is framed against a great red slab of steel sticking out of the twisted wreckage of civilization that stretches away behind him. Old fire engines, ambulances, and garbage scows lie abandoned, with weeds growing into their wheels. Truck tires form black dunes rising behind the two-story derrick of a dilapidated crane.

As I approach the razor wire for a look at the junkyard, one of the queens calls out, "Hey, Reporter! They's poison Ivory over there!"

I turn back but can't see the queen—it's just a voice in the crowd in the bright sunshine. Instead I find myself looking at a thin boy with a slight body, just barely able to grow the faintest moustache. His face has a narrow, sharpened aspect to it, as if designed to cut through something. He has an engaging manner, a friendly smile, and in another age he might have been an aspiring swashbuckler. It's difficult to connect his appearance with the tattoos that mark him as a member of the prisoner class. His name is Curtis Rimsky, and he has a tiger on his left breast. The lolling tongue of the Rolling Stones's logo licks his navel. On his right shoulder is a Nazi iron cross with a skull in its center. As he bends away and cups his hand to light a cigarette, I see the black widow spider that weaves its web between thumb and index finger. On his left shoulder is an impressionistic montage depicting a brick prison wall and, chained to the wall, a net thrown out in 3-D holding three skulls. It is a classic prison tattoo from the Big House. The legend above it says FTW, which means From the Wall (also, Fuck the World). The three skulls mean he has done three years. This is not a man filled with remorse and repentance, though there are signs that all is not certainty, even in his world. An 8-ball tattooed on his left wrist covers the name of an old girlfriend. The tiger disguises another. He has changed his mind about a lot of indelible matters.

We talk for a while, and I learn that he's been in detention homes since he was thirteen years old, and he's been down to Stateville several times during his adult life. He is twenty-four, has a three-year-old daughter, and his girlfriend is pregnant with their second child. I ask if he realizes that he is doing life on the installment plan. He has already spent a third of his life in institutions. "Well," he says with a smile, ticking his head proudly to one side, "I can't be doing too bad, I own a house and three cars."

Another inmate who is listening says, "Yeah, but you ain't living in any of it." (In prison there are always others listening, and people often appear out of thin air, hanging on my shoulder, reading as I write in my little notebooks.)

I ask this one, this apparition, a Cuban named Philip, what he is doing there. "Double murder," he says, naming one of the crimes considered a capital offense in most states. "They were Latin Kings, see, I'm a Latin Eagle." He shows his marks. I ask him why he killed. "They were talking crazy, disrespecting my nation." He doesn't mean Cuba, he means the Latin Eagles, or, in a broader sense, the nation of Folks. I ask how he killed them. "With a twelve-gauge shotgun. Executioner style. They didn't feel a thing. I mean, I *guess* they didn't feel a thing. I made 'em lie down on the ground, and then I shot each one in the head and the back. But I dressed it out and beat the case. I'm going home in a few days." I notice that he has been assigned to a psychiatric unit, and I ask him why. "Well, I'm in protective custody. There's a death warrant on me from the Latin Kings. They nailed a dead frog to my mother's door."

What does a dead frog mean? I ask.

"It means you better start jumping," he says with a laugh.

I ask Philip to tell me about his home life.

"I never knew my father," he says. He doesn't want to talk about it beyond that. He just says, "Tell them I didn't mean it."

"But," I say, "you killed two men with a shotgun. You made them lie down, and you deliberately shot them in the head with a shotgun."

"Yeah," he says, "but I was high on coke at the time."

I had gotten to the point where I felt it was essential to try to engage one of these men, these very young men, in a serious conversation about where he was going, what he thought life would have to offer him if he kept killing people and robbing them and throwing himself up against the cold implacable wall of the criminal justice system. Like the would-be reformers of old, I felt myself being swept into a rescue mission attitude, almost against my will.

I try to ask Curtis. He says he has had five fathers. (I met none who had two full-time parents. We can't go back and give these people parents, but perhaps there's a lesson here anyway.) But all Curtis can seem to focus on is that the joint, the Big House, is better than jail, where he is now. He says it's more mature in the joint. You don't have so much Mickey Mouse. You get treated like a professional. He can't wait to get back.

I ask Curtis why he did what he did, and he looks at me like I'm an idiot. He says, "We're human beings. We do what makes us feel good."

❖   ❖   ❖

If, on the broad social level, prison functions as a wall between two classes, what does it do on an individual level? The old theories of penal institutions, of carceral transformation, seem to have broken down. Is our action against the prisoner then a punishment (i.e., a torment), pure and simple? Is prison a time for the criminal to turn his gaze inward and contemplate his own conscience, thereby developing a disgust for his crime and a resolve not to commit it again? Is he to be captured and trained by progressive, ordered disciplines to live in the world once more? In my experience, little bits of each penal philosophy seemed to be in effect—for varying lengths of time and with varying degrees of intensity—depending upon which shift of guards happened to be on duty, which place I was in, and depending also upon the moods of the prisoners and the guards (e.g., while an easing of tension might result in the prisoners being engaged in useful or entertaining activities, confrontation between the two groups might produce repressive isolation, with "lockdown," or cellular isolation, becoming a permanent condition at some institutions). Even within the same institution several different penal methods were in effect in different locations or at different times of the day, and it was that very uncertainty, that very unpredictability, that became an essential part of the method, as one would teach a pit bull meanness through irregular and meaningless beatings. Any coherence of penal theory seems to be gone from our institutions now, which makes them, indeed, excellent schools for teaching warriors.

II

> *It is no accident that convicts speak of penal*
> *institutions for young men as* gladiator *schools.*
> *In such places, circumstances teach men* how
> *to kill one another. They are taught the way*
> *the bull is taught—through* torment.

—JACK HENRY ABBOTT, 1981

It is not necessary to look too deeply to find the proximate sources of violence in prison. But in most prisons I've been in it can be difficult to see the violence itself. It is, by necessity, under the surface, often far beneath an exterior that for all the world looks calm. In part that is because prison society is a subtle balance of forces, and in order to keep that balance only the immediate participants can be allowed to see the violence: those who perpetrate it and those who fall victim to it. Jack Henry Abbott wrote, "You *never* see violence in the open. And it's always with a knife or a piece of pipe (lately, here they use gasoline—dousing the enemy and igniting him)."

Most people, in fact, are struck, at least at first, by how seemingly normal many of the inmates appear. They look like any bunch of guys you might see on the street, but they are exceptionally polite—diffident even. That is because they know that any one of them might be about to kill someone. If a man interrupts a conversation and doesn't say, "Excuse me," he might be the next victim. By the same token, refusal to follow the order of a guard, however trivial, can mean that a group of five or six guards clad in battle gear will storm an inmate's cell and beat him into submission, chaining him afterward to his bed, naked, for an indefinite length of time—eighteen or twenty-four or thirty-six hours—without food or water or the ability to use the toilet.

I walked a tier of cells one day with an officer doing inspection tour. The bars formed a continuous web of steel a hundred feet long, which the inmates used as shelves. Magazines were interwoven with the bars. Cosmetics, bottles, cups, books were stacked on the spars. Wires ran from some cells out into the hall and up to the light fixtures—hot wires, which some inmates used to run their radios. They were illegal, but Officer Williams left them. He spotted several coffee heaters, plastic half-liter soda bottles in which inmates heated hot water over a pile of burning toilet paper to make coffee. Williams detached one from the bars and put it on the concrete floor of the catwalk and crushed it under the heel of his black patent leather shoe. The plastic, which had gotten brittle from repeated heating, exploded with a sound that echoed around the tier. A man under an army green blanket stirred and turned over on the metal bunk.

Like on days when I've been to the zoo and all the big cats were out of sight, many of the men on this tier were asleep in the middle of the day. Others milled around from cell to cell, standing, talking, waiting. It was as if something was about to take place, but it never quite happened, an incipience like escaping gas.

A man lay on his bunk, a rough blanket pulled over his head, a small transistor radio playing beside his ear. A group of five sat on bunks in one cell, and when the officer and I came past, their conversation stopped, and they all smiled up at us, big grins, and one with his back to us pushed something deeper into his lap.

A small group had gathered in the barred common room at the end of the tier, where the ubiquitous television made its diurnal grope through the culture. But most were simply waiting for their lives to resume. When we enter there, we find ourselves in the hiatus of someone else's life, which can be a deceptively quiet place. But this is not the quiet garden of monastic contemplation envisioned by the reformers of the eighteenth century. This is the eye of the storm.

❖   ❖   ❖

Beneath the dungeons are deeper dungeons; in each institution I visited, there were special places where an inmate could be put to bury him further. I saw Jack Henry Abbott huddled in a corner in K-house at Marion—the only Level Six prison in the country. K-house is the basement of the basement of the old hospital complex. Deep underground. It is virtual entombment.

But would even a quiet garden of contemplation do any good? Most of the people I've met in prison were not Cistercians; they were men with chains tattooed around their wrists and "Fuck the World" hammered with hand-made needles into their shoulders. My singular impression was that they were not getting any better, and maybe they were getting a lot worse. (Bringing someone back from this abyss can be difficult and dangerous. Jack Henry Abbott became the object of national attention when Norman Mailer helped him to get released from prison, where he was serving a life sentence, and helped him get his book, *In the Belly of the Beast*, published by Random House. Abbott, a highly intelligent, analytical person, a talented author, reflexively stabbed a waiter in a restaurant a few months after getting out of prison. So profound was his deconditioning to conventional social signals and systems that he took it as a threat when a waiter in a restaurant tried to lead Abbott to the washroom. The waiter died, and Abbott was returned to prison.)

❖   ❖   ❖

Property and territory become paramount in prison. Some men hoard paper milk cartons as if they were gold. As in very poor countries, nothing is thrown away, and so the cells pile up with what looks like trash but more likely is a man's property—picture frames made from paper plates, or a spigot made from used-up ball-point pens, melted and welded to form complex curves and then inserted into the tap. The sink may be full of plastic packages of Buddig's sliced ham and turkey from the commissary; water runs over them to keep them chilled. A toilet may be stopped up with a rag and there may be a carton of milk keeping cool in the water collected there. We may not understand what we see, but it has meaning. A man with a package of Kite tobacco may spend half a day rolling cigarettes. His improvised rolling machine—a pencil and a piece of cellophane laid over a paperback book—makes perfect cigarettes. Then he may tear the tobacco packet carefully and refold it, origami-style, to make a cigarette case with a flip top that he can neatly tuck into his shirt pocket like a real package of cigarettes.

Such seemingly trivial activity has great significance for man in captivity. It makes his world his own. It confers status. A man who can make himself a cup of coffee in the middle of the afternoon is no longer just a dog in a box, he is somebody. He's a human being. The men who bother are still maintaining order, still struggling, refusing to give in and be swallowed by the yawning void that is at their feet every moment of the night and day. And so to wreck those things that make up a man's world is to step upon his brittle soul and cause it to explode.

Some let go and drown. When compassion is finally killed, so is self-worth. You can tell by an inmate's cell, when nothing has been decorated, not even with the rude adornment of magazine women. Such a man's cell is steel, flesh-colored steel, and nothing else. His soul, too, is steel, and while he can't feel anything, he is also protected by it. Such a man doesn't even leave when he is called out for recreation or commissary. Such a soul can no longer be crushed. But his invulnerability is an imperfect and temporal illusion. He sleeps better than most at night, but he sleeps all day as well. Such a man eventually finds himself forced into activity again or else finds himself fashioning drop line out of braided bits of bed sheet, and then the officer on his rounds finds him hanged in his cell. If that's how much he values his own life, how much will he value mine?

❖   ❖   ❖

People who lock people up call their work "corrections," one of those spooky, Orwellian sins of language. Corrections is big business today. Stateville Prison in Illinois has an annual budget of thirty-four million dollars. "We're not about rehabilitation," the warden told me.

Social response to crime has taken two main forms throughout history: penal justice and corrections. The first sought to erase or efface the crime by punishment of the individual. The sentence—usually death or banishment or torture—was meant to reassert authority and to extract payment for the crime. But "Penal imprisonment," wrote Michael Foucault, "from the beginning of the nineteenth century, covered both the deprivation of liberty and the technical transformation of individuals."

We imagine an equation in which society with one hand gives life to the individual (through the benefits of commerce, fellowship, and social order) and with the other withdraws it from those who transgress. Life is withdrawn in increments proportional to the seriousness of the crime. At one end of the scale is the minor offense, such as disorderly conduct, for which a person is denied one day or week of his life. At the other end of the scale is death. In between those two poles, the criminal can spend months, years, decades in an institution.

But the beauty and simplicity of equations often fail to represent the messy circumstances of real life. For one thing, this pristine view of prison comes unburdened by fact or first-hand experience. It does not allow for the fact that most of the people in prison today are culturally distinct from us and do not respond to the signs and symbols we recognize. Moreover, this view does not take into account the way people (any people) respond to torture and torment, the normal condition in penal institutions.

❖   ❖   ❖

This is the Big House, the Steel Chateau. Loops of razor wire cascade in glittering tresses down the glass block walls above the concrete floor. Bright yellow steel stairs run up at one end of the cellblock. Hands flick out of the bars in ranks, flashing mirrors to give the prisoners a view of those on the catwalk. Opposite: Men with Remington Wingmasters, twelve-gauge shotguns cut down to pistol grips and full-bore scattergun barrels in combat slings. Death is real and ever-present. (This is no mere artifact; it has a profound effect on people: It is not like spending a weekend in some other culture. Big House sentences range into the decades, and the Class-X felony has made natural life a commonplace.)

Stateville Prison in Joliet, Illinois, is cast in the original mold of the grand panopticon. Even in the mess hall a centrally-located control tower looks out into the surrounding, glass-enclosed dining rooms. The tables are round. The circular rooms are brightly lit. There are two black ranks of canisters fifteen feet up the wall on two sides of each room. They are loaded with CS military tear gas. The doors can be locked, the tear gas fired, and everyone inside incapacitated in seconds. If that doesn't work, there is the shot box. The guards used to fire their shotguns into the ceiling as a warning, but ceiling repairs were getting expensive, so now there are black boxes with bullet traps in them so that warning shots may be caught and deflected harmlessly.

"How often does that happen?" I asked the warden.

"Not too often," he said. "Couple of times a week." Incidents happen; it's just that you try to cut them off at the lowest level. But sometimes that firebreak tactic can backfire.

The lockdown at Marion was instituted in an emergency (two guards were murdered) and was meant to be temporary; now authorities hesitate to unlock it. They fear that it's like those landmines that don't explode when you step on them. They explode when you walk away.

Prisons, like societies, exist in the balance of forces. People are ruled only because—and only as long as—they agree to be ruled. The power of government can push only so far before the people push back. Iran is an example of what happens then. Firepower means nothing once the decision has been made no longer to be ruled. The people simply walked into the guns (we watched it happen on television every night) until the guns stopped. People died, to be sure, but ultimately the Shah ran, his empire collapsed, and not all the fighter planes the United States could donate and not all the machine gun bullets the army could fire could have stopped those people.

When police and authorities push too hard in response to a threat (such as urban crime wave, drugs, terrorism, anti-nuclear demonstration), the result is to push people on the margin of society outward, not to draw them inward. Authority can therefore have a disintegrating effect on society—it does not promote a whole and healthy condition. It is premonitory to the condition in which the people begin to push back. It is precisely because of those dangerous and disordering effects that we ought to fear the people who are building new prisons now, expanding police powers in the name of law and order, and lobbying for multi-billion-dollar military efforts to stop drug traffic. They are the forces of escalation and disintegration, not of correction.

❖   ❖   ❖

I went back to say goodbye. In one wing, the toughest inmate was a twenty-one-year-old black man about five feet tall named Charles Ocean. He had the face of a middle-aged prize fighter. He'd been in institutions since he was thirteen, mostly on theft charges, "but this is just a mistake. This is a misunderstanding," he assured me of the current beef. When I asked how much time he'd done during his whole life, his face went through contortions, and for a moment it appeared that he was going to cry. I don't think anyone had ever made him think about that before, not all at once. "The longest jolt was thirty-three months," he said tentatively, as if that seemed like a very long time now that he'd considered it. But then he got tough again and had to act like he didn't care, and I got busy saying goodbye to other inmates and I forgot, for a moment, about his problems.

As I was leaving, Ocean was mopping the floor, and he slid his mop up next to me at the glass control booth, the interlock where I had to go through one door and let it lock behind me in that special way prison doors do, and then wait for the officer to open the next door before getting out into the corridor and going through a dozen more sets of doors before I was really out. As I was waiting for the first door, he mopped past my feet, and he whispered, "Hey, will you call me on the outside?"

I asked him what for.

He said, "Because I want to work for you. I've got talents. I've got to get my life straightened out. Can you call me?"

I didn't know what to say.

"Do you even remember my name?" he asked. And again, just for a moment, he looked like he was going to cry.

"Yeah," I said. "Ocean. Like the deep blue sea." And he smiled and slipped me a piece of paper with his phone number on it.

❖   ❖   ❖

One day at a penal institution I met some ladies coming out as I went in. They had on expensive clothes and their hair was done nicely, and the price of the sunglasses they wore might have bonded out almost any man in jail. I was with an administrator, and we stopped to talk to them. It turned out they were from Lake Forest College. They were in a class in deviate sociology—I think that's what they said. They kept saying the word "deviate" or "deviant," and when I asked what they thought about being in there, one of the ladies—she looked like a businesswoman, neat and aggressive and emphatic and intelligent—said, "I think they need a new paint job."

"What?" I asked.

"What?" the administrator asked.

"The colors in there are not calming. They're not soothing colors. They need mauves and pinks."

The administrator, a practiced hand at dealing with emergencies, launched into a discussion of the number of foot-candles of light required by law in each cell and the number actually being provided in *his* institution, and he added something about the emergency generators they have if the power should fail and how well the whole system works. I had to admire his energy and sincerity. Even so, before the lady left, she came back to her point: The real problem in prisons today is the colors. The colors of the walls were enough to make anybody irritable.

III

Construct an iron cage or dig an impenetrable dungeon that would serve him as an eternal retreat.

—A. DE MOLENES, DE L'HUMANITE DANS LES LOIS
CRIMINELLES . . . 1830

The locking and unlocking of old-fashioned prison bars is not like anything people on the outside ever get to experience, unless we're buried alive in an avalanche while skiing. The locks open with great brass Folger Adams keys, as big as Buck knife blades. The effect is explosive, like the metal-crack of pistols on a target range. The sound flees down cave-like corridors and ricochets around inside the catacombs, and then the door locks, finally, closing us into a space between two grilles. Then the next barred door is opened and locked after we pass through, and the next, with attendant waves of thunder; then, unbelievably, still another door, and another, until we are contained absolutely. It is as much symbolism as it is security: Punishment, once the great symbolic spectacle by which the sovereign power of a monarch was publicly reconstituted following the affront and defiance of crime, now acts in total secrecy, on the individual level, but still with pomp and ritual. It is made to seem, therefore, that there is nothing so final as the moment when we are put inside a prison, nothing so all-possessing of our body and soul, perhaps not even death itself. Nothing could be farther from the truth. Most people who are in prison today will be out within the next few years. Each day there are many who get out. But whereas the sentence is not forever, the experience is. And for someone on the margin of society, it may be enough to push him all the way outside, never to return. Prison is contagious; we take it to the streets like disease.

The first time I entered a prison I could hear a rumble, which, as we descended into the bowels, grew to a thundering subterranean vibration, and which gradually modulated into a continuous roar like that produced by a hydroelectric dam. As a guard led me along, bars and cells and the people within them became discernable in the darkness of those catacombs, and all at once I felt the transformation of my heart into a clenched black tarantula as I realized that the portentious, unearthly noise I heard was the sound of human voices—thousands of them. More amazing still was the fact that the inmates, jeering, laughing, catcalling at me from their cells, did not even seem to hear it.

I was at Brushy Mountain Prison in Tennessee, not as a prisoner but as a journalist, and I couldn't help wondering what this ritual would do to someone who, unlike me, would have to stay. I could wave my hand and be led out into sunlight the moment my job was done. But what would I be like now if I had had to stay there for a month? A year? Ten years?

In part at least, my answer came immediately, though I didn't recognize it right away. I was interviewing James Earl Ray, convicted murderer of Dr. Martin Luther King, Jr. A guard brought him his lunch while we were talking, but Ray did not seem to notice. It was spaghetti with tomato sauce on an institutional tray. The spaghetti was in one compartment, a green vegetable in another, a block of jello in another. Two slices of white bread and a plastic spoon had been thrown on top of the tray.

As we talked, time did its silent work: The sauce congealed on the spaghetti and the jello slowly came to room temperature and lost its shape and melted into a pool of Kool-Aid that leaked blue dye into the bread. I was hungry and kept looking at it, but Ray didn't so much as glance that way. It was summer when I visited him and the stone edifice with its old black bars was oppressive—dank and hot at the same time, like a corpse only recently expired.

Ray and I talked for a long time, and when we were through, I had the impression that I had been in the presence of evil, a man who had lost his soul. Ray wasn't, of course, a gang member, but he was just as much a part of a different culture. How did he get that way? Did God make him evil? Did society destroy him? Was he bad from infancy? And if he went wrong somewhere along the line, can we ever learn to define that point and intervene? (Even as I write this, I realize that the very concept leads us toward a new set of traps: to devise a method of preventive personality modification that would selectively destroy behavior, or perhaps to type criminals through genetic means and then to use preventive abortion the way we sometimes do with Down's syndrome.)

By the time I left, the meal had already started to putrefy in the galloping advancement of time and the summer heat that sweated through the stone. The year was 1977, and I still believed that crooks were locked up to protect society. Ray was the first real prisoner I'd met, so it wasn't until years later, after I'd been in many prisons and known many prisoners, that it dawned on me to ask whether prisons contained people who were that way by nature, or whether society made people that way and then prisons helped them to become even more that way—that icy, soulless way.

I have now eaten many prison meals and spent many days inside those living cells. I now know that (whether or not we can intercede in the Devil's work) if a man hasn't lost his soul when he commits his crime, he's certainly in danger of losing it when he serves his sentence. I know now that one's relationship with food, sex, pleasure, with the whole panoply of gratifications that guides us like a trail of crumbs through our social journey, changes in prison. A man may have been distant from his own feelings when he committed the crime that got him into prison, but not nearly as distant as he'll learn to be while he's inside.

Whether or not man is good, walls are bad.

Psychologists report that certain animals give up pleasure, even sustenance, in captivity. It takes an unusual kind of moral and spiritual fortitude to survive the prison experience—not the kind of qualities we expect the ordinary street criminal to possess—yet we send him there, where he is most vulnerable to further destruction of those qualities that might make him fit to live with.

❖   ❖   ❖

The message appears to be simple, self-evident (some would say tautological), and not a hopeful one: We select for prison those on the margin of society. In prison we teach them, through a system of disciplines, that they can never enter the normal social world, and we equip them with a set of reflexes that will drastically increase their chances of being imprisoned again. Jack Henry Abbott wrote, "So we can all hold up like good soldiers and harden ourselves in prison. But if you do that for too long, you lose yourself . . . and I am not even conscious about how my dissolution is coming about. Therefore, I cannot stop it."

There is a build-up of rage in confinement. We don't get mellow sitting in jail, watching our food congeal, while a bolus of hunger calcifies in our abdomens. We may learn to hold our-selves in check to avoid immediate physical pain, but we do not become better citizens, learn our lessons, pay our debt, and then return to society ready to contribute to the common good. That is a myth. Prison is punishment, vengeance, retribution in its purest form. Every prisoner also reports that it is torture, but we dismiss that as self-serving hyperbole. Most important, prison is an instrument of social control.

James Earl Ray is certainly one of the people on this earth I believe has earned the right to be locked up, but we can't even keep Ray. Anyway, that is not the point of prison. The ritual of captivity is seen for what it is: When I went to visit him, he had just escaped, and it was only by accident that he'd been found at all (after several frantic days) before he got clean away. Ridge-runner that he is, Ray knew how to go to ground for good, and when I sat with him in that red hot room with his blue jello soaking into the white bread on the institutional food tray beside us, I noticed that his arms were scratched and scabbed over from running through the woods, flying through the branches, the wind in his ears; and even as I hated him, I felt my heart go out to that moment of freedom. Of course, I didn't really want him to get away, but I couldn't help thinking how good it must have felt, after all those years behind bars, just for a day or two . . .

Many more like him, of lesser political status, don't even have to escape. They simply walk out. (I've stood in the parking lot at Joliet Prison and watched them go in their knitted caps with their plastic garbage bags full of belongings.) The "crime wave" is a misleading metaphor, as if one great storm surge de-scended upon us, when actually the way the prison class in-trudes upon middle-class society is more the way the tide in-trudes upon the land, gently going in and out, and only along the margins we call the beach. It remains to be tested whether the crime rate would go up or down if all the prisons doors in the nation were suddenly thrown open. Would we suddenly, overnight, as it were, see a sharp rise in crime? Or would nothing happen, nothing at all?

Most people are surprised to learn that the majority of prisoners are not incarcerated for serious crimes. (Roughly eighty percent of all people in prison are there on drug charges.) Most murders between unrelated people go unsolved. Many of the real criminals never see the inside of a jail cell, because police can't catch them, the courts do not convict them, and even if they're convicted, there's no more room in prison to hold them (or if they do go in, someone else comes out). "In recent decades," writes penal sociologist John Irwin, "criminologists have begun to discover that the most serious crimes, measured by loss of money and loss of life, are committed by reputable people whose actions are not usually scrutinized by policing agencies; these people are rarely prosecuted, and they almost never go to jail."

Prisons are being constructed at a record rate, yet no amount of construction that can be accomplished in the foreseeable future can contain what law enforcement agencies refer to as "the crime problem." The reason for that preordained failure is that the crime problem is in reality not a series of crimes, but a class of people.

These questions remain, then: Is there any hope for those souls? That may seem a concern secondary to our own protection, but it is not; it is paramount. Because they are not mere individuals, and the fact that they are in the lower class does not mean they are apart from society. They are merely *cut off* from it by the shuttle system that runs between prison and ghetto. They didn't invade us from Cuba or Haiti or Mars. They are home-grown. The rituals of prison betray our belief that the criminal is like a tumor that can be cut off, leaving the body healthy. But he is much more than that. He is an expression of the very heart of our civilization. And if he can't be helped, then God help us.

THE EXECUTIONERS

The Death Room

There are two handles for the electric chair at Stateville Prison, but only one of them works. That way if two executioners operate at once, neither need ever know who threw the killing switch. That arrangement is in part symbolic, in part a practical consideration. Symbolically, a man does not take a life; he only allows his hand to act for the spirit of the eleven million people of the state of Illinois. The executioner's hand becomes the hand of the law and therefore blameless. And in practice no man can say, "I did it," or take satisfaction or despair from his act.

The handles are thick and black. They look like old-fashioned beer tap handles of polished ebony. When I visited our death room, I put my hands on them and began to pull downward, one hand on each handle, to make sure that it was me and not the state hitting those contacts. I wanted to know what it felt like to be the one. The heavy handles moved slowly, resisting, as if driving a piston in oil. So, after all, killing someone is not as easy as it sounds. Not even the switch itself could be flicked with a fingertip; it took some muscle. I pushed down harder, and the handles slowly inched toward the bottom position, where contact would be made to send twenty-five hundred volts of electricity up over the partition separating me from the condemned man and down through the wires to the base of his skull. It would fire through his tissues and exit explosively from his ankle, where the other wire was attached. It would leave grotesque burns. Smoke and fire would issue from the wounds, but that wouldn't matter: The man would be dead. When the warden, who was across the room from me, saw what I was doing, he jumped. "Don't do that!" he said, rushing to my side and gingerly taking my hands off the switches. He repositioned the handles, putting the heels of his hands beneath them and shoving upward.

"Is it hooked up?" I asked, surprised.

"No," he said. "But, but . . ."

"But what?" I asked. "I just wanted to see what it was like."

He made a vague remark about calibrating the equipment, but we both knew that it probably wouldn't be used again. Executions would be carried out by lethal injection now. Yet the warden was nervous, distracted by my actions. "Are we about through here?" he asked.

There was a sense that we had come into the presence of a force that was ill understood, made even more fearsome by the control that he had over it. The warden did not decide who would die, but he moved the process along. He'd dispatch someone to get the chemicals. He'd make the arrangements. And when the time came, he would sign the papers, wave his hand, make it all happen. He was not faint-hearted about it; he would only do what was right; that much was clear. But he did not relish dwelling on it—that was my job, to bear witness.

Witness the death room: fifteen-by-fifteen feet, more or less, with floor and walls that look something like kitchen tile. A blue door. A gray box on the wall in a corner. It looks like a circuit breaker box, but it was made by American Engineering in Boston; it's designed to give poison injections. Since many condemned men (Illinois has condemned no women) were sentenced under an old law that specified electrocution, the chair has been kept in case someone mounts a successful lawsuit on that point.

"We'll do him either way, if it comes to that," the warden told me.

In fact, even after the death chamber was refurbished, the

fume hood remained in working order above the electric chair (although the chair itself is disassembled and stored in a room below). The stainless steel restaurant hood is about three feet square. It has a powerful blower to evacuate the smoke and smell of burning flesh.

There is no smell when someone is killed by poison. There is only the sound of a man clearing his throat. And then he is dead.

On the wall near the gray box is a small two-way mirror, and behind that is a room, like a closet, in which the executioners will stand to do their job. It is cluttered with the equipment for the electric chair—old stuff, with lots of black and glass fittings and thick cables. But a small space has been cleared for the new instrument, the latest development in the long struggle to sanitize the process of state-sanctioned killing. In societies where morality is rigid and well-understood, there is no need to disguise official retribution. Killing certain members of society is seen as a necessary evil: To let those people survive would be as preposterous as arguing the rights to life of cancer cells.

We are not so sure of ourselves. (And it is certainly not clear that being so sure would make ours the kind of society we'd want to live in.) We like to pretend to moral certainty, while our methods betray us. The poison machine stands amid the electric chair clutter, a clean and compact box with lights and dials and switches appropriate to our current image of ourselves as a culture: solid state. The two people operating it could be setting off an atomic bomb or tuning in signals from other galaxies for all the character this box has. A randomly selected button, or plunger, when pressed by one of the anonymous executioners, sends a metered lethal dose through the IV tube, through the wall, and into the arm of the condemned man on the other side. How does he die? Instantaneously, they say, or nearly so.

From the witness room adjacent to the death chamber, selected people will see for themselves. One wall of the death chamber is glass. Black curtains can be pulled closed across it. The witness room is as plain as the death chamber. Its floor slopes to a drain, "for people who lose their lunch," the warden told me. The floor can be hosed down after the execution.

When Evil Is Necessary

For all the debate that the death penalty generates, it is over a punishment that is meted out to relatively few individuals— few at least when compared with the damage they do to society. We are a nation of violence. There are about twenty thousand murders committed in the United States every year (about half with handguns). Yet we don't execute nearly as many people as we could: In the bloodiest year for official retribution, 1935, only 199 people were executed in the United States. (Iran, by comparison, reported executing six hundred people in 1982.) By 1950 that number was down to one hundred a year, and in 1967 legal execution was suspended in all states, pending a decision by the Supreme Court on the constitutionality of capital punishment in general. That decision came in 1972, stating that the death penalty as applied by virtually all states constituted "cruel and unusual punishment" due to the amount of discretion judges and juries had in deciding who did and did not die, as well as the clear prejudice shown against poor and black defendants. That decision effectively outlawed the death penalty.

With that decision in the wind, Illinois stopped executions in 1962 and has executed no one since. But many states rewrote their laws, and in a 1976 ruling, the Supreme Court found Florida, Texas, and Georgia to have legal death penalties. Guidelines were set for how to apply the capital punishment— usually for murder with specific "aggravating circumstances."

Other states, including Illinois, based their laws on the approved codes.

The first man to go was Gary Gilmore, celebrated in Norman Mailer's best-selling book *The Executioner's Song*. Gilmore received national attention, not only because his was the first execution after the Supreme Court's decision, but also because he was a volunteer—someone who stopped his own appeals and agreed to be executed. In fact, he had to sue the state of Utah, which responded January 17, 1977, with a squad of riflemen.

Since that time, Texas has led the way with twenty-six executions as of this writing. Although there have been as many as twenty-three thousand arrests for homicide in some years, fewer than three hundred death sentences were handed out each year from 1979 to 1985. Only fifty-eight prisoners were executed in the United States between January 1977 and May 1986, while some 1,720 others were on death row (110 of them in Illinois). The fact is, it's very difficult to get someone sentenced to death and more difficult still to get that sentence carried out.

Interestingly, some of the objections to the death penalty stem from the very fact of how few people are sentenced to death. The law, its detractors say, is applied unfairly and unequally. In fact, there is hardly anyone who will deny that if you are white and wealthy and have a good lawyer, you will never be considered for the death penalty—not in Illinois, not in any state, not in a million years. When the U.S. Supreme Court struck down the death penalty, the decision said that it was "freakishly applied." Leroy Collins, a former governor of Florida, one of the leading states when it comes to execution, said, "Who gets executed is still a freakish thing, and depends on wealth, power, and many unusual circumstances. Most who are killed are poor and friendless."

And, he might have added, black. Two-thirds of the people executed from 1930 to 1967 were black. In the 455 executions carried out for rape, an astonishing 405 of the condemned were black, which means either that whites don't rape women or that the application of the death penalty is discriminatory. Most of the victims of those crimes were white women.

Some people worry that an innocent person will be put to death. Others complain that mentally ill and juvenile criminals are executed. (A retarded boy, James Roach, was executed in South Carolina in 1986.) But the most illuminating debates are not the ones that shed a merciful or vengeful light upon the criminal. They are the ones that go to the more fundamental question: How far can society go in protecting itself from its members?

Vigilante groups take justice into their own hands. The rest of us expect society to fulfill its obligation to protect and defend us, even to seek retribution for us. Society must draw the line somewhere—that's what being civilized means—and without the resolve to carry out the death penalty, we refuse to draw the line; and that invites anarchy to rush in.

But the same argument is used against the death penalty. The Bill of Rights was set up to prevent the formation of a police state, and executions are one of the trappings of a police state. Yes, we do draw the line: If we are civilized, we don't torture people for information, for example. And we certainly don't set up systems for exterminating people we don't like. If we are civilized, we don't do that even if we really want to. There is a high cost attached to being that civilized, but we are willing to pay it. That's what makes us different from the criminals and puts us above the animals of the forest.

Supreme Court Justice Arthur Goldberg said, "The deliberate, institutionalized taking of human life by the state is the greatest conceivable degradation to the dignity of the human personality."

Michael Ficaro, executive director of the Illinois attorney general's office, has prosecuted everyone from mass murderers to the FALN to the sado-sexual Grant Park killer Lester Harrison (who not only dragged women into the bushes in front of the art institute in broad daylight, but bit off and chewed and swallowed their flesh in the process of murdering them). Ficaro's life has been threatened by notorious murderers. He keeps a gun in the house and impresses those who visit him as a man who would not hesitate to use it for the defense of his family.

Ficaro said that the death penalty as a deterrent had not been tested, because no executions were being carried out here. (Others, such as prison wardens I've talked to, say that it is most certainly not a deterrent in the outside world, where most people who commit murder don't stop and think, and those who do are beyond deterrence anyway.) Ficaro, who is a national spokesman for prosecutors who favor capital punishment, uses Henry Brisbon as an example of the ultimate riddle facing the nation. What do you think we should do with Henry Brisbon?

Brisbon was sentenced to serve one thousand to three thousand years in prison for murders he committed in 1973 when Illinois had no death penalty. It's an absurd sentence on the face of it. Making it even more absurd is the fact that he could have been eligible for parole as early as 1987.

During sentencing, Judge James M. Bailey told Brisbon, "You made the poor woman strip. . . . You made her leave that car; you made her crawl across the barbed-wire fence nude. You brought her down by the pond after she crawled over another fence and, the coward that you are, stuck the gun up her vagina. As the doctor testified, it was all the way in her before you pulled the trigger."

But Brisbon wasn't through for the night. He and his friends stopped a teenage couple driving on I-57. Ficaro, who prosecuted the case, told me, "Brisbon told this young couple, this boy and girl seventeen years old, to kiss their last kiss fifteen feet from the side of the road, and then he blew them out of their shoes with a shotgun." Brisbon was also seventeen at the time.

Judge Bailey told Brisbon, "The easiest sentence I could possibly give you, of course, would be death. But I can't. . . . You are lucky there because I would have no question about it. I tried over two thousand cases and you are by far the most evil coward I have ever seen."

Brisbon smiled throughout the proceedings at the Cook County Courthouse. He smiled after he murdered Betty Lou Harmon and went home to describe it to his cousin in front of the family's children. Harmon had begged for her life, saying, "You can have anything I have, my body, anything; take anything, just don't kill me." Brisbon shot her anyway and later smiled as he described the way she "flopped around like a chicken."

Brisbon did not repent. His behavior did not even improve slightly. He stabbed a trustee to death in prison. More than a dozen attacks on staff and prisoners followed. And the death penalty returned to Illinois after a fifteen-year hiatus.

On death row, Brisbon stabbed fellow condemned prisoner John Wayne Gacy nearly to death. He attacked a warden, attempted to destroy a courtroom, and single-handedly started a prison riot. As the seemingly endless appeals process dragged through the courts, the Department of Corrections was forced to build a special cage for Brisbon and put him under twenty-four-hour-a-day closed-circuit TV surveillance.

Brisbon became something of an unofficial symbol inside the halls of justice in the state of Illinois. He was used as an emblem, flashed like a badge whenever a reason was needed to explain why a nice Midwestern state such as ours has to have a death penalty. Wherever I went within the bureaucracy that exists to carry out executions here, I heard the name Brisbon, and it was often said with a shrug of the shoulders, as if to say: You tell us what to do with him.

Brisbon could be removed from his cell only in the presence of six guards and a captain. He was kept on a leader chain, "like a panther," Ficaro said. When Brisbon last appeared in court, there were four DOC guards and two Will County sheriff's police positioned there with shotguns to bring him down if he went wild. Still, Henry Brisbon threatened to cut out Michael

Ficaro's tongue for prosecuting him and threatened to cut off the head of a witness who testified against him.

During a hearing, an Illinois Supreme Court justice privately asked Brisbon's lawyer, "Isn't this case what the death penalty was made for?"

Ficaro said that society, by executing Brisbon, would make plain its revulsion and outrage at his acts. In fact, he said, it is precisely the ghastly and calculated nature of our retribution— the systematic, implacable, plodding inevitability of it—that makes the death penalty work. It is customary that death penalties be carried out only when the condemned man is conscious and able to understand what is happening to him. (Should he be sick at the appointed time, we will heal him first and then kill him.) Where people are too faint of heart to carry out such measures, then the strong must act on behalf of the rest. Barbarism means that the strong prey on the weak. Civilization means that the strong protect the weak and prevent evil from preying upon them. And where prevention does not work, symbolic retribution must suffice.

The Last Bargaining Chip

The warden at Stateville, where the execution of double murderer Charles Walker may one day take place, is a mild-mannered man of thirty-eight years, trim and congenial. He jogs and skips lunch and is concerned about such modern things as whether or not his inmates are comfortable. The warden (he asked that I not use his name) started out as a counselor in college. It was a practical requirement for his degree. He could have just as easily done his counseling at a mental hospital, but he ended up, for no particular reason, at the Menard maximum security prison in downstate Illinois. Somehow he never left the system. He didn't claw his way to the top. He drifted up through the ranks until he found himself working for a warden who left, and then he was the top man. He cares about people. He wants to do the right thing.

"What are you going to tell your little daughter when you go home the night you execute your first prisoner?" I asked him.

"Listen," he said, undaunted by my question, "I've resolved this in my mind. I don't know exactly how I'll feel, but I've resolved it. Because the death penalty is the only thing I have with some of these people." We were taking a walking tour of his prison, and it was a rainy day, and we were ducking in and out of buildings, shouldering through sprawling groups of prisoners wandering loose in their cellblocks. Prisoners said hello as the warden walked by. "Hey, there go the gang members," he said to one group. "Excuse me; *social organization*," he corrected himself as they gave him a funny look. When they were past us, he whispered, "That's one-two-three of the Black Disciples," meaning the top-ranking officers of that gang. Then he asked me what I would expect him to do if one of them grabbed me; how could he get them to let me go without cutting my throat?

"A lot of these guys are doing natural life," he said. "They've got nothing to lose. The only thing I have to bargain with is the death penalty. And I can say to them, 'If you let that man go, maybe I won't see you in that death chamber.' That's all I've got, and believe me, I think I need it."

We walked back to his office, and he showed me some weapons he had collected on a recent shakedown. "This has got to hurt," he said, holding up a jagged-edged blade about two and a half feet long cut out of solid steel. He showed me a dart made out of a hypodermic needle, weighted at the end with steel washers, a Bic pen for a shaft, and paper fletching. At about a quarter of a pound, it could be fired by hand across a tier and do some damage. Another inmate had made a gun barrel from a radio antenna and gunpowder from urine and match heads. The radio battery made the spark to set off the gunpowder. Lead from the print shop made a bullet.

"But we found a .32-caliber revolver in the women's washroom in the visiting area the other day. That's escalation," he said. "That's like nuclear war." To men in his position, losing the death penalty would be unilateral disarmament.

The Volunteer Paradox

Charles Walker has been on death row since 1983. Not only did he plead guilty; he asked to be executed. Walker has had problems since he was a teen-ager. He would get drunk, go out and rob people, and then get caught. He was a big-time loser, an alcoholic without any self-control when drinking. He was a classic American drifter who couldn't hold a job. He spent twenty-two out of thirty years as a prisoner. A model prisoner.

One summer day in 1983, on parole, Walker was fishing and drinking beer at Silver Creek just outside Mascoutah, Illinois, when a young couple came by, Kevin Paule, twenty-one, and Sharon Winker, twenty-five. They were engaged to be married. Sharon wore blue jeans and had shoulder-length brown hair. Kevin and Sharon set up lawn chairs by the river and began fishing a short distance from Walker. Walker is a friendly fellow, always ready to tell a joke, so he struck up a conversation with Kevin and Sharon. "It was at that time that I decided to rob them," Walker said. Kevin gave him forty dollars. This, in Walker's own words, is what he did next:

> I then took them into the woods, north of the bridge, about thirty to forty feet. I had gone to my car to get a roll of packing tape. It was white with nylon threads running through it. This was just before I decided to rob them. I tied Paule to a tree with his hands taped behind his back. He was standing up when I tied him. I also tied Winker to another tree about seven or eight feet away. While I was tying Winker, Paule said to me, "I know your name is Walker." After Paule said that, I knew that I was going to have to shoot both of them. So I wouldn't be identified.

There is something in us that cries out: Stop! Let them go! Do anything, but for the love of God, don't shoot them. But that voice is silent in Walker's heart. Perhaps he was born without it; perhaps it was washed out by alcohol. But without it, he is as dangerous as an automaton:

> I then finished tying her and turned and shot Paule in the right front part of his head. When I shot Paule, he slid down the tree to the ground. I then turned and shot her in the right rear part of the head. Winker then slid onto the ground.

When I visited Walker, I was put in a bulletproof glass room no bigger than a closet with a table and two chairs and bright fluorescent lights. When Walker was escorted in, wearing an orange jumpsuit and a red armband that identified especially dangerous prisoners, he was carrying two Pepsi Colas in paper cups. He handed one to me, saying, "You want one of these?"

Walker is in his late forties and wears a scattering of prison-made tattoos. He is a large man, and his black hair is waved into an old-fashioned 1950s pompadour cut. He wears a neat moustache and sometimes puts on glasses to read. He lost an eye in a shootout with police in 1969. (His father was killed in a drunken shootout in 1963.) He was shot in the face at point-blank range. The bullet went through the windshield of the car that Walker was driving, which slowed the projectile considerably before it lodged beneath his eye. Surgeons had to remove it through the roof of his mouth, and Walker lost the sight in that eye, which now stares dead, while the other one, lively and brown, moves around to fix on me as he talks and laughs.

"I told a screw here this ball-and-chain deal made my tally-wacker an inch and a half shorter," he said, and then laughed merrily. He was referring to a weighted restraint the guards sometimes put inside the pants leg of a prisoner to keep him from running. Walker's Cheyenne and Cherokee heritage show in the lines of his face, the blackness of his hair, and even the color of his skin. There is something about Walker that recalls the previous century in the Middle West, when outlaws like Jesse James—wild, jubilant, homicidal, impulsive men—

roamed the countryside, sowing the wind and reaping the whirlwind. They're still out there. But when you meet them face to face, there's nothing heroic about them. They're just losers, men who never matured beyond emotional infancy, reflex killers, as dangerous as a rattlesnake and about as useful to society. There's nothing very calculating about Walker. Even his crime was stupid, useless, and unspectacular. His life is just a long series of such events; ending it will not diminish society by what is lost.

According to an exhaustive set of psychological tests that he has been put through, Walker is in the top five or six percent of the population when it comes to intelligence. But that intelligence has never been put to good use. The only systematic project he has ever tackled is his campaign to get himself executed. And yet he has keen creative instincts and a superficially gentle nature. It's too bad that the bad parts of Charles Walker can't be put to death, leaving the rest intact.

Walker chain-smokes straight Pall Malls and has emphysema, which sends him into wracking fits of coughing now and then. "What am I going to do, quit for my health?" he asks with a macabre laugh. The subject of his own death is not taboo for him. It's his occupation now. He talks about it with ease. He hopes they "do" him, as he puts it, by spring.

"Watch out what you wish for," I caution him. "You may get it."

He laughs again. "I've been dead since October 19, 1983," he says, referring to the date on which he was sentenced to death. Once condemned, Walker waited until the mandatory appeal was denied and then wrote a letter to the Illinois Supreme Court, saying, "It is my desire that you reject the Appellate Defender's motion and by the order of the Circuit Court finding me fit issue a mandate setting my execution date. . . . Please have mercy on me and grant me my right according to law to make my own choice."

Walker explained his decision to his sister and mother, and although they disagreed, they said they would accept his wishes. He then called his brother Douglas, who is a volunteer fireman in a nearby town, and had him make funeral arrangements. A burial plot was purchased.

Without intending to do so, without fully understanding the issues involved, Walker threw the covers off of a well-kept secret in Illinois: Although Governor James R. Thompson tells us he favors capital punishment, we, the People of Illinois, may not be ready to carry it out.

Up until now, we could pretend we wanted capital punishment, but we didn't really have to do it. But Walker has narrowed the options: We have to go ahead and kill him or commute his sentence or change the law or find constitutional flaws in his trial or sentencing that will postpone our decision about who we want to be once again. There are plenty of people lining up to try each of those options, but there is nothing like a consensus on holding executions in Illinois.

What Kind of People Are We?

Killing a man presents problems that most of us don't have to think about. Like making sure to buy the tape that has the little fibers in it, as Walker did to hold Kevin Paule's hands securely while he shot him in the face. The face of death is painted in small strokes. These are the details, ultimately, that make killing so ghastly. When we, as a society, submerge ourselves in such details in order to kill, we are transformed. The question is this: Are we transformed for better or worse?

Some countries separate the head from the body, as in this description of a Saudi execution by David Lamb, author of *The Arabs: Journeys beyond the Mirage*:

> Fakieh, the man, was the first to kneel and bend on the cardboard, as though in prayer. . . . The executioner's assistant jabbed his ribs with a sharp stick. Fakieh's body stiffened and

jerked upward in response just as the glistening sword came down with a whoosh.

The crowd watched wide-eyed, but made no sound. Moments later, the curved sword, held by the executioner like a woodsman's ax, struck again, and Sasbie, too, was dead. A doctor stepped forward to confirm the obvious. Two medical attendants tossed the heads and the two bodies onto a stretcher, placed it in an ambulance and drove off.

In Saudi Arabia, a death sentence is retribution, pure and divine. The victim's next of kin can offer forgiveness and set the condemned free. In this case, the court waited fifteen years until the victim's son reached majority, at which time he said: Cut off their heads. In Saudi Arabia there is very little crime (ninety-seven murders in a country of seven million in 1982).

In Illinois, our next execution will not be public, and it will not be spectacular. But that doesn't mean it won't have its moments of drama. Compare this Associated Press report of a Nevada execution:

> Cole, unable to move because of the straps, asked the officer to please scratch his ear, "which I did, and he thanked me. The way he said, 'thanks' and the look in his eye stopped me for a moment. . . ."
>
> An innocent IV solution circulated in Cole's veins.
>
> Cole nodded to friends among the witnesses. From the needles in his arm, a tube extended to the alcove where the executioners waited, each with a syringe containing a different poison. The syringes were connected to the tube through three pigtails or shunts off the IV.

The executioners injected the poisons, and ninety seconds later Cole was dead. There was no fanfare. The heavens did not open up to punish those who did the deed, nor did hell open up to receive the soul of Carroll Cole, who murdered five women. The doctor pronounced official death. The techs carried the remains away on a stretcher. And no one thanked the executioners for keeping society whole.

Most people agree that injecting poison into someone's veins is a pretty clean way to go. Electrocution was seen as a way of bringing death into the realm of modern remedies, but it was tragically misconceived. Frying, as it became known, turned into a macabre sport fraught with misadventure; and ghoulish stories followed the procedure wherever it was tried. The unintentional black comedy of our death room restaurant fume hood testifies to the legacy of the electric chair.

Shooting was the choice among military men—a manly way to go—and probably as good as any, even if there is some blood to clean up. Instantaneous and certain, it brings one of the essential activities of the living organism to a crashing halt. Several states still have firing squads. Others still have hanging, which most agree is fraught with possibilities for bad press. Sometimes people's heads pop off unexpectedly. Defecation, slow strangulation—all make for untidy executions.

Although execution by poison is not a new idea, lethal injection was the latest attempt to bring execution into the modern age. At first it was conceived of as carrying the full weight of science. It was a brilliant thought: Have a doctor give the injection. Death would thereby become just another medical procedure. Unfortunately, doctors were not so eager to become the new executioners. In fact, the medical profession wasted no time in reminding the Illinois Department of Corrections that the Hippocratic oath clearly states, "Neither will I administer a poison to anyone when asked to do so nor will I suggest such a course."

Dr. Ronald Shansky, medical director of the Illinois Department of Corrections, told the American Medical Association, "Murdering someone is not a medical procedure. I was trained in medical school to protect the health and welfare of humans. I was not trained to be a butcher."

When it became obvious that doctors would not perform executions, DOC modified its position: Two physicians would be present during executions, but the medical technicians—the surrogate physicians—would do the actual work. Doctors objected even to that, saying that simply having an underling help to do the deed did not exonerate the presiding physician of guilt. And more to the point, no one is volunteering. Doctors and even technicians at Stateville won't do it, they say, calling it "absurd."

Even though the DOC procedure now calls for a doctor only to certify that the condemned man is dead, he could be thrown into a quandry should he examine the man and find that he is not, in fact, dead yet.

The American Nurses' Association issued a policy in 1983, saying that any participation in an execution would be a breach of its code of ethics. The AMA policy also forbids participation by technicians or even pharmacists who might prepare or issue the drugs used to kill a condemned man.

The question then is this: What are the People of Illinois really like? When we tell pollsters we are in favor of the death penalty, is it because we really want to engage in the ritual practice of killing people?

Dissent in the Highest Places

"I don't believe so," said Seymour Simon when I asked him if the people of Illinois want executions carried out on a regular basis. The Illinois Supreme Court Justice told me, "I know people who say 'Kill all criminals,' and they are moderates. But as to whether they would actually do it if pushed to sign the paper, I don't know."

Sitting high atop the city of Chicago in the Daley Center in an office large enough for test-flying model airplanes, Justice Simon was well-dressed and looked fit. He was obviously a man of deep learning and had given the issues long study and serious thought. If he could not quite remember something, he did not hesitate to pick up the phone or go to the shelves of law books that covered one wall of the room.

His concerns seemed to come down to these points: "If there is a constitutionally proper death penalty, I'd have to vote for it," he told me. "But I don't think we have that yet." He wants the law tested in Federal court. But that cannot happen unless Walker files a writ of *habeas corpus* as part of his appeals process, which he has failed to do. So Simon believes that Walker's appeal should be filed for him by a court-appointed attorney. Currently, only the first appeal is mandatory and automatic in Illinois. All other appeals the condemned man may make (and there are many) are up to him. Theoretically, any time he stops his appeals process, the state is free to go ahead and execute him. But although Walker fired his attorney and stopped his appeals, the theory has not worked; Illinois hasn't executed him, and that is largely because of Illinois Supreme Court decisions on the matter.

Walker believes that the delays are a violation of his rights, a kind of torture. Simon insists that the carrying out of a capital sentence is none of the business of the condemned man. (The logic is unassailable: If the prisoner had something to say about his punishment, it would be a topsy-turvy system, indeed.)

"We don't do this except under the authority of law," Simon said, "and we don't do it on demand. It is not an agreement between the Department of Corrections and Charles Walker. Eleven million people can't execute someone just because he wants to be executed. 'Give it to me,' they say, 'I want to get the needle.' The court isn't going to do it. They're acting for the eleven million people of Illinois."

In a separate but equally important issue, Simon believes that improper testimony may have been given at Walker's sentencing hearing. If so, that could render the sentence invalid under a U.S. Supreme Court decision against testimony concerning the victims, which is thought to sway the sympathies of jurors. The logic is this: If the jury will give out the death penalty only when testimony shows what a nice person the

victim was, then does that mean it's all right to murder home-
less, unemployed, unimportant, and unattractive individuals?
No, the death penalty must be handed out on the basis of the
crime and the criminal, not the identity or personal qualities of
the victim.

I asked Simon to give his opinion about death as punishment, but he said he wanted to remain judicial and not voice
personal opinions, though he did offer this: "You know, we're
spending an awful lot of money to try to get somebody to the
death chamber. All the appeals, the lawyers, the state's attorneys. What's the point of having a death statute? People say it
costs a lot to keep somebody alive, but it costs a lot to kill
somebody, too."

In fact, because appeals typically take more than ten years,
it is more expensive to execute a prisoner than to keep him
locked up for natural life. If the purpose of law is to safeguard
society (and Simon believes it is), not to seek revenge, then
the death penalty makes no sense. Long prison terms would
suffice.

I found it telling that the first thing Simon said to me when I
mentioned that I'd been talking to Charles Walker was this: "Is
he still angry with me?"

I said that Walker believed that Simon was using his position on the Supreme Court to turn his personal, anti-death penalty opinions into law. But, I told Simon, it wasn't a personal
matter with Walker. It was a philosophical one. "Good, good,"
Simon said. "How's his knitting going? Did he give you any of
his knitting?"

I told him that it was crocheting and that I hadn't seen any of
it, though I'd heard he was making roses for the guards for
Christmas.

"Is he any good at it?" Simon asked.

Coming to Terms with Killing

Scott Graham talks to Charles Walker every week, sometimes several times a week. They are working hard together, and to hear them talk, poring over the paperwork, you'd think that Graham was a volunteer from the Illinois Coalition against the Death Penalty. He is not. He is assistant attorney general to the state of Illinois, and it is his job to see that Walker is put to death. Since Walker wants the same thing, they have teamed up to achieve their common goal, and in the process have become quite close. Alarmingly close. Distressingly close, Graham says.

It is said that a convict has to learn how to do time. He simplifies his life, hones it down to routines, and then sticks to them. Everything is streamlined and he slips through time like a stone passing through the body of a bird. Graham is not a convict, but his life is like that now. He gets up early and goes to the twelfth floor of the State of Illinois Building, where he is awash in the paperwork of Walker's case. He skips lunch to work out with weights at the gym. He puts a lot of himself into that part of the day. There's a lot to put in: Graham can bench 450 pounds.

He stays late at work. There's not much more to his life right now. He's just doing time. The outcome of his work is inevitable. Legally there's nothing left, except Seymour Simon's insistence that the law be tested. (Graham and others point out that Utah shot Gilmore without testing its law. Furthermore, the U.S. Supreme Court has declined to review any Illinois capital cases.) Only executive clemency could stop the execution, and James Thompson is not likely to commute the sentence.

Graham is a mild-mannered man of enormous proportions, a kind of Clark Kent figure who seems about to burst into another identity at any moment. I asked him what it was like talking to Walker. "It's very unusual to speak to someone about his own demise," he said. "In fact, it's about as weird as it can be, really. He certainly doesn't consider me the enemy, which makes it such an unusual situation."

Graham was a public defender for three years before he got the job at the attorney general's office. I asked him if he made the switch because he was pro–death penalty. "If we didn't have a death penalty, I wouldn't be rushing to start a movement to get it," he said. "But because of the horrible nature of the crimes, I don't feel any qualms about this as punishment." However, he was quick to add, "It is not a deterrent."

I asked Graham how he had come to terms with his role in killing someone. "For a couple of months," he said, "I thought about it all the time. I had to face the fact that it was my conduct that was going to result in his death. I have had many doubts. And every time I do, I think of what he has done. It is true that when he is executed, because of my job, I will probably be sitting in Springfield waiting for a last-minute stay. But I could live with being in the execution chamber."

Graham brought up Luis Garcia, who was convicted of several murders, the most notable being that of a ten-year-old Polish girl. Garcia and an accomplice killed her mother in front of the girl. Then they took the little girl to a basement, where Garcia repeatedly raped and tortured her, putting his handgun into her vagina. After they were discovered by authorities, Garcia's accomplice was shot. He had crawled into a garbage can to hide, and the police shot him through the can. The jury deliberated ten minutes before sentencing Garcia to death. He recently died of a drug overdose on death row.

Graham said, "I can't get the image out of my head of that little girl. To be perfectly honest with you, it doesn't bother me that these men have their lives taken for this sort of crime."

But even as he said that, he began telling me that he was going to quit his job when Walker is executed and go back to Michigan to become a defense lawyer. Even while he argued that there was a clear statute on what must be done with Walker, Graham told me that he was through trying to get people killed.

If society must have the moral strength to protect itself by having capital punishment, then Scott Graham is one of the men paying the very high personal cost of being strong. He sacrificed himself, doing what no one else would do, for the good of all.

The last time I talked to Graham a date had been set for Walker's execution. It was vacated within the month. Graham said, "I'm going to talk to Charles. I'm going to tell him that he can still start his voluntary appeals process now. I want him to understand that just because he's put us through all this work, it doesn't matter. If he has the slightest doubt, I want him to stop this and go ahead with the appeals. I'm just worried that he'll stick to what he said just for the sake of sticking to it. And the next thing he'll know, he'll be on that gurney, and then it'll be too late."

I asked Graham how he would feel when Walker was executed, because he had gotten to know him so well.

"Sad," he said.

The Poison Arrow

Several years ago, there was a conference of government attorneys involved with capital litigation—a death conference, if you will. A man from Texas Corrections was giving a man from Illinois Corrections some tips on how to do it. "You get rid of that gurney first of all," he said, or words to that effect. "You get a regular hospital bed, because it makes it seem more like a medical procedure that way, and you rehearse everything so that when you go in on the night of the execution, you can say, 'Now, Charlie, here's what we're going to do. We're going to go ahead and do this thing now.' And he gets right up on that bed and you wheel him on down."

There is a ten-day death watch in Illinois, and the DOC manual describes how the warden will have to notify everyone involved and assemble the supplies and equipment to be used in the execution, to select and instruct the "medically trained individual." The supplies are: a hospital gurney, four intravenous bottles, fifteen syringes, four catheters, intravenous tubes, and saline solution. Michael Lane, director of the Department of Corrections, selects the executioner. Insiders say that in some states, heads of correction departments themselves have acted as executioners.

Seven days before the date of the execution, the officer in charge at Stateville, the major, chooses his death squad: two captains and four lieutenants, one of whom has to be the same size as Charles Walker.

Five days before the date, the major drills the death squad, using the man Walker's size to play-act the ritual. The DOC manual calls this preparing the team to "deal with any behavior that might be demonstrated by the condemned person." Walker is a big man. The instinct to continue life is a powerful force.

Four days before the execution the witnesses and visitors are notified. Two doctors are added to the death squad.

Three days: "The physician will examine the condemned to determine any physical problems (collapsed veins, obesity, etc.) that may impede the execution process." New clothing is issued.

One day: Death squad drills intensify. Paperwork, such as the death certificate, is prepared. The telephone company installs a line to the death chamber in case of last-minute stays.

On the day of the execution, the "medically trained person" obtains the poison with which to kill Walker, while the dietary supervisor prepares his last meal. The institution goes on full lockdown. The corner wall towers are assigned extra officers in case of a prison break. Regular checks of the telephone line begin. The major sets up folding chairs in the slant-floored witness room adjacent to the death chamber.

At the front gate, the guards will bodily search anyone entering the institution. The official prison clock is calibrated by calling the time-of-day service.

Thirty minutes: The warden takes the executioner into the death chamber's control room—that crowded closet full of electrical equipment where the plunger box rests on a table behind a one-way mirror.

Walker is taken to the death chamber and the IVs are attached. A slow drip of neutral solution begins.

Twenty minutes: Visitors are brought into the witness room. The curtain remains closed, so all they see is black and the sloping gray concrete floor, the small drain near the wall, and two guards and a nurse in a corner with oxygen and smelling salts.

When the moment comes, it is the warden who makes the execution happen. Although he won't press the plunger that sends the poison into the IV tubes, it is the warden who says, "Go ahead."

The black curtain opens.

Walker receives an injection of sodium thiopental, a drug that rapidly produces hypnosis (but not analgesia). Then he is given pancuronium bromide, which stops the heart. To make doubly sure he's dead, a potassium chloride injection is also given, which disrupts cardiac function.

This all seems so modern and orderly. Of course, a physician who knows his literature will tell you that pancuronium bromide is synthetic curare. Curare is found on the tips of what we know as "poison arrows." It has been used on wooden arrows for thousands of years by primitive peoples.

The Man Who Went Looking for Death

I met with the secret emissary that the Department of Corrections had sent to witness executions. Let's say his name is

Janik. He sits now in a large carpeted office with a heavy prism of mahogany on his desk displaying his name in bronze letters. But he's young and energetic, in his late thirties or early forties, a man with a quick sense of humor and a deep sense of duty and honor, right and wrong. Janik is a veteran of the Vietnam War who served in combat with the marines, and he now wears gray suits and runs marathons and has a lot of responsibility in his executive position.

He remembered it as his own idea, though he admitted someone else might have suggested sending him to witness an execution. "It would have been back in the early eighties, when we still had electrocution," he said. We sat at a big conference table in his office with two chairs turned out facing each other, and when he talked, he leaned in close and squinted into the middle distance of the past to get the facts right.

"You see, there was no one around [at Stateville Prison] who even had the slightest notion of how to carry this out. And it looked like we were going to have to carry one out at about that time. A few of these guys [on death row] were getting close. So the first thing we did was we brought the old electric chair over from Cook County Jail. And we had our engineer, who was also an electrician, set them both up so we could decide which one to use." It was immediately obvious that the Cook County chair was in better condition than the one at Stateville. "The electrode for the head on our chair was stuck inside an old football helmet," he said. "The kind with the leather earflaps. And that's how it had been used the last time there was a state execution, in 1949. And that's the point at which I realized how little we knew."

Janik learned of an electrocution about to take place in Virginia and flew there on the appointed afternoon, arriving just in time to learn that a judge had passed down an order postponing the punishment. Since he was there anyway, Janik went for a tour of the institution with one of the wardens, and it was during that tour that someone came and informed them that another court had overturned the judge's order; the execution was on.

I asked him what it was like going to see a condemned man. He didn't hesitate. "It's like going to see someone who has a terminal disease," he said. "You know they're going to die, and that's all. There's nothing you can do about it, and it's nobody's fault; it's just a fact." He added, "You develop a kind of clinical detachment."

The execution was late in the evening. Virginia's execution chamber was set up the same way ours is in Illinois, "with one notable exception," Janik said. "There was no vent fan. I noticed that when I went in, but the significance of it didn't strike me until later."

The prisoner was a volunteer. He was white, about forty, "he'd had his head shaven, of course, but he'd kept his moustache, this big moustache. He showed no emotion at all." He calmly sat down, was affixed to the device, and then the switch was thrown twice, and he was pronounced dead.

"It was at that point that I appreciated the need for the vent fan and made a mental note to make sure that ours was in good working order when an execution took place," Janik told me. "Because there was a stench of burning flesh in there that was terrible. Just terrible. And I was really surprised to see how badly burned the man's leg was. I mean deep, third-degree burns. There were two electrodes, one attached to the back of his head and the other attached to his leg. The burn on the back of his head wasn't so bad, but the one on his leg was really big. A deep burn."

He was quiet for a while. Then he added wistfully, "I hope M—— doesn't have to go through this," thinking of his friend who is now the warden at Stateville.

I asked, "You mean go through the mental anguish of an execution?"

"No, no," he said. "I mean it's an administrative nightmare to carry out an execution." The job is Byzantine in its complexity. Repercussions are widespread. Prisoners are more apt to riot after an execution. In Virginia, staff members had become attached to the condemned man. There were emotional problems. "The warden's secretary, who had brought things to the prisoner on a daily basis, was visibly upset. The staff members experience transference, like they say happens between hostages and terrorists. This is why wardens go gray."

Janik had expressed no personal feelings, and so I asked him. He said in the marines at places like Khe Sanh, he had been exposed "to enough dead bodies" so that death itself was no stranger. As for the process, he believes that the death penalty is necessary, at the very least as a tool inside institutions. "When you have a twenty-five-year-old guy who's serving a mandatory thirty years before he can get paroled, he's got nothing to lose by killing a staff member or another prisoner. To him, serving thirty years—well, you remember what it's like when you're that young. The idea of coming out when you're fifty-five, you might as well be dead. So you can't threaten him with another twenty years. He's already doing life in his mind." The death penalty, Janik believes, is the only way to influence his behavior.

I asked again for his personal reaction to seeing a human life willfully terminated. His eyes did a slow tour of the room, touching on objects here and there. It was a cold November day outside, and gleaming pools of sunlight moved imperceptibly on the carpet in the quiet room. "My feelings are not available for public consumption," he said. I pressed him: Somehow, watching men die must have affected him. He said he took it as "a life experience," like many others he'd had, yet unlike any others as well.

Of course, as soon as Janik returned from his Virginia trip, he learned that the law in Illinois had been changed. Executions would no longer take place by electrocution. Condemned men would now be killed by poisoned arrows. Although he felt some valuable lessons had been learned about killing in Virginia, Janik now had to plan another trip to witness another execution in Texas, where poison was employed.

I asked him how he felt about being sent out again for another death mission. "I felt, This is my job. This has to be done."

James Autry, sentenced to die for murder, was another volunteer. When Janik arrived in November 1983, he was given complete access by the state of Texas, which took him in and treated him as their own. He was taken to Autry's cell but found that the prisoner was not talking to anyone except a minister, who, Janik says, "did a good job. He talked him down." He described Autry as "in total control, but he wasn't talking."

Autry walked out of the cell on his own, and they put him in restraints, and then he walked on his own to the death chamber. "They had three big guys there just in case he changed his mind, but he didn't fight. He hopped up on the gurney himself," and then he was strapped down with perhaps a dozen restraints from the neck to the ankles so that he couldn't move at all.

Once the IVs had been inserted and taped off, Janik noticed that he'd been left alone in the room with Autry, who was strapped down on the gurney with clear fluid running into his veins.

Janik leaned in close to me and narrated in a low, tense voice, "Autry just lay there, staring straight up at the ceiling and chewing gum. And he was sweating. I mean, he was sweating bullets." It was a warm night in Texas, but not that warm. Autry stayed like that for a long time, chewing and staring, chewing and staring. All in all the IVs were in his arm over an hour, Janik said. Then, about 11:30, the minister came in, and Janik stood there listening while they talked.

I asked what Autry told the minister, but Janik refused to say. "I . . . I just can't say. It's a matter of honor that I not say." It was at that moment that I realized that for Janik, helping to carry out the death penalty was not a choice he could make. It wasn't a philosophical position he had adopted. It was a matter of doing the right thing, and he could no more refuse to do the right thing than he could refuse to draw his next breath. I had certainly come across those in the chain of people leading to our next execution who were simply covering themselves, denying their roles in the process, or making believe they

weren't responsible. But Janik was doing none of that. And I became obsessed with the question of whether or not this process
could taint such a man. Could one be forced into a position
where the only thing to do was the right thing, and doing the
right thing left one morally tainted? It was a philosophical
question of profound consequence, one that I will live with the
rest of my life. It was what Joseph Conrad's novel *Heart of
Darkness* is about.

Janik stood in that Texas death chamber, watching Autry
sweat and chew gum and look at the light fixtures, and then
someone came and motioned Janik out of the room. It was a
quarter to midnight. Another judge had stopped the execution.
In his heart Janik said, *Damn those judges*, because he knew
Autry would have to go through all this again, and why not just
get it over with? Was there no quality of mercy even to this
cruel law in these modern times?

Out of sight of Janik, Autry was unhooked from the IVs and
returned to his cell. Then a door opened, and Janik turned and
saw the face of the executioner, and he realized that it was
someone he knew. "I was in shock," Janik said. "And the man's
face was as white as a sheet. I have no idea what he was doing
there."

Janik was led out to the balcony for some fresh air, and he
and the assistant warden stood and watched the crowd down
below. It was mostly students, and they were surging in the
tracer-round prison arclight, chanting, "Bullshit! Bullshit!
Bullshit!"

"You know," Janik said, "coming up through the sixties and
all that, that's the last thing you're supposed to be in support
of—putting someone to death. But there they were, chanting
'Bullshit,' and they were drunk and having a time. And over
to one side I could see these protestors with candles quietly
dispersing."

Janik went home to Illinois, and James Autry was executed
on March 14, 1984. If society is held together by those with the
moral strength to carry out these duties, then Janik is one of
our heroes. Reflecting on his experience and his new position

in life, Janik says, "I'm trying to sanitize myself from my Department of Corrections experience now."

Finding Ourselves

I had plunged myself into the world of capital punishment to come to grips with what I thought. I wanted to know the walking dead men, to know their lives so that I could understand what it meant to lose them—no, to take them firmly, with conviction, the way an executioner is supposed to. And I wanted to know their executioners, too.

In the middle of this, I went off to New York one day to do some business I'd been putting off. It was meant to be a relief, a vacation from death, and I decided to enjoy myself and go to the theater the night I was there. I was with an old family friend, and as we rode up the Avenue of the Americas, the towering Macy's Christmas tree lights glittered off to our left across Herald Square. In the window were Santa Claus and mannequins in fur coats, and on the sidewalk people passing up and down the island. Ahead, at Thirty-fourth Street, gridlock had us stalled, and I was sitting in the cab, wondering whether we were going to make the eight o'clock curtain of *Burn This*, when the driver, a diminutive Asian man whose English was not too good, said, "Look, they've killed a man."

Then the gridlock broke and we pulled into the intersection and saw him. The driver glanced, then looked away and began weeping. "Oh! Oh!" he cried softly, almost under his breath. His tenderness was almost as touching as the sight of the man himself, who was so alive in his attitude of crossing the street. Even his briefcase was swung out at the right angle, and his coat was aflutter and his legs akimbo, as if he hurried to an important appointment. But he had no head.

I looked, and it was like an optical illusion. I turned away, then looked back at the dead man, prostrate in the inter-section. He was just outside my window, which was rolled down to the unusually warm December air. People were start-ing to gather and lift their hands to their mouths in attitudes of casual horror. There was a coat collar, a neck, a startling splash of white, and then nothing. The street.

Traffic made a wide circle, and we made the eight o'clock curtain to see John Malkovich whirl the audience into flames over his brother's death. I kept seeing the headless man on the street, the circle of people who looked, lifted their hands, cried out faintly, "Oh! Oh!" and then went on about their business.

Sometimes I think that we can know how precious life is only when we see it lost. Then we know, if only for a second, how it must be to take it, the tremendous sadness it must gen-erate, even for those who believe that it has to be done. Even the executioner turned ghostly white at the moment when he thought he'd have to take a life.

On the plane going home, I read the Japanese novelist Takeshi Kaiko, who describes a Buddhist monk "so strict that he couldn't dig a stick into the ground for fear of killing a worm." As I ate my meal, I thought of the headless man in Her-ald Square. I knew it was just an accident, but I couldn't help thinking of it as an execution, like the headless man outside the Saudi mosque. I asked myself: How do I feel? To carry out an execution, the people of a society must link hands and create a chain. Each person has a job. My job is to bear witness. Will I do my job in society and bear witness to Charles Walker's death? Will I have to go away and sanitize myself when it is over?

"Some people overreact to this sort of thing," said Michael Ficaro, "because it's a first-time experience." But, he added quickly, under any circumstances "it's not easy to kill some-body. Signing your name to the line requires a catharsis." I know now that I will go to watch when we execute Charles Walker. And sign my name to what I see.

The Sky

THE FLIGHT OF THE CRYSTAL WITCH

It involves physics, metaphysics, and the weather of the human heart. Yet it is a sport, to be sure; my sore arms attest to that. When I fly the kite-that-has-two-strings, I am making a spectacle of myself. Yet I am hidden from view. It is not uncommon for people to come out onto the field, saying, "We came over because we could see your kite. It was amazing—what it was doing. But we couldn't see you." That is because when I fly the kite-that-has-two-strings, I become the kite. My soul leaves my body, flies out through my fingertips, through the handles, and up along the hard fiber lines, and there we (my kite and I) look down upon all creation as we go winging around like a barn swallow.

This kite is called the Hawaiian and unfolds from a bag, umbrella-wise. It is outfitted with fiber-wound epoxy spars and gleaming chrome fittings, a counterpoint of black and rainbow chevrons—so pretty, yet wedge-shaped and lethal-looking, with a wingspan as big as a Condor's and the gleam of a stained glass bat.

The first time I flew it I knew that, as with all kite flying, my feet were not supposed to leave the ground; but I'm not sure the Hawaiian knew that. The big nylon delta went ripping across the sky with a velocity and raw power that baffled and frightened me. It made a portentous noise as it split the sky. The Wicked Witch of the West Coast.

When we hear the word *kite*, we think of a pretty, diamond-shaped bit of tissue with a bow-tie tail, attached to a child on the end of a string. Now we hear the phrase *tethered aircraft*. This Hawaiian is no toy.

❖   ❖   ❖

I was at the Top of the Line kite factory in San Diego. Patrice is one of the people there who makes the Hawaiian and its sister kite, the Spin-Off. Patrice and Eunice and Laura and Francisco sew all day long in a great loft near the airport. "There is one mind in the universe," Patrice explained to me, as she measured the nose of a kite and carefully clipped off its beak with tailor's shears. "An individual's mind is the use he makes of the One Mind. How much good we can accept depends on how we are within." Patrice meditates upon these truths as she sews. She spent years of her life seeking heaven on earth, living in communes, working in natural food restaurants, but now she makes the kite-that-has-two-strings.

The factory is the size of a rugby field, an airy room with a beam-braced ceiling and sprayed-on, colorless concrete adhering to the walls. Pfaff sewing machines are set up on tables, and the seamstresses are hard at work. The machines do not sound like the ordinary sewing I heard at home as a child. Here the Germanic machines, whirring through that exotic fabric, make an insect sound, like locust gnawing on aircraft cable.

Wherever we walk, bits of fabric are blown this way and that. The cloth is not really cloth at all but some sort of post-NASA invention. Imagine what it would look like if we could spin diamonds into thread and then weave it into cloth; that might approximate the high scintillation, the crisp feel, of three-quarter-ounce ripstop nylon—spinnaker cloth, as it is called. It comes in a dizzying variety of colors, as if all the precious stones in the world had been trucked in one end of the factory and then thrown into a giant hopper and spun by the Great Spinner into this opalescent cloth: Amethyst, emerald, ruby, topaz; the scraps migrate across the floor in a dance of static electricity; geometric shining shapes, glinting in filtered sunlight, suggest their subterranean lineage.

In a distant corner, two men are cutting on glass tables; they trace their glowing red filaments around silver forms—diamond, isosceles, parallelogram. Rolls and rolls of the bright, brittle fabric—emerald, opal, garnet, jade—lay on racks awaiting the cut glass operating table, the annealing sparks, the fingers and needles of metaphysical mistresses. Out of this scintillating foil comes the trap to catch the strumming wind.

❖   ❖   ❖

Steven Edeiken is credited with the invention of what is now known in kite-flying circles as "team ballet flying." The very conjoining of terms suggests something strange and new. Things that fly do their flying in flocks, do they not? Or squadrons at the very least. And those who dance to music do so in troupes and corps, yes? Nevertheless: team ballet flying. Edeiken had invented a small two-line kite called the Rainbow. Graceful, highly-maneuverable, with a long tail, it could skywrite with the whimsical fluidity of a good ball-point pen. At kite festivals Edeiken flew Rainbows in stacks—tandem arrangements of six or twelve kites, one above the next, flown on the same set of lines. Then he would get a partner to follow his stack in the sky with yet another stack—follow him in swooping, diving, blazing cursive, like two towering skeletal birds of miraculous color, mythical creatures, chasing each other around the heavens, leaving their indecipherable floreated messages traced upon the surface of the clouds.

Kite makers and fliers are always pushing the limits. We're a small species of small animals bored by quotidians. Daedalus was a kite maker, and made himself and his son into human kites. The Wright brothers' first aircraft were modified box kites, and look where it has gotten us: flights every half hour to Chicago.

Bulfinch's *Mythology* says of Daedalus and his son, "As they flew, the ploughman stopped his work to gaze, and the shepherd leaned on his staff and watched them, astonished at the sight, and thinking they were gods who could thus cleave the air." We are told that since ancient times, man has dreamed of flying, but I'm not sure that's the whole story; I believe that since ancient times, man has had the dream to show off.

A corollary to that is man's drive to take everything to absurd extremes (whence kitefliers, aviators, and other dreamers come). In 1985, during an attempt to set some sort of world's record (it is no longer clear precisely what sort), fliers of the kites-that-have-two-strings came from all over the world to Chicago and connected their kites together in a long ladder-like tandem nylon nightmare such as might have been dreamed up by Cristo. Or Breughel. Only this one was made up entirely of Flexifoils. The Flexifoil is a fast and highly maneuverable kite that is a cross between a parachute and an inflatable wing. (It looks like a colorful air mattress.)

First they decided—these mad, metaphysical explorers of the human heart—to set the world's record for the largest sail area for a dual-line maneuverable kite. They arbitrarily picked their goal as a thousand square feet, and some hasty calculations showed that they'd need eighty-four Flexifoils to achieve that area. In setting various records with two-line, steerable kites, it had already been established in the world kiting community that "flying" meant doing one loop to the left and one loop to the right and staying aloft for at least five minutes. Instant airborne catastrophes did not count.

A pulley system (with a truck tire rim for a capstan) was used for steering this eructation of crystal cloth. The lengths of Kevlar cable, made specially for the event, were threaded around the capstan and attached behind the lone flier, Bill Werme, to two antique fire trucks for anchorage—a 1928 America LaFrance and a 1950 Mack.

Word of the feat went out in the kiting community, and Flexifoils began pouring in for the effort. Ray Merry and Andrew Jones, the Flexifoil inventors, donated thirty. The Kite Society of Wisconsin also provided thirty. But then people started bringing their own Flexifoils, UPS-ing and FedEx-ing them in, coming by car, on bicycles, on foot. A lot of people mailed Flexifoils— in singles and pairs and bevies and little flocks. In all, sixty people donated kites and stacks of kites. Each kite would be stamped to commemorate the event, like a souvenir that had gone into outer space. The stamp said WORLD'S RECORD FLEXIFOIL TRAIN, 1985 CHICAGO HOOK AND LADDER.

The Chicago Hook and Ladder—eighty-four Flexifoils on a single set of dual control lines—flew successfully on September 27, 1985. The pilot in command looped and dove the amazing high-colored   pink-and-black-and-green-and-orange-and-everyother-color-you-can-think-of stack, and the capstan system worked just fine for steering. And the new record was set. Which was when the trouble started. For another corollary to man's dream to show off is man's inability ever, ever in history, to leave well enough alone.

The truth was it was just too easy. Success breeds failure in metaphysical sports. If at first you do succeed, try, try again. The reigning kite doyens, discovering that they had not only the required eighty-four kites, but an excess, a virtual cornucopia of kites, hastily (and on the same afternoon) proceeded to go after the next logical world's record: the largest number of stunt kites ever flown on a single set of control lines.

At that time one Rick Bell held the record with, as one Chicago Hook and Ladder participant put it, "141 dinky little Hyperkite Starfighters." While a Hyperkite has perhaps an ounce or two of pull during flight, a Flexifoil can generate up to fifty pounds. In order to brush aside Bell's record, the Chicago Hook and Ladder crew assembled the 153 Flexifoils that eager participants had brought to the site. Someone had the foresight to calculate that 150 Flexifoils could generate up to seventy-five hundred pounds of pull—or nearly four tons. Think ahead; think big.

By and by, the requisite number of Flexifoils was linked up ladder fashion, and with the antique fire engines sitting by like two old red stegosaurs and hundreds of onlookers gaping in disbelief, with cars on the highway stopping and bumping into each other and nearly thirteen dozen kites-that-have-two-strings all tethered together and the custom-woven Kevlar control lines wound around that truck tire capstan, Bill Werme was once again ready to attempt the launch.

"We got into the air," said Al Hargus, who helped organize the madness. "In fact, they went up quicker than the initial eighty-five."

"I felt like I was steering a slab of concrete," Werme said.

And of course, he had to try to perform those compulsory loops. The pulley system worked well enough. The problem with doing loops is that, when the kites come directly across the wind, the force the air exerts on each is at least doubled—reaching toward that magic four-ton figure. As the stack of kites began turning at two minutes and ten seconds into its flight, the force lifted the front ends of the two fire trucks, like dinosaurs that wanted to sit up and beg. There was a sound like rifle fire far off in mid-space; the fire engines "literally jumped," Hargus said, and the thirty-five-hundred-pound lines snapped." This almost-historic event occurred at Ned Brown Woods in Schaumberg, Illinois. The stack was a quarter-mile long, which may in itself be some sort of record—it's difficult to keep track in the madcap world of kites.

But not all such jostlings of the limits end so happily. Back in the fall of 1983, a professor in Washington state was going for the overall record for the largest kite ever flown: 14,260 square feet. With eighth-inch parachute cord shrouds lying in a tangle all over the ground, Steve Edeiken, the safety officer for the flight, was walking among the lines, trying to keep curious onlookers away, when a gust of wind lifted the kite majestically into the air. The shrouds (the lines meant to keep the kite balanced aloft) snapped taut, and up went the kite. The record was underway, but so was Steve Edeiken, the father of team ballet stunt kiting, inventor of the Rainbow, and a favorite figure at kite festivals. Edeiken went whirling upward into the clouds upon which he had scrawled his name.

About 275 feet up, the kite (or Steve) let go. Edeiken fell to his death. Moments later the kite exploded, as if, gorged with the howling wind of the Pacific that had finally been trapped once and for all, it couldn't stand the strain.

People outside of the kite flying community wondered the next day at the sight of black kites here and there across the nation. Who would fly a black kite?

W. H. AUDEN WROTE OF ICARUS:

> The ploughman may
> have heard the splash, the forsaken cry,
> but for him it was not an important failure; the sun shone
> As it had to on the white legs disappearing into the green
> Water; and the expensive delicate ship that must have seen
> Something amazing, a boy falling out of the sky,
> Had somewhere to get to and sailed calmly on.

The mere fact that the Chicago Hook and Ladder experiment came *after* Edeiken's death says something about men who fly kites.

Don Tabor, inventor of the Hawaiian, questions the wisdom of going after raw power and big numbers. You can't beat the wind, he believes, so why try? Nature always wins. He doesn't even go in for large stacks of kites. One kite well flown—one kite for one soul—is enough for him, the interior dialogue of falcon and falconer. Oh, and while we're at it, how about a *team* of souls, flying in formation? When will we ever learn?

❖   ❖   ❖

Until about two years ago, the Flexifoil was the most popular dual-line kite in the world. The introduction of the Hawaiian and Spin-Off kites changed that. Top of the Line, Tabor's company, cannot seem to produce them fast enough.

Tabor first flew the prototype Hawaiian in 1982 in Detroit at the National Convention of the American Kitefliers Association. He won the Best New Manufactured Kite award. Before that he was an artist in search of an art form. He had tried everything, like someone seeking religious enlightenment, like Patrice with her metaphysics. Don tried acting, singing, guitar playing, piloting airplanes like his aviator father, the fine art of cooking, embroidery. He even tried to go on the bum and ran off to ski in Park City, then returned to become a boat repairman and outfitter. But one day his winged creatures came to him, and they have been with him ever since.

Tabor once baked enough chocolate chip cookies to fill his guitar case for a party. He just went on a jag and couldn't stop baking. Another time he baked two chocolate cakes a week for several months until he had perfected a recipe. Tabor seems to do everything that way: He is seized by an idea and driven to pursue it until he solves the riddle. That was how he invented the Hawaiian and Spin-Off kites.

Even now he can be found at two in the morning sitting over a glowing computer terminal in his living room (which was his kite-building shop before it moved into a real factory space) designing new color patterns for his kites, mixing and moving and shaping the stripes on the screen. He keeps swatches of cloth beside him and a fluorescent lamp lit so he can see what the kites will look like with sunlight coming through them. His wife, Patricia (not to be confused with metaphysician Patrice), gets up at dawn to cut material on a glass table just outside their bedroom. Someone at the factory could just as easily do it, but she is driven, too. She has a dream, and when she talks about it, her eyes light up and her hands move in the air like birds. It involves a team of kitefliers. But it's not like any regular three-man team. It is dozens and dozens—perhaps hundreds—of fliers, all maneuvering their Hawaiians in unison. . . . Sometimes she sits bolt upright in the still-darkness before dawn, and she can see the traces of kite patterns in the blue-black sky. At times like that, she goes to the glass table and cuts the crystal cloth, tracing around the silver form with her glowing filament razor. One day . . . some day . . . hundreds of fliers . . . maybe thousands . . .

❖   ❖   ❖

When Tabor showed up at the practice field in Detroit in 1982, what everyone saw was "A completely different shape and style from any kite we'd seen before," said Al Hargus, kite monger and long-time observer of all matters concerning kites. "Most two-line, controllable kites were diamond shaped and small with long tails," like the traditional kite that all children learn to crash. Only these had two lines to allow directional control.

"Not only was the Hawaiian different in design, but what Don had was much larger than anything we'd ever seen." Size was part of its secret. The great sail area could fly in a slight breeze as well as in a gale.

One witness to those first flights in Detroit called it, "The best stunt kiteflying I'd ever seen, a level of stability and control that was unheard of at the time."

That sort of precision made team flying possible for the first time—maneuvers akin to what the Air Force Thunderbirds do with jet fighter planes. Some follow-the-leader flying was done with Flexifoils, but they were too slippery (and frankly, too fast) for precision work. With the Hawaiian, a flier could outline a perfect square in the sky. Now teams of three and four fliers do cascades, starbursts, and girandoles with the greatest of ease.

At forty-five, Tabor is a compact and powerful man with a reddish-brown beard and bright eyes that seem to alternately express quiet determination and an impish propensity for mischief. It does not surprise those who know him to look away for a moment, turn back, and find that Don has put his glasses on upside-down and is wearing half a pretzel like a nose ring while reciting a Polonius soliloquy. When I came to Top of the Line to visit his new sewing loft, he greeted me with a pneumatic-powered rubber tarantula crawling down the front of his shirt and told me how Eric Streed freaked out in Hawaii when they put the mechanical mouse underneath his hat while he was sleeping. Eric ("The Red") is one of the three members of the Top of the Line Flight Squadron, Tabor's stunt flying team, which happens to be ranked number one in the nation, a position it has held for three years. This is a serious million-dollar growth business for Tabor, and the team takes competition and winning quite seriously. ("We don't like to brag, but the fact is that you don't just happen to win everything for three years running without really working your ass off," Tabor says.) Still, mirth leaks in all around the edges.

At the factory there is a room where they hot-cut plastic. Because of the odious nature of the work, it is a room so filthy and smelly that they keep the door closed. Don calls it The White Room, taking a gentle poke at his high-tech friends up the road in Silicon Valley.

Ten thousand yards of shimmering crystal cloth come in one end of his factory and slip beneath the filament knives on the glass tables, past the doors-on-saw-horses that are the measuring tables, through the Pfaff sewing machines and the fingers of the metaphysical seamstresses, and then out into the tile room where kite skins hang like flesh.

The old factory shower room has been turned into a kind of charnel house of kites. They hang on nails like boneless pelts, except that they are made of that strange sapphire fabric, so brightly colored that even in this dim cave they sizzle and dazzle the eye with ruby-tangerine, aqua-topaz, coral-sunburst rainbows.

The kite skins are taken into the assembly room where Dominic's crew frames them with spun glass bones. Those moonstone wings are then gently folded into the blue or red chrysalis forms of long tubular sacs, which are tied with a piece of Dacron string. Each is three feet long. Dormant, neat as cocoons, they hang on hooks all around the walls of Dominic's bone shop. When the day is done, they are taken down and packed in cartons and shipped around the world to unsuspecting owners.

Out in the sun they bring them, these innocents, to watch them hatch upon the water's edge. I've seen it happen: A lady walks by, sees the unfurling fabric, this hypnotic, glimmering, iridescent surface, like mercury tourmaline, shaking out its wings for the first time in the sunlight that flickers on the sand. She stops, entranced, and picks up the handles. The alarmed creature darts off into the sky, ripping the lady's soul out of her body, and she is caught there, flying, looking back down onto the beach, where her mystified body waits for her return.

One day while the Top of the Line team was practicing, I saw such a lady, Debbie by name, sitting on a bench nearby, chin in hands, watching forlornly. I went over to talk to her. "Are you interested in kiteflying?" I asked.

"Ron showed me two weeks ago," Debbie said with a sigh. "He let me fly." She was referring to Ron Reich, team captain, who also happens to be ranked the top individual precision flier in the nation.

"Did you enjoy it?" I asked.

"Enjoy it! I've been dreaming about it," she said, exasperated. "I can't think of anything else." Her soul had been stolen, sure enough.

That day she bought her first kite. There's another step. Debbie probably has no inkling of this yet. It's called Kite Lust. When I first started flying, I met a man on the field who must have had fifteen Spin-Offs and Hawaiians. I said, ironically, "Got enough kites?" And he looked at me deadpan and said, "You can never have enough kites."

He was right. Each new one I meet is like meeting a new elf—I want him to be my friend. On my visit to San Diego, Tabor lent me a pink and lime and blue Spin-Off to fly in my free moments, and I fell in love with it. I really fell in love. I'd be out at dawn, waiting for a wisp of air to come off the bay; and when it was dead calm, I'd just set the kite up on the beach and sit near it, and we'd talk. When it came time for me to leave California and go home, I had a serious moral battle to fight with myself; because I was going to steal that kite—that's how badly I was afflicted with Kite Lust. It's a passion, and one kite does not equal another anymore than one lover equals another. The supreme sign of friendship between kitists is the gift of a beloved kite.

It has not been necessary for Tabor to do much advertising.

But he has a magazine ad ready for when the time comes: A misty woodland scene at dawn. Gnarled trees, dew-wet grass, dappled sunlight, and his sapphire kites sitting out on the grass, hanging in trees, floating here and there. Twinkling elves are moving among the kites, gathering them up. And the copy says: "We make kites the old-fashioned way. With elves and magic."

❖   ❖   ❖

It sounds like a joke, but watch this, it's true; I saw it with my own eyes: The kites in formation skitter across the beach, then fly out over the smooth water of the bay. They skate along just inches from the water, then actually skim it with their wingtips, leaving a little sparkling wake. Back over the beach again, they make another approach to the bay: This time they actually land in the water, squatting like fowl, slowly sinking in, sinking, sinking, until nothing but their little beaks remains in sight.

Without warning, they leap out and hang for a startled, incredible moment in the air. This in itself is amazing enough, except now they wiggle their wings to shake off the diamond dew drops in the bright air, and then gently glide away across the bay, as calm as pelicans hunting for fish.

❖   ❖   ❖

Eric enters laughing—correction—roaring with laughter, blue eyes glinting, red hair flying. And then the roaring laughter doesn't stop, somehow, and he is pulling stunts, tumbling on the carpet, playing pranks, and generally amazing everyone with his humor and ability and his—well—lack of personal dignity. But when the team is ready to fly, a transformation takes place, and Eric becomes perhaps the most serious of the serious fliers. It's like the work he does, brokering for a paper company. Enter laughing, but when it's time to close the deal, the ink is on the page. When I talked to Eric, the team had just returned from the first major competition of the season, the Hawaiian Challenge, where they took five out of six first place trophies.

"We all want to win," he explained. "We are adamant about it. As a result, we do not compromise on practice time. Every practice is centered around winning. And we put aside ego, personal desires, to get to that point. We push one another and help one another to get what we want. In this past competition in Hawaii, I was all but shaking when the scores were posted. I'm saying we really care. And there is a difference between wanting to win and knowing how to win." They practice four hours at a stretch and spend as much time as possible judging other contests so that they can "think like the judges."

Dual-line kites are taking over the nation and unquestionably have already taken over most kite festivals. In 1986 about ten percent of the kites at the American Kitefliers Association convention were of the dual-line, controllable variety. The rest were traditional single-string kites. In 1987 the AKA convention was dominated ("about ninety percent") by two-line kites.

"The mood changed overnight," Eric said. "The atmosphere changed from some kind of quaint and stodgy craft show to an organized, happy, competitive event." It used to be like going to a pottery show. "Now it's like, let's go fly. Let's crank these suckers up and fly!"

Eric, like many kitefliers, started with the Trlby (sic), a fifteen-dollar stunt kite with a long tail, easy to fly to spectacular effect. It has so little pull that a child can learn (my six-year-old daughter has flown one). But it teaches the essential skills necessary to fly the more profound, awesome, and roaring Top of the Line variety. It's a bit like taking lessons in the Cessna 150 before you pull on your G-suit and step into the F-5.

Eric was largely responsible for bringing team captain Ron Reich back onto the team after he'd been flying for a competing kite manufacturer.

❖   ❖   ❖

Ron Reich smiled when I ask him if he'd like to go flying—I mean flying in an airplane, like perhaps a high performance fighter plane, rolling upside down sixty feet off the deck at half the speed of sound. "Naw," he grins shyly. "I don't get my feet off the ground," echoing the sentiments of the two other team members. Yet he is considered one of the best fliers in the country. He has won top honors in the biggest stunt kite competitions for the last two years running. In many of the events, he has outstripped the second best by orders of magnitude. Still, he does not like to leave the earth personally—or rather, bodily. He would rather have his soul leave the ground in the body of an amber pterodactyl kite with an eight-foot wingspan and a cruising speed of seventy miles an hour.

Ron and his wife were taking a walk at Mission Bay one day when they saw Don Tabor flying. They sat down to watch and within a short time, Ron said to his wife, "I have to do that." But he was too shy to go over and ask questions. "It took me two or three weeks to find them again. Then Don took me down and showed me how to fly, and he wondered if I hadn't done this before." That was in June. By September Don had asked Ron to join the team and fly with Top of the Line for the national competitions. Ron didn't want to pay the hundred-dollar fee for entering the competitions, so instead he choreographed the team's routines. With his background in skating and gymnastics, that seemed natural. What Don and the other Top of the Line team members didn't know was that Ron's flying skills came naturally, too. For years he had been handling a project that required him to guide remote underwater vehicles via a TV monitor, a couple of joysticks, and sometimes even foot pedals. He had the hand-eye thing down, and you couldn't fool him about depth perception either. Flying the Hawaiian on a set of 150-foot lines was as natural as walking. He had been doing the same sort of thing underwater while wearing scuba gear.

In those first chaotic days of scrambling among stunt kite manufacturers, Ron was asked to fly with another team, Skynasaur, and it seemed like a good idea at the time. Then one day at the Venice Beach tournament, he got out his Hawaiians again and went over to fly with Eric, just for fun. It was one of those moments. Eric the Red got serious about flying.

That day at Venice Beach, Tabor was watching Ron and Eric as one kite followed another, and a rhythm developed, a fluidity that can only be described in musical terms. The tune came alive and both people were playing it. Soon there was a crescendo (and sometimes this is even accompanied by a helpful cooperative rise in the wind), which literally set the kites singing as the lines stretched and hummed and the crystal fabric rattled with a sound like tambourines.

The tympanic pop of the sapphire skins, the scream of the high wires in the wind added to the climbing tension. The kites moved closer and faster, missing each other and the ground now only by inches. As the suspense and excitement grew, the anticipation of a cataclysmic crash, miraculously averted at the last possible moment, was palpable. And then the whole creation quietly unwound and settled to the ground, and everyone saw once more that it was only kites—sticks and string and colored cloth.

When Ron and Eric were done they turned around and two hundred people had gathered and were applauding. Something magical had happened that day. Eric and Ron had hit upon a formula. There was something about the size and sound of the Hawaiian kite, the trembling of the earth and wind, that awesome crackling of the fabric, the crisp performance of those spun glass bones, that made the magic roar out of the vortex like the demon wind itself, flung out of a long, dark cavern.

Ron sat down with Tabor, and they had a typical aviator kind of exchange. "You looked pretty good there," Tabor said, or words to that effect. Ron allowed as how it was awful fun. "I was beaming inside," Ron told me later, "but I couldn't let it show when Don asked me to join the Top of the Line team again." Typical aviator.

I know the feeling of moments like that, though, because

I've been there now. I had the thrill of flying with Eric and Ron and Don, all four of us together at once, as a team, and it's like dancing in the sky. My eyes—my soul—travel up with the kite and I can see down on myself. I and my world look so small, my petty concerns cannot possibly matter now. As I become the kite, I become god, demon, angel, by turns. In the team flying all that is amplified a hundredfold. We are up together living the dream to fly like the birds—not in machines, but like birds. A flock of birds closes with another and the two mesh some-how, magically, without any two colliding. So do we, and it is so breathtaking that we stop in amazement and have to think for a moment: Who are we? What are we? We scarcely believe ourselves.

AT THE STILL POINT
OF THE TURNING WORLD: FLYING JETS
WITH THE AIR FORCE

At a minute before seven each weekday morning, one of the pilots from B Flight stands at a wooden lectern in a long room under fluorescent lights in an old hangar on the flight line at Randolph Air Force Base and looks at his watch. The room is clean and plain, ivory-painted cinder block with a single brown stripe running around the circumference by way of decor. Behind the lectern is a blackboard. The pilots sit at aluminum desks, spaced at intervals around the room, like clerks in a bank. On one wall is a white erasable scheduling board that lists the name of each pilot and the flights he will make that day. Most pilots have two 60- or 90-minute sorties a day, one in the morning, one in the afternoon, each preceded by a briefing and followed by a debriefing. The normal day is a busy one, and the canteen down the hall provides a large percentage of pilot meals—nuts, apples, Grandma's brand cookies, Coca-Cola, and a few canned concoctions that can be "nuked," as the pilots say, in the microwave. Occasionally, if there was a hold on launching the fleet, a pilot might sneak over to the deli for a jalapeño submarine, which can be a risky item for a pilot to have on board when he's traveling upside down near the speed of sound pulling six or seven Gs.

The job of the Twelfth Flying Training Wing at Randolph Air Force Base just outside of San Antonio, Texas, is to turn out instructor pilots (I.P.s), who are then sent to air force bases around the country to train student pilots—the wellhead of young aviators to fly the planes the Pentagon builds. There are no student pilots at Randolph, only pilots who are learning how to teach. "Flying and talking," they call it. It is the Ph.D. program for aviators.

The briefer this morning, Captain Stuart Rodgers, counts down, "Five, four, three, two, one, hack," in order to begin his briefing at exactly 7:00 A.M. and to allow others to set their watches. "Could we please have a weather briefing?" A speakerphone call is placed to the civilian weatherman, who drawls, "Let's see here, I got some kind of scattered or broken clouds up here . . ."

"Where's the contrail level?" one of the pilots calls out. He'd been in tactical fighters in Iceland for three years before coming to Randolph for pilot instructor training, and he would appreciate a little precision first thing in the morning. A neatly lettered sign under the glass surface of Captain Rodgers's desk says "NO WHIMPERING! NO CIVILIAN BEHAVIOR!"

"Way the hell up there," says the Texas weatherman, and someone switches him off. That gets a big laugh all around the room.

Captain Rodgers begins, "OK, today we've got min turntime, so we're going to try to blast early. Maybe twenty minutes early." (That's how they talk; one day I asked a pilot what Bingo Fuel meant, and he thought for a moment about the best way to explain it, and then, convinced that he had it formulated so clearly that even a civilian could understand it, he said, "When you reach Bingo Fuel, you're supposed to RTB at that time." When no formal briefing is in progress, a flight room is filled with such talk, like Captain Melissa Ward saying, during a post-sortie debriefing, "We G'ed up a little to lose energy. Did you guys get spit out real bad?" She fingers the parachute knife pocket on the inside of her thigh, adding, "Say, do you guys at Reese really taxi that slowly?")

Captain Rodgers makes a couple of routine announcements: Volunteers are needed to take some brigadier generals on T-38 orientation rides—Boom Rides, they call them, when they go supersonic. (The T-38 is the training jet; it is supersonic, and thirty-one countries use it as their primary fighter plane.) Also, says Captain Rodgers, pilots are needed to make a two-day four-hop, which means four ships flying cross-country in formation on a trip that will take two days. Captain Rodgers has dark hair, strong features, and a serious demeanor. He (like most) is in his twenties. He is quick to smile or laugh, but he is fundamentally businesslike. Even his jokes are to a point. He picks up a piece of chalk and puts a single dot on the blackboard. "What's that?" he asks.

Several voices answer at once, "A T-38!" making the point that how the aircraft looks really depends upon how you look at it. Each morning a different pilot gives a briefing on a different subject. This morning Captain Rodgers explains a few of the tricks involved in maintaining formation.

"And how do you tell your relationship with another ship when you're flying formation?" Captain Rodgers asks. There are various types of formations the pilots have to fly, from fingertip (three feet apart) to chase (five hundred feet back) to tactical (almost a mile abreast). The problem is: How do you tell, with any precision, what those distances are? An aircraft, like a crystal, has many facets, and as you turn it and move in close—now far away—it changes its aspect. For example, a T-38 has two canopy bubbles—front seat and back seat. At six thousand feet abreast, you can't make out both of them; they appear as one. But at four thousand feet they are distinguishable as two.

While everyone listens carefully, no one takes notes. One of the differences between real pilots and bank clerks (or even real pilots and airline pilots) is this: air force high performance jet pilots memorize everything. They cannot look everything up, because there are no libraries in the air. (The critical checklists, which tell what to do if an engine fails on takeoff or a fire breaks out in flight, are painted on the restroom walls, so that no time is wasted.) Generally speaking, if something goes wrong in the jet, something big, the pilot has between four and eight seconds to decide to get out.

After Captain Rodgers's briefing, each I.P. pairs up with his trainee for an individual briefing before flight. After that there is a stop at SOF desk (supervisor of operations) to get assigned an airplane and a call sign and to pick up any last-minute notices or precautions (birds in the area, for example, or radio facilities that are not functioning). Just down the corridor is the restroom, where everyone pays precautionary tribute and sneaks a last glance at the boldface on the walls. ("In-Fire Flight: Eject," a very short checklist, easy to remember.)

Each pair of pilots is going out to do something different, dictated by the training syllabus and the individual's progress through it. Some will fly formation. Some will fly contact—loops and cloverleafs and Cuban eights. Some will go into a flight simulator—a fully-functioning cockpit mounted on hydraulic legs, which can simulate everything about a flight, including motion and the view outside. Sim rides, as they are called, teach procedures while saving money. Each T-38 flight costs about two thousand dollars, not counting the salaries of the pilots. There's only a certain amount of money appropriated by Congress, and although it doesn't happen often, if the money runs out before the end of the training month, flying stops until the new month begins. That is one reason (though by no means the only reason) that only people who learn fast can do this sort of work. And yet to hear the I.P.s talk about student pilots (every pilot was once a student) you'd think they were worse than coral snakes.

"We're teaching these trainees the only form of combat flying," one I.P. tells me, "where the enemy is going to be in the cockpit with you."

I ask how the air force selects student pilots.

"Well," he says, "you see, we go down to the Dunkin' Doughnuts, and we take everybody who's sitting at the counter, and we say, 'OK, you're pilots.' Then we send them out to an airfield somewhere real far away, and we put them in airplanes, and see if they can fly." This mythical creature, the freshly hatched venomous larva with no wings, is politely referred to as Joe

Bag-o-Doughnuts, the quintessential student pilot, sometimes also called Harvey (as in Milquetoast). And if there is to be any air force, then someone must train him. That intrepid someone is the instructor pilot, the I.P., who is taught at Randolph Air Force Base. "Essentially," an I.P. tells me, "we try to teach our I.P. trainee how the student can kill him and how to avoid that. But at the same time, you have to let the student fly the plane, and you have to let him make some mistakes, or he won't learn." I.P.s have to know how far to let a student pilot go before intervening in his destiny, and of necessity, they develop the virtue of polite, cautious calm.

To accomplish his task of training the trainee, the I.P. must pretend to be Joe Bag-o-Doughnuts, while the trainee (the aspiring I.P., who may be fresh out of undergraduate pilot training but may also be an experienced fighter pilot coming back to learn to instruct) must pretend to be the actual I.P. So the one who best knows how to do things correctly will intentionally make mistakes—some of them bordering on disasterous— while the trainee will attempt to stay one step ahead of that process, correcting the person who is instructing him. It is a dangerous game that involves a very high level of mental dexterity, not to mention flying skill. Being a good I.P. requires an ability to concentrate in a calm and detached fashion while roaring upside down and semi-out-of-control toward the misty green earth, and keeping hands off the controls when it would be a simple matter to set things right; so that someone who *doesn't* know how to get out of this fix very well can attempt to do so. At the same time, the aspiring I.P. has to explain in clear language what to do, while looking out the window for traffic, scanning his instruments to make sure he's not on fire, and projecting an air of quiet confidence and smooth discipline (and even the most experienced fighter pilots sometimes come to Randolph and find out that, although they can fly with the best, they can't explain what they do, and they can't talk while flying). Despite those tremendous demands, the high speeds, wind, worry, civilian behavior, whimpering, and the law of

averages, the safety record at Randolph is better than that of
the scheduled air carriers.

❖   ❖   ❖

One cannot, as in the movies, simply jump into the cockpit
and roar off into the W.B.Y. A T-38 jet is something like an
artificial heart, an iron lung, a bathyscaph of the empyrean.
There must be intimate connections made between man and
machine. A G-suit is zipped on over the flight suit, as tight as
an old-fashioned corset. It sometimes takes two men to get a
pilot into those so-called Speed Jeans. In the cockpit, a hose
connects G-suit to jet, so that when the pilot pulls Gs, a pneumatic system can inflate air bladders sewn into the fabric. The
force of inflation, like blood pressure cuffs on legs and abdomen, literally pumps the pilot's blood for him so he doesn't
black out. (In pilot terminology, graying out refers to a loss
of vision, not a loss of consciousness. The optic nerve is extremely sensitive, requiring a high rate of oxygenation, and
when blood is mechanically pulled away from the brain by the
centrifugal force generated while turning the plane, the first
physiological effect is "pulling the shades," as they call it. The
pilot remains completely able to function in every other way;
except he's blind. If he widens his turn a little bit, by relaxing
his pull on the stick, the G-force decreases and vision returns
instantly.)

One of the life support crew members helps a pilot fit his
helmet and face mask properly, measuring the distance from
bridge of nose to tip of chin with calipers, then adjusting the
straps and taping them in place when they're tight. Ordinarily,
it is not so important how the helmet fits, but if a pilot tries to
eject with a loose-fitting helmet, the 250-knot wind could blow
the helmet right off his head. (As a point of comparison, Hur-
ricane Gilbert's 175-knot winds destroyed big chunks of several
Caribbean countries in 1988.) Some of the pilots wear silk skull
caps to protect their heads from the cutting foam inserts in the

helmet and to absorb and carry sweat away. The ramp is apt to warm up to 110 degrees or so on a typical Texas afternoon. Inside the glass bubble of the cockpit, a greenhouse effect makes it even hotter, and, with the Nomex flight suit, gloves with leather palms, combat boots, helmet, and rubber oxygen mask, they say that those who get sick riding in these jets aren't getting motion sickness so much as they are reacting with claustrophobia to the unusually close environment and the heat.

A plastic flask of drinking water goes into the left calf pocket of the flight suit. ("Gentlemen," a safety officer warned, "do not freeze your water bottle before a flight. It may keep it cool for you, but in a crash it becomes a projectile.")

❖   ❖   ❖

Captain Rodgers said to me one day, "Why don't we go out two-ship, pick up some contact, then rejoin and recover two-ship? You'll get to see a lot that way." I said that sounded fine. There were two crews, Captain Rodgers and I in one ship, Colonel Dave Kirkland and Captain Greg Unwin in the other. As the highest ranking officer, it fell to Colonel Kirkland to give the preflight briefing.

Colonel Kirkland, a fit-looking, sharp-featured man of forty with a voice like Slim Pickens and a quiet, relaxed confidence, went through everything from precisely how he would signal the takeoff roll with two jets on the runway at the same time (and what to do if one of the ships lost an engine on takeoff), to what type of turns we'd do on the way out to the area, to how we'd split up and rejoin, and what we'd do when we came back for a landing (called recovery).

"We'll go out and pick up the freqs en route," he said. (Meaning: frequencies.)

"Do you want to get the humiliation vectors back to base?" Captain Unwin asked. (Meaning: should we let a mere air traffic controller put us on radar and tell us how to get home, or should we find our own way?)

They wrote nothing down. They did not sit and contemplate the plan. It just stuck the first time. And it all went exactly as Colonel Kirkland said it would.

There were a lot of birds in the area that day, so Captain Rodgers briefed me on what to do if he was killed by a bird shattering his canopy at three hundred knots. Since I had my own pilot's license and since the air force had been kind enough to give me two days of simulator flying practice, he knew that at the very least, I could fly the T-38 around in circles and talk on the radio at the same time. "But I wouldn't try to land it if I were you," he said. "Just turn the radio to channel eleven, that's the Guard frequency, and call for Copperhead. Tell him who you are and what happened, and he'll probably have you fly out and eject somewhere."

I said that would be a shame, crashing a nice plane like that, especially since Northrup was not manufacturing T-38s anymore.

He thought about that for a moment and then said, "Well, hell. I'm dead, and you're flying at that point. You can do anything you want."

Riding out to the flight line, the big, dusty, dark blue panel truck stopped to pick up crews waiting in the sun with their helmets under their arms and their thirty-five-pound parachutes slung over their shoulders. The pilots, two by two, got in and squinted in the darkness and sat down on the hard wooden benches, resting their parachutes between their knees, helmets in their laps, as the truck rolled down the ramp and stopped again to pick up another crew. They smiled knowingly, as if they shared a secret, but it was quiet in the truck. About a mile out, we stepped off the truck onto the hot ramp beside the ranks of white rockets gleaming in the sun, and Captain Rodgers handed me a stick of gum. "SOP," he said. "You gotta have gum."

If life were cut into snippets like a movie, then at this point we would jump into the jet and blast off. But the ground check, or walk-around, is one of the pilot's most important responsibilities. If he were to take off with a bird's nest in the air intake or with a tire that was flat, it would be his fault. So we set down our parachutes and crawl around underneath the plane for a while, inspe ːting everything that can be seen, looking for leaks, cracks, and unattached spare parts, lest we embarrass ourselves and cause the taxpayers a grave additional expense.

The T-38 is a simple, reliable plane based on a forty-six-foot-long airframe, a twelve-hundred-pound weight, and two rocket motors that were originally designed for guided missiles—throwaways, in other words. They each produce about thirty-five hundred pounds of thrust in burner, and one day I went to the maintenance base and watched some technicians test one on a stand in a specially-shielded room with a steel and concrete furnace flue pointed up at the heavens to direct the exhaust blast away.

I put in foam earplugs and then placed heavy ear protectors over them, and they locked me into the chamber with a technician for company. The naked, eight-foot-long engine was wrapped in whorls of tubing like a living body part that had been surgically flayed of integument. It was mounted on a steel stand that had been rigged to measure thrust and bolted to the concrete floor of the chamber. The technician signaled thumbs up to the operators at the control panel behind the thick glass partition, and they lit the candle. As they gradually ran it up, I began to fear that I was going to be blown apart by sound waves. The technician had come in with me to point out the danger zones, so that I didn't inadvertently walk into anything, such as the bleed air. He signaled again through the window, and the operator ran the jet up to full or military power. Then the tech put his hand out to show me where the hot bleed air was. (This is not the jet exhaust, which would have instantly burned his hand off, but simply the path of escaping air on the side of the engine; bleed air powers such things as the air conditioning.) I put my hand into it. Imagine that someone drops a fence post from a third-story window, and you try to catch it with one hand. It gives a very clear demonstration of how air can hold up airplanes. The column of air was as solid as hickory.

At another signal, they kicked the engine into afterburner,

and a four-foot-long blue flame grew out of the back of the black pipe known as the burner can. A ring of nozzles sprays a mist of JP-4 jet fuel into the path of the flame, and it ignites. "Increasing mass," they call it, for it is the mass of the exhaust that pushes the mass of the plane, according to Newton's third law of motion; and the bigger the mass, the greater the thrust. In some jets, water is dumped into the path of flame to increase mass (and therefore thrust).

I could feel the mass. With the afterburner going, the sound was no longer sound. The concrete room was like a maw, and I was a bit of gristle, being chewed up by unseen teeth. My bones rattled, and my flesh flapped upon them like ill-fitting clothes. I could not imagine how we could go unharmed, and yet we did; and then the tech made a neck-cutting hand signal, and they shut it down.

We climbed into the flue, a reticulated maze of rust-red-and-black-steel sculpture, like crawling into a giant auto muffler. The metal was still too hot to touch. Twenty feet back in the forbidding oven tunnel our channel took a vertical right-angle turn; and reaching that point, I could look up out of our man-made hell and see the sky like a tantalizing drink of water. It was in this blistering retort that the alchemy was worked to make the sleek white rocket pin itself against that high, clear, cool blue firmament. And it was atop two of those missile motors that I sat one day, out in the Texas sun, as our crew chief whirled our engines up to start them.

❖   ❖   ❖

After I'd climbed into the cockpit, the crew chief, (we've all seen him beside airliners, directing taxiing aircraft with hand signals) climbed up the ladder after me to make sure that I inserted the gold key into my seatbelt hasp. In the event that I had to punch out, that brass ring would automatically start my parachute sequence as I separated from the ejection seat. ("If we have to go," Captain Rodgers had told me during briefing,

"I'll say 'Bailout, Bailout, Bailout' three times. Don't delay. Just get a good position, keep your back straight the way they taught you, tuck your arms in next to your body, and pull the handles. It only takes two and a half inches, so don't touch them unless you're going to use them.")

The two days of simulator training could familiarize me with how the T-38 works, but nothing could have prepared me for the real ride. Even taxiing on the ramp, I felt I had hold of something titanic—that I'd reached inside my chest and grabbed hold of my own heart and squeezed. *They're not really going to let me fly this*, I thought. But they were, they really were. ("I'll take it from you if I have to for safety reasons," Captain Rodgers said in briefing, "but otherwise, you've got the aircraft.")

The microphone in my oxygen mask picked up the sound of my breathing—hiss-click, hiss-click. I could hear it speed up when the needle nose of the jet swayed left and right as I tried to steer it with the rudder pedals to keep it on the yellow taxiway line behind Colonel Kirkland's plane.

Relax, relax, I told myself, as the nose went all over the ramp, like a blind rat looking for a scent. I thought: *The ground crew must think I'm drunk. Or worse: a student pilot.* I consciously slowed my breathing and made my feet settle down on the pedals, and the plane began to track straight again. Captain Rodgers said, "That's OK, give it a little power. Good." The two planes took the runway side by side with Colonel Kirkland's plane slightly ahead of ours.

Colonel Kirkland swirled his finger in the air, telling us to run up to mil power with the brakes on. At that point we had a moment before blast off, when if anything was going to go wrong, we prayed that it would kindly do so now.

All four of us wore mirror green face shields, oxygen masks, and gray matte helmets, so expression should not have mattered; and yet it seemed we could see each other—somehow we were intimately connected. Colonel Kirkland tapped his helmet, meaning, *We'll go on my head signal.* He leaned his head back against his seat, and when he brought it suddenly forward, we tapped the afterburners, released the brakes, and were rolling. A moment later, a gentle pull on the stick lifted the nose. Another second on the concrete, and the planes flew away.

We tucked into fingertip formation, barely three feet away from and just behind Colonel Kirkland's plane. The Colonel's tail slab, flipping up and down like a whale's, signaled us to go to chase position about three hundred feet back; and as we shrugged off the green mantle of the earth, like birds shedding water as they struggle into flight, I noticed my world explode around me.

Streaming white mists and bright blue heavens poured out at me from the void, as the world pitched and swirled and turned suddenly into a boiling molten fluid of brown and green below. Solid referents were gone. We were in a realm of pure energy, with the only limits defined by the sharp seat under me, the solid pedals beneath my feet. Pulling back on the stick lifted the aircraft's nose and the centrifugal force made my world grow solid, like plaster of Paris setting. By pushing the pole, I could make the forces dissipate, as if I dissolved bodily into the fluid that sang to me outside the thin and glistening bubble of my canopy.

Here was my dream: A child in a soap bubble, rising into the sun. The high thin clouds streamed across the sky as if a mysterious, celestial spider weaved its web unseen somewhere beyond the horizon and spewed the tangle of its shiny lanyards out at us as we came, on and on.

At first I was so excited that I forgot how to fly. Following Colonel Kirkland, I just about flew up his exhaust pipe, and Captain Rodgers had to grab the controls to prevent me from scorching our nose. I was suffering what they call brain lock, when the sensory overload freezes you. I shook myself awake and took the controls again.

"Ninety right—now!" the voice said. I moved the stick and felt the plane and my body galvanize, pumping blood, and heard the hiss-click of my graphite insect lungs. I remember being locked mouth to mouth with my lover, breathing each other's breath until we nearly blacked out, never more intimate than in this titanium embrace.

After a time, I no longer particularly noticed when the aircraft was upside down. That is, I was aware of it, but no more so than the fact of going 450 knots or the fact of being at fifteen thousand feet or of the tactical crossing maneuver my wingman was making far beneath me as we closed and descended into the immensity of West Texas.

We were switching positions, putting me in the lead, and now the white jet, forty-six feet long, sucked up beside me and sat there as if we were parked, and I could see Captain Greg Unwin, in the back seat behind Colonel Kirkland, duck his head and roll his fists, as if he were punching an invisible speed bag in the cockpit. His head, of course, was concealed by the dragonfly compound eye of glare shield and rubber mask, but I knew he was grinning underneath. I returned his sign of joy and exuberance, boxing the air with my gloved hands. This was not in the official lexicon of sign language, but I could read it just as clearly: Rock and Roll! Light that fire!

It was much easier flying lead, because Colonel Kirkland or Greg Unwin, whoever was flying at that moment, could make me look good simply by staying right on my wing. No matter how sloppily I flew across the sky, they were right with me as if we were welded together.

With a solid pull on the pole, I made myself, all at once, weigh about 765 pounds. My oxygen mask pulled down on my nose and my hands grew heavy as my G-suit inflated to supply additional pressure for my puny cardiovascular system so I wouldn't black out. The airplane knew, even when I didn't, how much to squeeze.

I had become one with the aircraft. Not metaphorically but actually. Nothing of my former, mushy, flesh-and-blood self showed anymore. I was covered, every inch, in Nomex fireproof nylon, with gray and green fireproof gloves, with heavy black jump boots, and the helmet that made my head look like a machine bearing, a spare part stuck on, painted with rust-inhibiting matte gray primer. Finally there was my rubber oxygen mask and sun visor to give me that quality of medieval knighthood.

I sucked my breath out of the lungs of my rocket—a hose attached my arteries, my very hemoglobin, to its oxygen supply. I flicked the white switch to get a blast of oxygen for more speed inside. I flicked the black switch to get a blast of JP-4 fuel for more speed outside. I just kept them matched up, and we were good to go.

My whole environment was processed and filtered and reformulated, within, without, until man and instrument were one, and that was how we flew. I could stretch my fingers out and feel the hummingbird tips of my wings. But here's the best part: It was my will that drove the rocket, will and imagination and the hand and eye. I had been able to transfer my soul out of my body and into a superhuman instrument and then send us skipping along, tracing the silhouette of the absolute.

We rolled the fingertip formation over on its back and let it fade out of the blue and down toward the steaming skin of the earth. We were deep in the distortion zone, where up and down no longer mattered, as long as we kept it somewhere between the green and the blue: Touch either one and you die.

I reached over and hit the switch for a blast of pure oxygen directly into my brain. The profusion of beatitudes engulfed me in a giddy exhilaration. Between my right thumb and forefinger I held the black magic crystal: By gently tickling it left and letting the needle nose of my white rocket drop just off the hazy green horizon, I could perform a dance with my wingman in a lazy S across the sky, three feet apart, thudding across the waves of light like stones skipping off the stratosphere, so frail and yet so heavy, like the froth of air itself.

The wings of a jet, when they are loaded up, smoke like the advancing crest of the great breaking ocean waves. The sky inhaled, then spit us out, exhaling steam like a mythical beast. "Look," my instructor said, "contrails." Hard rays of sunlight hailed on the origami wings as we shuttled down the vortex of gravity, the centrifugal spiral howl of a vertical dive into the earth.

❖   ❖   ❖

We split up the formation and went our separate ways so that I could practice my acrobatic maneuvers—contact—and it was somewhere out over Hondo, Texas, that I decided to try my first loop. I'd done a hundred of them in the simulator, but I had a feeling that this was going to be different.

I reached out with my left hand and checked that my throttle was set at mil-power—the full throttle stop just before afterburner. Then I pushed the stick away and watched as the airspeed climbed toward five hundred knots—the prescribed entry speed to give us the kinetic energy necessary to get us around and over the top. (It works like a roller coaster: You gain speed before you reach the next hill.) The altitude bled down to nine thousand feet, the hard deck, and I gradually pulled back on the pole, pulling, pulling, as I felt myself grow heavy. My Speed Jeans inflated, and I started pumping my muscles, hauling the stick in toward my stomach, clenching my whole body against the forces, as I pulled into the first half of my ten-thousand-foot loop. As I drew the stick in, something Captain Rodgers had told me before the flight came back to me: "Incidentally, when you get the aircraft up to five hundred knots," he had said, "it *is* possible to rip the wings off, so be gentle."

I was so gentle.

I topped out the loop upside down at eighteen thousand feet, and the Gs let off, and my G-suit deflated. I drifted up there for what seemed an hour, just looking around the leviathan immensity of my domain. The sapphire blue was floreated with spider web clouds, a great tarantula of light and energy that encircled the double dome of earth and sky. I felt I was in the center of a spherical lens, refracting all existence through the focus of my being. I felt so intensely happy and secure at that moment, the calm in the center of my psychic storm.

I would have cried out for joy, but the mike in my mask was

hot, and I didn't want to hurt Captain Rodgers's ears, so I just whispered, "Rock and Roll," and I heard him chuckle softly. "Nice maneuver," he said. "Now pull through."

I fingered the pole back until I saw the horizon rise from below into my field of vision. Over the top, I pulled down into the emerald sphere of man. I stole a glance at my instruments (no warning lights) then directed my vision back outside, and as I pulled the stick back, the Gs built steadily once more, and I felt the pre-stall buffet—the burble, they call it—when the stick and then the whole plane began to shudder. That's what we hear engineers talk about: pushing the outside of the envelope. The performance envelope is a curve on paper, but how do you find it in the air? You know you're max-performing the aircraft when you have the pre-stall buffet, the burble. That's the ragged edge.

My G-suit inflated again, and I grunted and puffed and strained against the centrifugal mastodon growing within me.

Going ballistic, into the very earth, vertical at five hundred miles an hour, and doing it with two fingers, I rolled my head back and took in the sky, and my head cleared of all the rubbish of the mud below: my outstanding MasterCard bill. Mother's Day. The dental work I ought to have done. Being forty years old. Like a good journalist, I had attached my notebook and pen to a knee board Velcroed to my leg. At one point, I even began to take notes, but then I just laughed and ripped it off and stuffed it all into the map pocket. Writing is for losers; let's fly jets!

Thus my life fled into a great gray backdrop from which the act of flying stood out in such sharp relief that I did not even hear the engine noise—the bone-shuddering concussion of nearly six thousand pounds of thrust coming from just behind my head. Even when I pushed the throttle past the detent of mil-power into Max, afterburner, I heard nothing as two four-foot-long blue flames shot from my tail. I felt the kick in the seat, the strain of the plane, but all I heard above the sleeping earth was the hiss-click of my breathing as the blinker valve opened and closed and Captain Rodgers talked me through maneuvers, teaching me, "Pull a little more now, that's it, that's it. Now add power. OK, unload the plane now." I leveled out at the hard deck.

Aileron rolls: With less effort than I'd use to apply a postage stamp with my thumb, I flipped over and over. As I rolled, the blue globe was swapped with the green one, and then they'd flip back again. The T-38 rolls so fast (720 degrees per second) that there's scarcely time to consider it. Blue and green, the sapphire and the emerald, only their ratio mattered: Half and half meant I was straight and level. More blue-and-white meant I was climbing, but I didn't care if the sky was on the top or bottom. I could even do it all while on my side.

Colonel Kirkland, miles away in his practice area, interrupted my reverie with his "Joker-plus-one-hundred" call on the radio, and my heart shut off for a moment until I could stick my gray glove down into my chest again to restart it manually. Joker is a code name for the fuel level at which preparations must be made to return to base. All my life I had been searching for the place where my restless soul stood still, and high above the earth and time, I found it. I didn't ever want to go home now.

"Do you see him?" Captain Rodgers asked me. Out over Hondo, Texas, we were trying to rejoin with Colonel Kirkland's plane at the rendezvous point.

"No joy," I said, having trouble locating his white rocket in the glare of the sun. Then I saw the glint of his wings winking as he turned, and I called contact—I had him in sight. We turned north to rejoin.

Returning to base (RTB), we made a low approach in formation, and Captain Rodgers flew down to within an inch of the ground before popping the afterburner, retracting the flaps and gear, and taking us aloft again. We went back out and switched positions, putting Colonel Kirkland in the lead for an overhead pattern. That is the standard military way of coming in for a landing, maintaining altitude as long as possible in order to avoid fire from the ground in enemy territory. The turns are hard and tight, to keep turning time to a minimum and expedite the descent to the runway. I flew that one, coming in high over the runway, about eighteen hundred feet, and then performing a maneuver called a pitch out. As we passed above the approach end of the runway, Colonel Kirkland turned into a sixty degree right bank and swept around for a landing. I delayed my turn about four seconds for spacing and then pitched out some three thousand feet behind him, pulling perhaps four Gs in the process. The aircraft slid down the approach to the runway and sat on the numbers obediently, and we rolled on out.

When we are walking away from the plane, Captain Rodgers said, musing, as if to himself, "You know, I always swallow my gum somewhere in the flight. I never can remember where, though."

❖   ❖   ❖

Randolph Air Force Base is unusual among bases, because the town—the complex of Spanish-style housing, the tree-lined streets, the commissary, the gym, the gas station, and all the people—is situated between the two runways. When you enter the base, you are driving (or biking or jogging) down a long road with jets taking off and landing on either side. In this way, the element of manned flight, the fact of being *inside* a churning, boiling cauldron of aviation activity, is enhanced to its maximum effectiveness. Randolph is, was, and always will be about flying. This fact permeates life at every level. I asked directions one day on the base, and my would-be Samaritan, wishing to suggest that I follow him in my car, said, "I'll take you there two-ship."

Everywhere on base, the audacious fact of aviation asserts itself. One night a captain invited me to the officers' club bar and said, "Let's go shoot down our watches." If you stand at the bar at nine o'clock on a weekend night, as far as the eye can see there are pilots in green bags (flight suits) with their hands making airplanes in the air. (Thus the right-hand fighter plane shoots down the wristwatch on the left.) Pilots cannot talk without their hands. In fact, a document known as AFR 60-15 lists hand signals used by pilots. They are meant to allow pilots to communicate without radio contact in flight, but they are also used at the bar, at the gas station, and in the classroom. The one most familiar to civilians is the "O" made with thumb and forefinger. It means Outstanding. Another, seen often, is a cutting motion made back and forth rapidly across the neck with the hand flat, palm down, fingers together and pointing at the neck. It means cut your engines, or stop. Also if someone says, "Would you like a blind date with Melanie tonight?" or "Do you want me to check that oil, sir?" you make this signal.

Even kids use those hand signals. The base is a desirable place to live, cheap and convenient and pretty, and people move in with the mower and the dog and the water skis, and they raise their families there, between those two roaring runways. Children grow up knowing that to amount to anything, you have to be a pilot, just as surely as children on a river will grow up wanting to be riverboat captains. At the flight line, kids on bicycles cruise around and watch the blue panel truck with its special commuters inside and wait for real pilots to talk to. Whenever someone in a green bag comes within range, the kids surround him on their cut-down, knobby-tire bikes and ask him what he flies and if he has any extra patches to give them. I talked to some of the kids one day and learned that most of their fathers were not pilots; they were mechanics or clerks or accountants or even (gasp) civilian workers. They fiercely insisted that they were going to grow up to be pilots. Each had a substantial collection of flight patches and an extensive knowledge of aircraft types and technical specifications. Since Randolph is a popular stopping-off point for aircraft from all over the world, the kids who hung around the flight line, like greedy space-age bird watchers, could see virtually anything they had the patience to wait for, from base-hopping NASA astronauts to the evil, camo, droop-nosed, rat-faced F-4 Phantom jet whistling in for a landing with drag chutes whirling in the wind like a witch's skirts.

The kids more than anything made me wonder what it was that made them want so badly to be pilots. And what it was that distinguished these special pilots from all others.

One day sitting in Beaver Flight during a weather stand-by, when no one could fly because of thunderstorms in the MOA, I heard a fighter pilot named Chuck, who'd left Iceland and his F-15 Eagle to learn to teach at Randolph, shout out to the room, "Anybody who's doing this for the money, raise your hand!" Everyone laughed. (One pilot told me that the civilian driver of the blue panel truck made more than the pilots, though perhaps he was exaggerating to make a point.)

Chuck had been doing what they call dissimilar air combat training virtually every day for maybe three years. He and three other F-15 pilots would take off and fly out over the Atlantic, not knowing what they might meet. Somewhere out there they'd run into a bunch of navy planes of various kinds, whose job it was to simulate bandits and bogies. All the planes carried computer equipment that allowed game planners back at the base to record through telemetry who killed whom, along with nearly every other element of the encounter. When the dog-fight started, with planes closing at supersonic speeds, all aircraft turned in on one another at once. Everyone was trying to get on someone else's tail, creating a mess they call a furball. On that rainy day, we sat watching a film of two planes colliding in just such a simulated dogfight. The pilots in B Flight gathered around the video recorder and watched the sequence over and over, listening carefully to the radio transmissions, which told the story of what those pilots did in an emergency of amazing proportions—a mid-air collision in a dogfight.

The first transmission I heard was the leader, calling "Knock it off! Knock it off! Knock it off!" the standard signal for disengaging from the furball. Emergency transmissions are always sent three times.

We could see the two planes on the screen glide past each other, shearing off silver body parts. Smoke splashed on the air like the strokes of a Japanese sumi-e brush. Then one of the pilots who was hit called, "Bailout! Bailout! Bailout!" And: "Mark." Then—bang—his ejection seat fired, and he was out. "That's just pure polish," Chuck told me. "In a situation like that, your only responsibility is to get out. But he said 'Mark' so they'd mark his position when he ejected, to make it easier to find him. That's just pure professionalism."

I asked Chuck, "What are the qualities that make a true fighter pilot?" I had asked a lot of people that, and most didn't know what to say, but Chuck didn't hesitate at all.

"He's the kind of person who, when you tell him something, he gets it right away," he said. "He's a good athlete. He's competitive. He can stand up in front of one hundred people and speak on something he doesn't know about. He'll just do it. He won't hesitate. He's a creature of habit and a perfectionist."

In undergraduate or primary pilot training, those pilots who are selected for the good jobs—flying fighters or P.I.T. at Randolph—are taken from the top rankings, which are based for the most part on academics and flying skill. That is not surprising. What is surprising is that all those pilots place in the top five percent of their class. The grades have to be carried out to two decimal places to get the rankings. In other words, like Olympic speed skaters, virtually all of them are "the best." They are highly competitive, but it's not like in the movies.

The image of pilots that has become so popular—as if our government runs a sort of Hell's Angels of the air where the motorcycles cost thirty-eight million dollars each—was not what I found. But there have been so many movies and books about it, that the pilots themselves—the real ones—have become a bit self-conscious. Most of them today studiously avoid anything that would connect them with the odious popular image. In fact, if such a nasty, godawful thing as *the right stuff* were mentioned, most of the pilots would stand up and try to brush it off, like brushing crumbs out of their laps. *Right whut? Get that stuff off of me!* Real pilots do not strut around on the flight line grabbing fannies, one and all. For one thing, a few of those real pilots are women, and such a gesture of questionable manly camaraderie could be considered sexual harassment on the job.

One day on the way out of the flight line in the blue panel truck, I saw some pilots laughing and slapping high fives, jabbing around and joking like the actors in one of those movies. I thought: Well, maybe they really are like the guys in the movies, until I realized that they were actually *making fun of* one of the movies.

"I feel the need," said one of them. Another answered, "The need for speed!" and everybody cracked up. It was a line from *Top Gun*, which got a rating of five doughnuts for the biggest Bag-o-Doughnuts of all the jet jockey movies.

"If a pilot here acted like Tom Cruise acted in that movie," Captain Rodgers told me, "he would have no friends. He'd be an outcast."

But there is a problem with *The Right Stuff* and *Top Gun* and *The Great Santini* and *An Officer and a Gentleman*. In each case, someone bothered to do enough research so that some portion of the image projected by those books and movies had the feel of reality about it. That sensation of reality, while not being real, is the problem, like those mirror buildings that reflect the sky but are not, in fact, anything like the sky at all. Birds fly straight into the illusion with perfect confidence and die.

In part, the public image bestowed on military pilots is dangerous because it ignores many traits that are crucially important, while playing up those that are handicaps, such as arrogance, impudence, low self-esteem, boastfulness, alcoholism, and reckless disregard for safety.

Tom Wolfe was correct in observing that to be a good pilot one must have an attitude. But he was incorrect about what that attitude was. The correct attitude is more like that of the missionary going into the company of dangerous cannibals— humble, deferential, calm, confident, and well-briefed.

❖   ❖   ❖

There are crossing trajectories in the life of an air force pilot. The air force has adopted what it calls the Whole Man Concept (which the pilots call the Manhole Concept). "We are officers first, pilots second," they kept telling me. The pilot is not merely a pilot, but a whole man (says the air force). And therefore he must do what the air force wants and needs, not just fly planes. He must also increase his rank and responsibility. They all come in with a bachelor's degree, but they are encouraged to get a master's. Suddenly they are qualified for executive jobs. Soon they are on a career path that inexorably takes them away from the cockpit. By the time they're thirty-five, they're so valuable as leaders and managers and administrators that they're lucky to get in any flying time at all. The very fortunate ones may, like Colonel Kirkland, get to be squadron commanders or assistant commanders and fly several times a week. But most of the pilots, in their twenties when I met them, would inevitably face the day when they are pulled unceremoniously from the cobalt sky. I know now what it must feel like. Not even when I was fifteen, talking my first girlfriend into that first unforgettable embrace, was I more eloquent and convincing than when I begged, cajoled, and pleaded to be allowed to fly the T-38.

A lot of pilots leave the air force to fly for the airlines, but I wasn't very convinced by the ones I talked to that it was a fitting alternative. One, who had just left the air force because his days of supersonic flying were over, said, "I don't even like to go out to the field anymore. The pilot thing is short-lived, but I'd do it again in a heartbeat." He was scarcely twenty-nine and had flown jets for seven years. He was a test pilot, part of what he called the "pigs in space" program. "Light 'em and let 'em roll," was how he described his work. "Kick the tires and light the fires."

We sat in the living room of his suburban house one afternoon, and as he got to talking, his blue eyes went far away, and his feet kept working on the white carpet the whole time, like he was pushing rudder pedals. The drapes were drawn against the Texas heat, but outside, every now and then, we could hear a jet go whistling by. Randolph Air Force Base was only seconds away as the T-38 flies. "I could take off," he said, as if it had happened years ago, "and in five minutes be at forty-five thousand feet going supersonic sixty miles from the field. I got to where I could do it in my sleep, seven hundred and twenty degrees-per-second roll, like a bullet. It's wonderful to take off and leave the ground going five hundred knots straight up. I get seventeen thousand feet just like that," he snapped his fingers.

I couldn't help laughing. I knew what he meant. I'd done it, too—earlier that day, in fact. But it all grows dim so quickly. The end of his air force life was less than twenty-four hours behind him, and yet it seemed ancient history already. Still, he did not want to stop talking about flying those jets, and when we went onto his deck, as the sun was going down, he looked out at a section of sky and said, "That's where they fly by, right there in the pattern." Eventually he'd have to move.

Now, while admitting that flying for the airlines was a poor, almost preposterous, second choice, he had no real idea what else to do with his life. "My mind has deteriorated with respect to the rest of the world," he said. "All I've done is fly jets. I started when I was sixteen years old."

I told him I wasn't sure what I was going to do with the rest of my life, either, and we had a laugh; but I wasn't exactly joking. After the T-38, I went on to aerobatic training in the T-34, an old navy prop plane, and there came a time when I'd close my eyes at night, and my bed would roll and roll, as it used to when I was a child, living by the ocean, and we'd spend all day playing in the surf and steal the feeling home with us when we went to sleep at night. Flying my bed into darkness, I got a chance to glimpse that life I might have lived if my father, who was a World War II bomber pilot, had not been shot down in Germany. If he had gone into fighters, as he had planned to after that last mission, he would have been a career air force officer, and I would have been one of those kids on the bikes by the flight line. As hard as I've tried not to try to be like him,

I know now that I would have become a fighter pilot, too—another one of those minor paradoxes that rule our lives while we're out there, busy making other plans.

❖ ❖ ❖

My instructor, Captain Rodgers, had just been assigned to fly F-15s, and he was leaving to become the minister of death. I asked him why he had gotten the assignment—was it because he was the best? "No, no," he laughed, embarrassed by the question. "I was just lucky. Real lucky." In fact, the most evident and overpowering quality about those men was their sincerity and honesty and directness. They pretended not to be that way. They laughed if it was suggested and made lots of jokes about how dumb and awful pilots are. But of course it's obvious that their lives depend upon those very qualities: They must trust each other absolutely, three feet apart going five hundred miles an hour. Mutual support, it's called. They must communicate with each other instantly, directly, and with total candor. Any attempt to conceal, dissemble, or embellish could cause the independent clause of death to take over the sentence.

On the eve of his departure, I asked Captain Rodgers how he felt about the idea of killing his fellow man.

"We always hope it won't come to that," he said. "Of course every pilot wants to test himself against the enemy, to see what he's like in combat." As with the pyrotechnic beauty of a bomb going off, there will always be that paradox. "But as far as the people down there go," he added. "Well, the Russians are just ordinary slobs like the rest of us."

Every few minutes we had to stop talking while jets took off, drowning us out. A four-ship taxied out under the tumbling clouds that blew in and had tornadoed Seguin, Texas, the previous night. The ships wasted no time taking the runway in sequence and plunging into afterburner. And then as we stood mid-field and watched, a hosanna of jets peeled back the scalp of the earth and rose on pillars of fire into the sky. We watched until they were just barely chalk marks on the sky, and then Captain Rodgers said, "But, God, I love the ramp. The smell of JP-4. The whole thing. I just love it."

As I was leaving on my last day, I got lost on the base in my little Chevrolet, and I ended up in one of the quiet residential streets. In among the Spanish-style stucco houses shaded by live oaks, a mother played with her son on the lawn in the early morning hours. A jet took off with a whistling treble growl over the complex, and the toddler stopped what he was doing and pointed. The mother smiled and pointed, too, *See the airplane? See Daddy fly?*

WORLD WAR THREE IN WISCONSIN

I was tucked up in the tail of the KC-135 jet, going north out of O'Hare with the 126th Air Refueling Wing of the Illinois National Guard. There was a window in the floor, and I was lying on my stomach, looking down, watching little lakes go by. We were on our way to World War III.

It's not common knowledge, and it's not really advertised, but every July American soldiers stage what they hope is a realistic enactment of World War III on a simulated European battlefield about two hundred miles northwest of Chicago and just twenty miles east of LaCrosse, Wisconsin, at Camp McCoy. There is a 240-square-mile government range there, which for years has been the battlefield for mock warfare.

The KC-135 is a Boeing 707 outfitted as a giant fuel tank. It carries some thirty thousand gallons of kerosene, which is used for refueling fighter aircraft in flight. A long nozzle comes out the rear, and the fighter must fly up behind the tanker and hook on to receive fuel. In order to accomplish that amazing feat of engineering and pilot skill, there must be one man flying the fighter, one flying the KC-135, and a third, the boom man, in the rear to operate the nozzle.

The boom man has a little nest in the tail of the KC-135 where he can lie down on a red leather pad that looks like something invented for brain surgery. There is even a padded chin rest, because neck fatigue results from lying face-down looking out and down through the tail window for a long period of time. Lying thusly, the boom man has an instrument and control panel before him with which to operate the nozzle. And that's where I was on the trip up north: Flat in that cranny like a cockroach behind the molding, I watched as we headed past Pal-Waukee Airport, where the private pilots and bizjets go, then up along the lake shore.

At 350 miles an hour, it was only a moment before I could see Fox Lake below, while Waukegan came past on the left. It was familiar territory to me, because I fly small aircraft out of Pal-Waukee and Grayslake, Waukegan Airport, and Galt up near Wonder Lake. It looked to me just like any little Thursday morning joypop I might take in a Cessna-172, and it was a beautiful day for it. So it was difficult to get my mind around the fact that we were trying to go to war. Or something that was meant to be very much like it.

Behind and above me, the inside of the aircraft was naked and functional. Wires, conduit, tubing, switches, great banks of electrical gear, switching boxes, circuit breakers, and hardware were exposed throughout, and the fuselage walls were covered with silver-gray padded fabric that could be unhooked and removed. Canvas cots folded down from the walls and hung at eye level to make sleeping racks for long flights. Parachutes were hung on steel yellow coat hangers from a rack on the starboard side of the ship. As we floated in air above Wisconsin, the green-painted wooden knobs and orange metal knobs dangling from the chutes bobbed about as if for a festive occasion. The green apple, as they call it, is for emergency oxygen in case you have to jump at high altitude. The orange knob deploys the chute. Even though the ship had some ordinary airliner seats installed in its vast empty spaces, there was no mistaking that it had been designed with one thing in mind. Some of the silver padded panels on the fuselage were marked in stenciled red lettering: RADIATION SHIELD.

There were only four tiny windows the entire length of the cabin of the ship—those in the exit doors—and so those of us who sat in the airliner seats had to take it on faith that we would fly at all. The plane's interior was dark, except for a few emergency incandescent lights in the ceiling and the intense white bars of sunlight that swept the rubber floor as the aircraft turned left or right.

At Badger VOR, which is a radio navigational facility west of Milwaukee, we were cleared by air traffic controllers to turn northwest toward our destination, out over Lake Koshkanong, past Madison, along the Wisconsin river past Portage and Dells, and out over Castle Rock Lake into Volk Air Base.

The lake and woods came up beneath my chin at two hundred miles an hour on the landing run into Volk. As we descended lower and lower, the land rushed by, quickening its pace and deepening its nap from a soft green felt to the clawing fingers of the evergreen trees, reaching up to dice me up like a cantaloupe. Finally, as we passed the middle marker on our instrument approach (a tiny white building filled with electronic navigational equipment), the world hurtled past so fast that my eye could no longer focus on it, and the tree branches were like the whirling blades of a saw. We breached the runway; yellow, displaced threshold arrows flickered past, and the scarred black, tire-black concrete ripped along just a few feet from my face as the pilot set it down softly and hit the thrust reversers.

❖   ❖   ❖

Volk Air Base presented itself to us as woods, wind, rock outcroppings, a handful of red-roofed tan buildings bleaching in the sun, a control tower, a lone Tweet close support jet parked out on the ramp, and ten Huey helicopters with their M-60s drooping earthward and their rotors tied down. As I boarded the number three helicopter, the crew chief pointed at the machine gun and said, "That's a Rambo Special." Soon the ten crew chiefs had untied ten rotors and we were all starting our engines at once. Warriors of old had many methods of making themselves seem like the winds of Armageddon, by make-up or magic, by rattling spear upon shield as the Zulu do, or by hoisting singing men on singing kites, as the Chinese did in battle a thousand years ago. Today we have the winds of Armageddon all wrapped up in a neat bundle, a jet engine powerpack with two gigantic popsicle sticks attached on top. And when ten of those contraptions get going all at once, it is a fearsome experience. For an unprotected man to stand and fight against the approach of such a thing as this weed-green, bulbous eruption from the earth, with its elephantine awkwardness and immense weight, its guns and mass and the fracted thunderous voice of hell—it would require a courage or a desperation that is hardly imaginable. But even so, to fly one into combat also requires a good bit of skill and self-control. The fact is that in Vietnam more than one Huey helicopter was brought down by men throwing spears.

Taxiing in a helicopter means hovering very close to the ground and then maneuvering along. But the effect, especially in formation flight, is an eerie, nimbus, ghostlike squadron that has suddenly lost its corporeal reality and gone all floaty. There is something positively unnatural and spooky about a thing as big and blob-like as a Huey simply floating in the air like a tar-pit, slime-green soap bubble, but as I watched the pilot with his delicate green Nomex hands and gray leather fingertips caress the collective lever and steady the movement with his smallest finger on the metal edge of the nearby console, then gingerly pull up with three fingers, it all became real, as real as an animation. I couldn't help thinking of Walt Disney and Steven Spielberg and then, of course, of the wonderful world created by Francis Ford Coppola in *Apocalypse Now*, for there is nothing in real life that can be compared to this improbable defiance of gravity, this sepulchral ballet of flight.

Ten feet off the ground in close formation, the first five helicopters taxied out to the runway from the ramp. Our ship bobbed and ducked, dipped and turned, as the pilot held the stick, which came up from the floor between his knees, controlling the left-and-right, back-and-forth movement with gentle pressures from his fingertips, and all the while pushing hard on the left rudder pedal to keep the ship from turning against the torque of the great rotor spinning above us. Higher above, where the clouds began, I watched a flight of two A-10 Thunderbolt aircraft in formation as they pitched out and came around.

As soon as we had all made the runway and the A-10s were out of the way, we were cleared by the tower for takeoff. There was no race down the runway, such as there had been in the KC-135, no building of great momentum for the upward swing. We simply lifted, and something unseen, a force with no name, sucked us into the sky.

The second formation of five took off behind us, and we flew like that across the landscape of Wisconsin toward the west, announcing our dragonnade with explosions of the air upon Interstate 90 below. I saw a Shell gas station, small and orange, pass between the pilot's feet, where a window showed the whirling world, and thought of how easy it would be if that were a target. Push a button and it would disappear in a crackling nitrate flash. Suddenly, in this machinery, in this spell of unconscionable magic, all the world below became a target. I remembered when I was a child with my first .22 rifle, going out into the Texas prairie and understanding, suddenly and with a quickening sense of excitement, that everything around me was subject to my will. That anything I could see, I could shoot. No wonder people like to be combat troops, helicopter pilots, tactical units, green berets—it's sort of like being God. No, it's a lot like being a god. And by our mood alone—now benevolent, now the destroyer—we decide the fate of others. Personally, I liked it a lot. But it's like taking drugs; it's so short-lived. And back in the world, it becomes a real burden.

We swept into the treetops, down into the woods, and found a clearing in the forest where we could see a few soldiers in camouflage bearing M-16s and radios. As the first five helicopters in our flight sank down into the drought-blond grass, the world whirled up from the bottom in the circling trees, and the chopper blades churned it all—dust and grass and men and arms—into the sky. Dust rose so thick it blotted out the sun.

The Hueys came to rest easily upon their skids, and hunched-over men ran toward the treeline, where now we could see what we could not detect from the air: a whole encampment operation—men and arms and Jeeps and Chevy Blazers painted in camo-black and tan and green, with radio antennas tied back—all under camouflage netting. Scattered throughout the woods around us were six thousand combat troops, and they were having a little war. I could hear the distant punch of 105 Howitzers and eight-inch guns and mortars, firing into the impact zone to the west.

All the men had painted their faces. It was difficult for me to fix eye to eye with someone who looked for all the world like he might be my lawyer or editor, except that his face was smeared with green and black grease. Some of the men had only a token smudge here and there, but others clearly took their make-up seriously, applying clean-edged swirls of different colors in deliberately hideous patterns across nose, eyelids, forehead, cheeks, and down into the neck and chest area. This was not high-tech, but it was effective theater. Not incidentally, it made them difficult to see in the bushes.

Amid shouting and waving then, in the blowing wind of dust and strawgrass, with helmeted, painted men clutching rifles and radios and running and waving, grenades and canteens bobbing on their chests, we moved out into the woods to meet the unseen forces.

Every emplacement of equipment or encampment of men was covered with camouflage netting. More than just protection from aerial detection, the special material diffused infra-red radiation so that satellites and high-altitude reconnaissance equipment could not get a "signature." A cubical metal generator cover, for example, which is the size of an automobile, would show up clearly in an infrared picture. Once it is covered with the netting, it appears blurred at the edges and has no identifiable shape. Its temperature appears as the temperature of the forest. In other words, it becomes invisible.

The men's fatigues and combat clothes were also impregnated with a chemical that diffused infrared and made them all but invisible. It was an improbable and brilliant idea, in the insane way that so many things are in war: invisible troops. Who would have been audacious enough even to consider it? But when other men are looking not with their own eyes but with the eyes of gods, all mythology can come true.

The troops were also pretty well hidden from our own mortal view as we crunched along the rutted tracks through the woods in a sage green Chevy Blazer with a radio mounted on a steel rack next to my head in the back, the steel speaker screaming out static and the orders of the firing battalions, whose shells crackled over our heads as they went through the air at 194 meters per second, about sixty-two percent of the speed of sound.

Our escort, a major, reached for the hard black microphone and called, "X-Ray sixty-seven, X-Ray sixty-seven, Whiskey six, who's hot?"

"Charlie Company." The answer came over the speaker an inch from my ear with a sound like a chainsaw cutting sheet metal. The silent driver, an enlisted man who had been dishonorably discharged for smoking dope a few years back and decided to give it a second try to clear his record, drove on through the lime green, burned-out world, churning yellow dust into the yellow sunlight. As we passed the cool flanks of the forest, a darker green, which lay around us like a sleeping beast, the major said, "They're all out there. Six thousand of them. You just can't see them." Every now and then we'd pass an intersecting set of rutted paths where we could detect a cool and quiet M-60 barrel poking out of the brush, mounted with a laser scope, the gleaming golden cartridges, a lethal jewelry dangling from its craw into a dark ammo box. Here and there men surveyed the land with tape and transit.

We finally managed to locate Charlie Company, the Howitzer team that was firing. We pulled up on a go-nowhere tractor path and were challenged by a guard with an M-16. The day's password was Harbor, and there was the definite sense that if we did not know it, we would wind up with our heads on pikes, like Kurtz's victims in *Heart of Darkness.* To our right as we walked in we could see the five Howitzers dug in underneath camo canopies. The material looked like jigsaw puzzle pieces of rubber, mud-green and snakeshit tan and carbon black, interlaced through the holes in a great spreading fish net.

We stopped by the computer truck to check on the mission sequence, which told us who was going to fire next, and to pick up a helmet for me. No one could go into the artillery area without one. The computer operator explained that his system took everything into account—virtually everything—wind, air temperature, humidity, muzzle velocity, and then calculated the proper elevation, azimuth, "the angle of the dangle," and even the powder charge for propelling an explosive projectile accurately to a target that was anywhere from six to thirteen kilometers away. That information was passed down the line by wires laid out on the ground to each artillery location, where another on-the-spot computer operator, sitting on the ground at a terminal, massaged the data and came up with what he needed for his own firing team.

Each artillery piece was manned by five or six people. We went under the netting at Gun Two so I could learn how to blow up a tank five miles away. Permission to fire is called Mission. A soldier received word over a field telephone and called out, "Mission!" to which everyone responded, "Mission!" like a high school football team coming out of the huddle. (In fact, the camo-faced men, who were suddenly rushing around me in a flurry of urgent activity, were not much older than high school or college age.) They put in orange earplugs, which hung around their necks, as one barked out deflection and elevation figures, and a pair of soldiers repeated the call while cranking the tube into the correct position. The barrel of the gun, the tube, can be moved by rotating cranks, which operate gears. The sights of the artillery piece are focused on a stationary spot a few meters ahead of the barrel and just to the left of it, and each movement of a gun tube is calculated based on that fixed reference point. If we know where we are and we then know where you are, then you are dead.

Meanwhile, the powder man cut the proper load. Each artillery piece was dug in—that is, a pit was dug so that the barrel could be deflected fully upward (at which angle its breech won't clear flat ground). A few yards behind the pit, a duece-and-a-half truck with equipment and ammo was parked, the open back facing the gun. Underneath the tailgate was a rack that held half a dozen live rounds—bullets, they call them.

Each bullet is assembled from four components: the brass casing, the propellant, the high explosive projectile, and the fuse that screws into the tip of the projectile. That day they were using PD fuses, which means point detonate, which means they go off when they hit the ground. There are also mechanical time fuses, which detonate after a certain length of time, producing an air burst; and radar fuses ("They got an eye in 'em," one soldier told me. "They can see the ground").

The powder man, who handles the propellant, checks to make sure the correct components are being used, and then (based on the computer's calculations) cuts the proper charge. Each brass casing is delivered with seven bags of black powder in the bottom. The powder comes in white, elongated, tubular cloth bags sewn up with a thread running continuously from bag to bag, linking them like sausages. When the charge is called out (say, "five-bag"), the powder man reaches into the open shell casing and pulls out the unneeded bags, cutting the thread on the brass edge of the casing. He gives the extra bags to a man who stands outside the artillery pit and holds them up so that everyone can see them. That way they cannot inadvertently fire a shell with too much powder and overshoot the target, which could be potentially fatal for friendly troops, who are somewhere beyond the target, watching to see if the explosions are actually destroying the tanks and trucks they're meant to destroy.

Since this is Wisconsin (and not the Germany where we envision fighting an actual World War III), and since this is only make-believe war, there is another problem with overshooting the mark. There are farmers beyond the limits of Camp McCoy. They are real farmers with real lives, and they have real barns and cows. The major told me of one farmer just a mile beyond the limits of the battlefield whose place has been hit more than once. Fortunately no one has been killed yet. "If I was him," the major said, "I'd move."

We moved. With shouts all around and a scrambling for equipment, the breech was opened, the sight was checked, and the forty-pound bullet was slipped, clink, up into the high-angle gun, while everything was checked yet again. After all that, after the computer and the ritual, the care and caution and complexity, it was surprising to learn that the actual firing of the piece was accomplished by pulling a bit of cord with a wooden knob tied on the end, like closing the drapes. Death comes in modest guises. The cord was of a non-descript earth color, and the knob was black or brown and worn smooth from a million thumbs. It would be a comfort to detach it from the cord and keep it in one's pocket and worry its lovely polished surface. Such a noble wooden bead as that one could make a good amulet, or even be put on a line and bob on the calm surface of a north woods lake to alert us to a biting fish.

But instead I grabbed it and when the man called, "Fire!" I yanked the cord. The concussion was like being hit in the side of the head with a flat board, but which was actually a wall of air moving so fast that it became solid. For a moment I was stunned, trying to determine if I'd been injured: Surely something must have fallen off of me in the blast. But I was not. I was whole. Six miles away a truck was about to disappear.

Flight time: thirty seconds. Almost instantly the radar picked up the projectile and calculated the muzzle velocity, feeding those numbers back into the equations in order to adjust for the next shot. Across the range on a rise ten miles away, the fire support team observers had heard the call over the field phone that my shell had left the tube, and they picked up their attention. When the observer timing the shot called, "Five seconds," the others picked up their binoculars for a look at the tanks and trucks to see what I would hit.

When you watch the rounds come in from the fire support team (FST, pronounced "fist") location, the first thing you see is a flash and a ball of dust rising out of the land. The flash seems like a momentary hallucination. It doesn't seem real because there is no sound. The smoke—black washed in with yellow and white—billows and boils up from the ground like sediment stirred from the ocean floor. There is no sense of the actual violence and calamity of the device—the intense flame and power of a blast that would whip a truck into a froth of metal tailings. The FST officer, whose name was Winston, told me with a certain pride, "We're responsible for the most kills in combat. Anybody gets it in the field, we get more than anybody else, direct fire, machine guns, grenades, you name it. Artillery gets more kills."

Only a long while later, when it seemed to be an awkward afterthought to the event, did the sound of the explosion come crawling up the slope toward the observers, rumbling like an old bear through the scrub pine and sumac and poison ivy. But by then everyone was through with that story and on to the next, and the sound didn't even register with most of the men.

Hustling through the woods, I saw a small green snake, bright green in that dry land, slithering away. I approached him, but he seemed confused. He seemed to be trying to escape from the earth itself, which leapt each time the guns fired. He could not find a place to hide.

We ate in back of the FST post up on the ridgeline so we could watch the incoming while we had our picnic. Mortars and eight-inch guns were firing now, in addition to the 105s; every now and then one would land on target, and a rusted vehicle in the wide valley below would disappear in turbulent dust and smoke, as if an unseen hand erased it from a chalkboard.

My lunch consisted of "spiced beef," which was actually chili and not half bad, though it could have benefited from a few minutes over a small fire. Everything was vacuum shrink-wrapped in heavy plastic that looked like the stuff they use for body bags, but it was a surprisingly palatable meal. Even the dehydrated peaches, reconstituted with canteen water, were pretty good. I suppose the problem would come if you had to eat that same meal three times a day for a month. Each ration package (they no longer call them C-rations) came with an army green book of moisture-resistant matches, two white pieces of Chiclets chewing gum wrapped in clear plastic, and a folded sheaf of toilet tissue packaged in brown kraft paper.

Later that afternoon I sat in the command post, two deuce-and-a-half trucks parked back to back. They were parked under camo netting in the woods and surrounded by armed men. A plywood plank between the tailgates made a walkway from one "office" to the other. This was the nerve center of the artillery operation of the Thirty-third Infantry Brigade. The operation was being conducted by the National Guard (which would compose most of our nation's fighting force if we ever "got a mission," as they say when they mean to say, "went to war"). Elements of the Eighty-second Airborne had come up from Fort Bragg to observe, teach, and ultimately grade the guard on its performance. One of the key elements in the performance was the command post, those humble trucks, crammed with radios and radar and computer gear, where it reached 130 degrees in the middle of the day, where the men worked sometimes all day and all night without a break and had to move the whole operation down the road or across the forest sometimes two, three, four times a night for security reasons, with only catnaps for sleep, eating and living in the stunning, fatiguing heat and human closeness. "If your headache goes away," the major told me, "then you know something's probably wrong."

We drank warm diet Coke ("They didn't deliver no ice today, Sir") and listened to the dispatchers direct the fire. Three men in wooden folding chairs faced the back of one truck, shoulder to shoulder with no room to spare. Before each man was a rude green radio like the one that had blasted my ear during our ride through the woods. The radios sat on a plywood plank. Each man wore headphones and held a hard black microphone. ("Bravo Company wants to go dry, Sir. Yeah, I already told you that.") Everything was functional, absolutely unadorned, stripped down to the point where it almost seemed to reach a poignant and strangely brutal statement of style. I kept searching for the meaning of the statement but it eluded me for a long time until I realized where else I had seen such a style, such a cleared-off, naked, raw, bone-raked leanness. It was on death row. That was when I understood what I was seeing.

Earlier I had asked the major what a high explosive shell was for, and he had said without qualm or hesitation or any evident embarrassment about his purpose, "Kill people. That's the only thing it's for. To kill people." Now, as I baked in the oven truck, my shirt aflame with my own sweat, sipping the thick black nauseating syrup of a diet Coke and feeling the radio traffic on the steel speakers claw at the inside of my ears, I realized that I was seeing the bland adornment of death, as plain and rude and awkward as a body bag.

❖   ❖   ❖

Out in the hot white field, in the dust-dry, drought-dry grass valley, surrounded by wooden hills that looked a lot like southern Germany, I boarded my Huey helicopter again, put on my helmet, and pulled my tinted glare shield over my eyes so that I looked like a faceless, emotionless, high-tech gladiator, and we hovered in that magic, bobbing crouch over the whirlwind grass that flew up and around us and through the open doors and back out the other side again, and then we sucked ourselves up into the white-blue empyrean and flew at treetop level, thundering out over the north woods, going 130 miles an hour, fifty feet over the reaching fingers of the trees, listening to Elvis Costello on my Walkman, rock and roll over silent herds of white-tail deer scattering beneath our combat boots.

"Not a bad way to spend an afternoon," the pilot said.

I remembered that while I was standing on the ridgeline with binoculars, watching the mortar and artillery shells blow up trucks in the valley below, Winston, who was directing the FST operation, studied my nametag and said, "Don't I know your work from *Playboy?*"

I said he had the right man. I was a contributing editor.

"But, Sir," he asked with a smirk, "aren't you a bleeding heart liberal?"

"Negative," I said. "I just like to blow things up and fly jets."

"Yeah," he said. "Destroying things is a lot easier than building them."

I think he was probably doing the same thing up there that I've been doing for the last quarter century: searching for manhood. Sometimes finding it. Chasing it. It never holds still for long. It's not the Holy Grail, something we can catch and put in a bag and bury for safekeeping. It's different for each one of us, but personally, I have to get going real fast (or else get very close in) to catch a glimpse of it. The major told me that he'd gotten out of the military for five years and worked in a civilian office. He did well. He made money. But life was black. Life was death. And then one day he realized that death was life. It was like a revelation. And he returned to the military and went full-time in the guard. Now he has a smile that won't quit, and he talks about his job with an enthusiasm that is difficult to find in the civilian world in any profession. He is charged and alive with his work. And I'd find it difficult to deny that scraping around out there in the woods, banging away over laser sights on a Rambo Special, blowing up tanks, is a lot more interesting than writing for network television, which pays about forty times as well. I can't argue with the major: Death is life. I just don't know why.

❖   ❖   ❖

Ten choppers swept over the forest in a wobbling line, stretched out over the hills, and we flogged the air into Volk and picked up the KC-135 for the ride back to Chicago. During the flight there was a brief detour for an air refueling mission of two F-4 Phantom jets over Milwaukee, and I was the eager witness to one of those feats of technique, imagination, and engineering so astonishing and improbable that we are apt to call it a miracle, perhaps even art, like quadruple bypass heart surgery or the American Ballet Theater.

Out the window, where the tail boom lowered, I could see the two men in the first F-4 coming up twenty feet behind us. The pilot gave us a little wave with his left hand as he held the stick with his right, guiding his plane gently up toward us. And then he parked there in the air at twenty thousand feet, going three hundred miles an hour. His jet nuzzled up to the mother ship and sucked itself onto the twenty-foot nozzle, and I thought: He's there, right at the meat of the matter. We were all there at that moment of fusion: the boom man, the F-4 pilot, his backseat man, and the KC-135 pilot, (and I, to bear witness) all together in triumphant unison, our hearts and muscles thrilling to the test, the skill, the will, and just how radically cool it all was. What spoil-sport would think of little children dying in flames at a glorious moment like this?

The F-4 tanks filled, and when the pilot popped off the nipple, the valve closed, spraying jet fuel back across the fuselage of the fighter plane, a white disappearing ghost of kerosene that left a bright clean pennant stain on the misted aluminum behind the canopies. The ash gray F-4 fell away into the angled afternoon sunlight. The pilot rocked his wings at us, bye-bye. Then he pitched out to the east as the second ship came in and sat underneath waiting to feed.

There are many ways to make the quest. I know a man, a westerner, who is a Zen priest in Michigan and heir to a family fortune. He has done all the adventures, including flying into the sky, diving beneath the sea, mountaineering, making safaris in Africa with the Masai. Today he has come to this adventure: Sitting at dawn in lotus position in his Zendo.

He told me a Zen story about a young man who wants to become a master swordsman. The youth goes to the Master and begs to be taken as a student. When the Master accepts him, the student is put to work in the garden, hoeing and weeding and planting. He protests, but the Master ignores his complaints. Moreover, whenever the student isn't watching, the Master sneaks up behind him and hits him with a stick. The student gets the idea that this is some kind of test, and he carefully does his work and waits, and watches, but no matter what he does, the old Master manages to sneak up undetected and whack him with the stick. Then one day the Master sneaks up to hit the student, and just as the Master swings, the student ducks, causing the Master to miss. Overcome with joy, the student leaps up and shouts, "*Now* will you teach me swordsmanship?"

The Master smiles and answers with a bow, "Now you don't *need* swordsmanship."

8   3/09

7 1/95